The Sagebrush State

Wilbur S. Shepperson Series
in History and Humanities

MICHAEL W. BOWERS

The Sagebrush State

Nevada's History,

Government, and Politics

University of Nevada Press   Reno   Las Vegas

Wilbur S. Shepperson Series

in History and Humanities No. 38

Series Editor: Jerome E. Edwards

University of Nevada Press,

Reno, Nevada 89557 USA

Copyright © 1996 by

University of Nevada Press

Manufactured in

the United States of America

Cover design by Erin Kirk New

The paper used in this book

meets the requirements of

American National Standard for

Information Sciences—Permanence of

Paper for Printed Library Materials,

ANSI   Z39.48-1984.

Binding materials were selected

for strength and durability.

First Printing

05 04 03 02 01 00 99 98 97 96

5 4 3 2 1

Library of Congress

Cataloging-in-Publication Data

Bowers, Michael Wayne.

The Sagebrush State : Nevada's history,

government, and politics /

  Michael W. Bowers.

p. cm. — (Wilbur S. Shepperson series in

history and humanities ; no. 38)

Includes bibliographic references (p.   )

and index.

ISBN 0-87417-249-7 (alk. paper)

1. Nevada—History. 2. Nevada—Politics

and government.

  I. Title. II. Series.

F841.B593   1996

  979.3—dc20   96-15678

CIP

This One's For

A. L. S.

Contents

Preface

When I first began discussing this book with Nicholas Cady and Thomas R. Radko of the University of Nevada Press some years ago, I had in mind a relatively short work that would provide readers with an overview of Nevada history and government. I thought then, as I do now, that many Nevadans and non-Nevadans would be interested in a concise work that would allow them to understand Nevada's intriguing past and its effects on the present and future direction of the state. A work of that type could be utilized as a supplementary text in the state's universities and community colleges and would, perhaps, also find a niche among high school students and members of the general public.

These thoughts and discussions brought about *The Sagebrush State*. Throughout the writing of this book I have attempted to be true to my original intent to provide a concise work that could be revised on a regular basis to reflect changes in the state and its politics. Certainly this work does not pretend, nor was it ever intended, to be a comprehensive volume on every detail of Nevada history and politics; for that degree of thoroughness, the reader is directed to the bibliography. A great debt is owed by this author and all others in the field to those pioneering historians and political scientists who have taught us what we now know about the state: Hubert Howe Bancroft, Eleanore Bushnell, Don Driggs, Russell Elliott, James Hulse, Effie Mona Mack, William Rowley, Elmer Rusco, and many others too numerous to mention.

In addition, I would like to specifically thank Eugene Moehring of the History Department at the University of Nevada, Las Vegas, and Michael Green of the Community College of Southern Nevada for their assistance and counsel during the research and writing process. Were it not for their insights, this book would be the poorer. Brian Davie of the Legislative Counsel Bureau and Sidney Watson of the Government Documents Division of the James L. Dickinson Library at UNLV provided regular assistance in my quest for obscure facts and figures. I would also like to thank Leonard E. "Pat" Goodall for providing me with a draft of his forthcoming omnibus book with Don W. Driggs, *Nevada Politics and Government: Conservatism in an Open Society*. I am grateful to Trudy McMurrin of the University of Nevada Press for her unflagging devotion to seeing this work in print and her regular phone calls to ask, "So, how's the book coming?"

I would also like to thank Dean Guy Bailey of the College of Liberal Arts and the staff of the Dean's Office (Joyce Nietling, Leslie Marsh, Judy Ahlstrom, Jeremy

Wirtjes, and Mike Comstock) for all they have done to ease my burdens as an administrator. Without them, I would be unable to pursue the joys of research, writing, and teaching.

Any errors to be found within these pages must, of course, remain mine alone.

Chapter One

Nevada

Origins and Early History

Early Exploration

Although archaeological excavations indicate the migration from Asia of prehistoric peoples to the area now known as Nevada as early as 12,000 years ago, the state's written history can be said to have begun in 1776, the same year the American colonists in the East launched their war for independence against the British Crown. In the spring of that year, a Spanish Franciscan missionary, Father Francisco Garcés, and two Indian guides broke off from the second expedition of Captain Juan Bautista de Anza at the present-day site of Yuma, Arizona, to discover a shorter, more direct route between Santa Fe and the Spanish military presidio at Monterey. During the course of his exploration, it is believed, Father Garcés crossed the southernmost tip of what is today the state of Nevada.[1] It is also possible that a Spanish expedition of fifty-five soldiers led by Gabriel Morara entered the southern portion of what we now call Nevada in 1819. Morara's aims, however, were not quite so benevolent as those of Father Garcés. Morara's party set out to the northeast from the San Gabriel Mission in an unsuccessful attempt to wreak revenge against a band of Mojaves who had raided one of the Los Angeles–area missions.[2]

The Spanish, however, had little interest in exploring and developing the vast, barren region that eventually came to be identified as the Great Basin. In 1822 the area was transferred to Mexican possession when Mexico gained independence from its Spanish conquerors, thus following the earlier course of the American revolutionaries in throwing off the yoke of European imperialism. Within five years, however, British and American commercial interests were routinely violating Mexico's sovereignty in the furtherance of fur trapping and trading, concomitantly beginning the first serious explorations of the Great Basin. As one noted Nevada historian has observed, "Nevada's written history [began] with a struggle to exploit the resources of land as rapidly as possible. . . . [It is a] struggle [that] has recurred several times throughout Nevada's history."[3]

In 1826 two fur-trapping expeditions entered the Great Basin, one American and the other British. Although the two parties entered the region from different directions, they both had the same goals: to trap as many fur-bearing animals as they could and lay claim to the area for their own companies. The first English-speaking person known to have crossed into the Great Basin was the leader of the British expedition, Canadian-born Peter Skene Ogden. Ogden and his party, representing the Hudson's Bay Company, most likely ventured slightly into the northeastern corner of Nevada in the spring of 1826. Ogden's major explorations of Nevada, primarily in the north, did not occur until his later ventures into the territory in 1828 and 1829. He is generally credited as the first Anglo to discover and explore the Humboldt River.

The first American expedition, which started out in present-day Utah in August 1826, was a fifteen-member team led by twenty-seven-year-old Jedediah Smith, one of three co-owners of the Rocky Mountain Fur Company. Smith's party entered the area from the east and traversed present-day Clark County, in the south, reaching San Gabriel Mission in November. Mexican authorities, understandably anxious about new colonial threats so soon after they had gained independence from Spain, requested that Smith leave Mexican territory by the same route on which he had entered. Instead, he turned north, taking his party to an area along the American River in central California. The inhospitable nature of the snow-covered Sierra mountains made Smith decide to leave most of his party in California and attempt the mountain passage with only two other members of his expedition. Smith's three-person party successfully crossed not only the Sierras but also central Nevada, eventually reaching the Great Salt Lake. Smith's place in history is secure as the first Anglo to actually cross the hostile Nevada landscape. Although he retraced his original path through southern Nevada in 1827 to meet up with the members of his expedition whom he had left behind in California, Smith did not afterward return to the Great Basin.

The Ogden and Smith expeditions were the first to explore the region now known as Nevada, but they were most assuredly not the last. Other fur-trapping parties, originating in Santa Fe and traversing the southern part of the state, were led by Ewing Young (1829), Antonio Armijo (1829–1830), and William Wolfskill and George C. Yount (1830–1831). The path blazed by these hardy trappers eventually established an overland route known as the Old Spanish Trail.

One of the last fur-trapping expeditions, and one of the more famous and significant, was the Walker-Bonneville party of 1833 to 1834.[4] Although the group was putatively on a fur-trapping expedition, there is some evidence to suggest that its leader, U.S. Army Captain Benjamin L. E. Bonneville, sent some members of the party, led by Joseph Walker, on an excursion into California to spy on the Mexicans.[5] During their trek through central Nevada, Walker's party killed some thirty to forty Native Americans, establishing an unfortunate precedent that would haunt later relations between the region's oldest and newest inhabitants. Walker is perhaps best known for the "discovery" of the Yosemite Valley in California and

Walker Pass over the Sierra Nevada mountain range, although native inhabitants had clearly known of these for many years.

Explorers and Immigrants

Spurred by the desire for land and the American creed of Manifest Destiny (that is, that the United States had a duty and an obligation to inhabit all land lying between the Atlantic and Pacific oceans), emigrants on their way to California began to cross, but not settle in, the Great Basin. Unlike their forebears, who traveled in this region to pursue fur trapping, these individuals were interested in establishing a new life for themselves and their families in the Far West. The first group to do so was the Bidwell-Bartleson party in 1841. As head of the Western Emigration Society, twenty-year-old schoolteacher John Bidwell organized the six-month journey from Missouri to California's San Joaquin Valley; John Bartleson served as the group's captain. In addition to its distinction as the first of the emigrant parties, the Bidwell-Bartleson party is noteworthy for including Nancy Kelsey and her young daughter, the first Anglo woman and child to cross the Great Basin. While the Bidwell-Bartleson party crossed the Nevada frontier in the north, a second emigrant party in 1841, the Rowland-Workman party, traveled through the Las Vegas Valley, following the Old Spanish Trail and the 1826 route of Jedediah Smith from Santa Fe to San Gabriel.

The hardship of the terrain and desert conditions along the Old Spanish Trail, however, led later emigrant parties to cross the Great Basin through the north along what became known as the Humboldt Trail. The discovery of the latter trail is credited to the aforementioned Joseph Walker, who led the 1843 Walker-Chiles party along the northern Nevada route he had discovered during his 1834 journey out of California. Other emigrant parties followed that route through the Great Basin over the next several decades, including one in 1844 led by Elisha Stevens, Martin Murphy, and John Townsend—an expedition famed for its successful crossing of the forbidding and deadly summit that would tragically become known a few years later as Donner Pass.

The Donner party left Missouri in the spring of 1846 to pursue dreams of land ownership in California. Following generally the path of the Humboldt Trail, the party took an ill-advised cutoff in northeastern Nevada that put them woefully behind schedule. Their tardiness caused them to reach the Sierras in October after winter storms had dumped snow on the mountains, which were difficult to cross even under better weather conditions. Trapped at Donner Lake, slightly more than half—forty-seven—of the eighty-seven people who began the trip survived, but only by cannibalizing the remains of their less fortunate companions. The misfortune of the Donner party caused a temporary slowdown in emigration to California, a hiatus that would end with the discovery of gold in California in January 1848 and the February 1848 cession of what is now the southwestern United States by Mexico at the end of the Mexican War.

In addition to the informal and unofficial explorations of the Great Basin area by fur trappers and immigrants to California, a number of official expeditions were launched by the U.S. government in the early 1840s into what was then still Mexican territory. The leader of these expeditions was a member of the U.S. Army's Topographical Engineers, Captain John C. Frémont, whose destiny was most assuredly not harmed by the fact that his wife, Jessie, was the daughter of influential Missouri senator Thomas Hart Benton, one of the most fanatical of the Manifest Destiny zealots. Frémont headed two expeditions into present-day Nevada, the first from 1843 to 1844 and the second in 1845. The former traversed the western edge of northern Nevada to central California and back along the Old Spanish Trail in the south. The latter expedition, on which he was accompanied by Joseph Walker and Kit Carson, explored the central portions of the state. The lasting significance of the Frémont expeditions can be seen to this day. Although Frémont "discovered" little that had not already been explored by others, his parties, unlike their predecessors, painstakingly and accurately mapped the area and gave names to its features, names that adhere today: the Humboldt River, the Walker River, the Carson River, Pyramid Lake. Indeed, it is Frémont who first identified this vast area of interior drainage as "the Great Basin."

Settlement of Nevada

The fur trappers, California immigrants, and explorers who visited the Great Basin in the 1820s, 1830s, and 1840s had no intention of settling in the region now known as Nevada. To them it was merely a place where they hunted or passed through on the way to a new land or to an adventure, respectively. Permanent settlement of Nevada would not come until the latter part of the 1840s. Political scientists Eleanore Bushnell and Don Driggs, among others, have noted that the settlement of Nevada came as a result of three contemporaneous events:

(1) the cession by Mexico of vast territories to the United States in the Treaty of Guadalupe Hidalgo in 1848; (2) the migration of the Mormons into the Salt Lake area and later into much of the region that now comprises Nevada; and (3) the discovery of gold in California.[6]

None of these momentous events had much to do initially with Nevada. No Mexican War battles were fought here, the Mormons first settled in what is now Utah, and the first discovery of gold came in California. Like the fur trappers, California immigrants, and explorers who had traveled the land before, few among the next groups of travelers through the Great Basin saw it as an area of inherent desirability. Yet these three milestones ultimately conjoined to lead to the permanent settlement and eventual statehood of Nevada.

The Church of Jesus Christ of Latter-day Saints (the Mormons) was founded in western New York State in September 1830 by Joseph Smith, who claimed to have received from the angel Moroni a set of golden plates containing scripture and the Urim and Thummim to interpret them. Conflict with and persecution by more traditional Christian groups led Smith to move the Mormons to Ohio, Missouri, and Nauvoo, Illinois. The murder of the Mormon prophet in a Carthage, Illinois, jail led his successor, Brigham Young, to move the group once more. The journey, from 1846 to 1847, of 15,000 men, women, and children eventually came to rest at the Great Salt Lake, an area still within the sovereignty of Mexico. By March 1849 Young had proclaimed the independent State of Deseret, a region encompassing present-day Utah, Nevada, southern California, and parts of Arizona, New Mexico, Idaho, and Colorado.

While the Mormons were on their way to the Great Salt Lake, the United States was engaged in a war with Mexico for control of California and what is today the southwestern United States. Following the doctrine of Manifest Destiny to its logical, if bloody, conclusion, President James K. Polk launched the war in 1846, a war that ended successfully for the Americans in 1848 with the Treaty of Guadalupe Hidalgo. The treaty gave the United States control over California, Utah, Nevada, and portions of Arizona, New Mexico, Wyoming, and Colorado. The Great Basin was now firmly and legally ensconced in the hands of the United States.

Simultaneous to the end of the Mexican War, gold was discovered in California at Sutter's Fort on the American River near Sacramento. Beginning in 1849, thousands traveled from the east to California in search of riches; some came by sea around South America (the Panama Canal was yet to be built), while others traveled overland along the routes used by earlier California immigrants through the northern Great Basin.

As already noted, none of these three events initially had anything to do with Nevada. However, each in its own way contributed to the region's development. After 1848 the Great Basin was no longer foreign territory, the Mormons aggressively moved into its northern and southern regions to proselytize and establish settlements, and the influx of California gold seekers through the region created a need for supply stations along the overland route, including the area now known as Nevada.

The cession of California and the southwestern United States in 1848 by Mexico forced the U.S. government to deal with political issues of statehood and territorial boundaries. Rejecting Brigham Young's massive State of Deseret, Congress approved the Compromise of 1850 to establish some order in its newly acquired territory. That act, debated by Congress for two years over the heated issue of slavery, established California as a free, that is, nonslave, state (even though it had, unlike other states added after the original thirteen colonies, never been a territory) and divided the remainder of the Mexican Cession of 1848 into the territories of New Mexico and Utah, which could, upon statehood, determine for themselves whether to allow slavery. New Mexico Territory included not only New Mexico but also most of Arizona and the southern 10 percent of present-day Nevada. The newly created Utah Territory included all of present-day Utah, small parts of Colorado and Wyoming, and the northern 90 percent of present-day Nevada. Congress thus not only changed the name of the Mormon territory from Deseret to Utah but also included only half of the area Young and his followers had earlier claimed. It is doubtful that the Mormons would have achieved even that but for the death of President Zachary Taylor in July 1850. Taylor opposed the Mormon cause and was unsympathetic to state or territorial status for them. His successor, Millard Fillmore, however, was favorably impressed by the Mormons and their representative, Dr. John M. Bernhisel, who had been dispatched to Washington, D.C., in 1849 to lobby (unsuccessfully) for congressional recognition of the much larger State of Deseret. Not surprisingly, Fillmore appointed the Mormon leader, Brigham Young, as Utah's first territorial governor.[7]

Mormon settlement in the western Utah Territory (now Nevada) began that same year, 1850, when a party led by Joseph Demont established a temporary trading post in Carson Valley near Utah Territory's western border with California.[8] The post, named Mormon Station, served the needs of emigrants and gold seekers crossing the Great Basin on their way to California. Although abandoned with the onset of winter, the post became a permanent settlement the following year when a party led by John Reese sought to establish a farming and trading community and fort. In 1856 the name of this first permanent settlement in Nevada was changed to Genoa.

Once the Mormons had established the feasibility of survival, agriculture, and commercial enterprise in the Carson Valley, they were joined by non-Mormons ("gentiles") who also opened trading posts in Carson, Eagle, and Jack's Valleys and Truckee Meadows. Gentile population in the area was augmented by the discovery in 1850 of gold in Gold Canyon just east of the California border. Gold miners from California and new gold seekers from the East soon established residence in the region as well, although they generally had no intention of making the place a permanent home. The combination of Mormons and non-Mormons in the Carson Valley was from the beginning a volatile one and was partially responsible for Nevada's eventual separation from Utah Territory in 1861.

The area that is now southern Nevada was also being settled during this time. Although the development of the south did not have the same profound effects on Nevada's becoming a territory and, later, a state that the development of the north did, the settlement of both areas exhibited many of the same characteristics. Settlement of the Las Vegas Valley (then part of New Mexico Territory) began in 1855, when Brigham Young sent a group of Mormons led by William Bringhurst to establish the Las Vegas Mission. The mission was to serve a dual purpose: establish supply stations along the Old Spanish Trail (just as Mormon Station had in the north) and convert the Native Americans, primarily Southern Paiutes, to Mormonism. Their task was, in many ways, a hard and thankless one, performed in a hostile environment. One of the missionaries, John Steele, observed in an 1855 letter that "the country around here looks as if the Lord had forgotten it."[9] Later in that same letter he noted that there was a "general weakness" among the Mormon missionaries because

> the weather is very hot; and not having light, suitable clothing fit for the season; and the last and principal reason is, they have nothing (with a very few exceptions) to eat but dry bread, as the cows are mostly dry. But we still are not discouraged, for we hope for better times ahead; and if we don't live to see it, maybe our children will.[10]

The Las Vegas Mission eventually was abandoned as a result of a split in the community between Bringhurst and Nathaniel V. Jones, whom Brigham Young had sent to the mission in 1856 to mine lead ore in the area. This division was part of a larger conflict within the Mormon community over whether its primary purpose was to proselytize or mine. By 1858 most of the missionaries had returned to Utah, leaving only a small band under the authority of Benjamin R. Hulse. Hulse's group soon followed, and the Las Vegas Valley was left to its Native American inhabitants until 1861, when small traces of silver were found in the old Mormon lead mine and a large gold strike was made near the current site of Hoover Dam. A permanent settlement in Las Vegas (named Los Vegas Rancho) did not take root until 1865, when Octavius Decatur Gass took ownership of the Old Mormon Fort and established a station to supply Las Vegas Valley miners and the settlers passing through to California.[11]

Establishing a Government

From the first moments of their arrival in the Carson Valley in 1851, the settlers agitated for separation from the Mormon-dominated Utah territorial government. Separated as they were by five hundred miles from the territorial capital, first in Fillmore City and later in Salt Lake City, and ignored by Brigham Young, who concentrated on organizing that part of the territory that was nearest to him, the western settlers were left with no established government and no protection from bandits and Indian attack. In response to this lack of law and order and Utah's *de facto* policy of benign neglect, settlers held three meetings in Mormon Station on

November 12, 19, and 20, 1851, to establish order.

During the course of these meetings, the settlers created a squatter government to establish bylaws and regulations for the community and to create public offices. Ten resolutions were adopted dealing with the survey and recording of land claims, while an eleventh established a committee of seven officers to act as the region's governing board. In addition, a magistrate's court, made up of a justice of the peace and four others, was to serve as the area's judicial body; appeal could be taken to a court of twelve citizens who had final say on matters brought to them. Notably, the group also adopted a petition to Congress seeking "a distinct Territorial Government" for the western Utah Territory.[12]

Displeased by the Carson Valley settlers' petition, Brigham Young intervened and attempted, at last, to establish territorial control over the area. Seven Utah counties were extended to the California border in order to include the western Utah Territory. County seats remained in present-day Utah, however, and with such a distance between them, county officials persisted in their failure to exercise any authority over their newly acquired western lands. The ineffectiveness of the squatter government in achieving law and order, combined with the objections by many non-Mormons to the possibility of control by Salt Lake City, led forty-three settlers in 1853 to sign a petition to the California Legislature requesting annexation by California "for judicial purposes until congress [*sic*] should provide otherwise."[13]

Although the settlers' petition was ignored by California, Utah took great note of it and attempted once more to bring its western territory into the fold. In January 1854 the territorial legislature created Carson County, an extremely large new county in the western Great Basin. It encompassed what is today Carson City, Washoe, Douglas, Storey, Lyon, and Mineral Counties and parts of Esmeralda, Churchill, and Humboldt Counties. Once again, however, no immediate attempts were made by the Utah authorities to exercise control over their newest creation.

Utah's lack of action led the squatters to once more endeavor to establish an organized government in what was now Carson County. In 1854 they hired attorney William A. Cornwall to write a constitution for the Carson Valley. Very little is known about the Cornwall Constitution, and most Nevada history books fail even to mention it. What we do know is that the powers of government were to be exercised by an elected group consisting of a sheriff, a president, a secretary, and a three-member court. The Cornwall Constitution was, apparently, never adopted, and "there seems to be no evidence that it was ever presented for a vote."[14]

In January 1855 the Utah Legislature took several actions that indicated a serious desire to maintain territorial control over the Carson Valley. It established Carson County as Utah's Third U.S. Judicial District, and George P. Styles was assigned as presiding judge. Orson Hyde, a member of the church's governing board, the Twelve Apostles, was appointed as probate and county judge to organize the county. In response to the settlers' complaints that they were without representation in the territorial legislature, Carson County was also given one vote in the Utah Territorial Assembly.

In May, Hyde, Styles, and thirty-eight others left Salt Lake City to once and for all establish territorial (and Mormon) control over Carson County. In those terms, Hyde was incredibly successful. Arriving in Carson Valley in June, Hyde first commissioned a survey to ensure that Mormon Station and Carson County were within the boundaries of Utah. Determining that they were, he called for county elections to be held at Mormon Station on September 20. All but one of the victorious candidates in the 1855 contest were Mormon, thanks to the immigration of Mormons into the area.

Not surprisingly, non-Mormons in the area were displeased with the now-realized Mormon domination of the Carson County government. The gentiles were convinced that the law was not administered fairly to Mormon and non-Mormon alike and were particularly dissatisfied with the practice of polygamy exercised by Hyde and others. They looked "with disgust upon the prospect of raising their daughters among such associates, and they ardently desired that their homes in their pleasant valley shall not be 'defiled' by the horrible favoritism and deception of Mormonism."[15]

Mormon domination of the Carson County government led non-Mormons in the area to petition once more, in November 1855, for annexation to California. Unlike its February 1853 predecessor, this petition was looked upon favorably by the California Legislature. Unfortunately for those seeking annexation, Congress failed to act on their plea. Hearing of the settlers' continued attempts at secession, Brigham Young ordered fifty to sixty more Mormon families into the Carson Valley. "By the middle of 1856 Carson County was organized politically, economically, and socially in the firm and able hands of the Mormons."[16]

Territorial and Mormon control over the western territory, however, was not destined to last. Probate Judge Hyde left Carson County to return to Salt Lake City in November 1856; whether he was frustrated with his position or recalled by Young is open to dispute. In January 1862 he illustrated his contempt for the people of the Carson Valley when he wrote to seek compensation for the sawmill he had left behind in his hasty departure:

> You shall be visited of the Lord of Hosts with thunder and with earthquakes and with floods, with pestilence and with famine until your names are not known amongst men, for you have rejected the authority of God, trampled upon his laws and his ordinances, and given yourselves up to serve the god of this world; to rioting in debauchery, in abominations, drunkenness and corruption. You have chuckled and gloried in taking the property of the Mormons, and withholding from them the benefits thereof. You have

despised rule and authority, and put God and man at defiance. If perchance, however, there should be an honest man amongst you, I would advise him to leave; but let him not go to California for safety, for he will not find it there.[17]

Hyde's departure from Carson County left the area once more bereft of organized government and law and order. He was followed to Salt Lake City by a large party of Mormons in July 1857, and all of the faithful were officially called back to Salt Lake City by Brigham Young in September of that year to fend off what Young believed was an imminent invasion of Utah by federal troops in what became known as the Utah War. Although characterized by some historians as a series of misunderstandings and miscommunications,[18] there were real causes for the federal government to be concerned with goings-on in the territory, including antagonism between Mormons and gentiles in the Carson Valley and an incident in 1856 in which a federal judge had been "driven from the bench" in eastern Utah by "an armed mob of Mormons."[19]

The official beginning of the Utah War came in July 1857 when President James Buchanan removed Brigham Young as territorial governor and appointed a new, non-Mormon government headed by Alfred Cumming. The anticipated arrival of the new territorial government, accompanied as it was by 2,500 federal troops led by General Albert Sidney Johnston, struck fear into the hearts of the Mormons. It was then that Young called upon all Mormons, including approximately 1,000 in the Carson Valley, to return to the capital to fend off the anticipated federal invasion. In addition, Young issued an order prohibiting an armed force from entering the Salt Lake Valley and declared martial law. The Mormons prepared for war, but the federal forces eventually were allowed to enter the valley peacefully after successful negotiations between Young and Buchanan's representative, Colonel Thomas L. Kane, who had made friends with the Mormons when they had lived in Nauvoo. In April 1858 the Utah War, such as it was, officially ended when Buchanan granted amnesty to all who swore allegiance to the Union. Although the returnees were, thus, not ultimately needed, they did not go back to the Carson Valley, and the land, homes, and businesses they had spent years building into profitable enterprises were often simply taken by the remaining settlers—a situation that led to Hyde's curse upon them.

In apparent anticipation of the September call by Young for all adherents to return to the Salt Lake Valley, the Utah Legislature in January 1857 repealed the act creating Carson County and put the area under the nominal control of Great Salt Lake County, headquartered in Salt Lake City. Although no doubt happy to see the Mormon exodus, the western settlers were once more left without any organized government, and the Carson Valley was again in the grip of the same lawlessness it had suffered prior to the Mormons' arrival in large numbers in 1856.

The period between 1857 and 1861 has been described as an "era of anarchy and confusion." The phrase is an apt one. In 1857, after the Utah Legislature's dissolution of Carson County and Judge Hyde's return to Salt Lake City, the settlers held a series of mass meetings in which they once more petitioned Congress for status as a separate territory within the shortest time possible. The new territory was to have its capital in Genoa and would be called Columbus, after the explorer whose birthplace in Italy had served as the source for Mormon Station's 1856 name change. The settlers' representative to Washington, D.C., James M. Crane, predicted in a letter to his constituents that Congress would act favorably on the petition in order "to compress the limits of the Mormons and defeat their efforts to corrupt and confederate with the Indian tribes."[20] Crane's optimistic prediction was wrong. A bill granting territorial status, which included a change of name from Columbus to Nevada, passed the House Committee on Territories, but the full Congress adjourned before acting on the petition. The congressional failure to act was based in part on the pre–Civil War sectional strife over slavery that was even then dividing the nation: the territorial bill was held up in the House by Speaker James L. Orr of South Carolina, who feared that the new territory would not support slavery. Of lesser, but still significant, importance, the federal government hoped that the newly appointed non-Mormon government of Alfred Cumming would resolve the antagonism in the western territory between Mormons and gentiles.

In addition to petitioning for separate territorial status, the settlers attempted to establish a more immediate mechanism for protecting law and order in the region. A committee of twenty-eight men was created during the 1857 squatters' meetings to serve as a provisional government. The committee proved ineffectual, and in March 1858 the settlers met again, this time to establish a vigilante committee to maintain law and order. The vigilantes were equally unsuccessful in holding the criminal element in check, although they did try, and sentence, several people. One of those, the ironically named William "Lucky Bill" Thorrington, was a prominent member of the community who had served on the twenty-eight-member provisional committee of 1857. Thorrington was hanged for being an accessory after the fact to murder, although there is substantial evidence to support his innocence.[21] Thorrington's hanging had the unfortunate consequence of creating a serious rift in the Carson Valley community between those convinced of his guilt and those who believed him innocent.

Once again, Utah Territory attempted to establish control over its wayward western province, this time by appointing, in 1858, John S. Child as probate judge to reorganize local government in the Carson Valley. Child called for new elections in October, elections noted for such intense conflict and voter fraud that the results in four of the six precincts were discarded because of charges of fraudulent voting. In January 1859 Utah officially reestablished Carson County, gave it a single representative in the territorial legislature, and combined it with two other counties to form the Second U.S. Judicial District. John Cradlebaugh was appointed as the district's judge.

The failure of Judge Child to effectively reorganize Carson County led the settlers to call for a mass meeting in Carson City on June 6, 1859, to take up once more the issue of separate territorial status. At that meeting an election was called for July 14 to choose a delegate to represent the interests of the Carson Valley in Washington, D.C., and to select fifty delegates to attend an unauthorized constitutional convention.

Nevada Territory

James M. Crane was again elected to serve as the settlers' representative to the nation's capital, although his election was surrounded by more charges of voter fraud. The convention delegates met in Genoa on July 18, 1859. Again, support for separation from Utah Territory appeared to be based primarily upon a desire to be freed from the Mormon authorities, who, according to the settlers, "so [mixed] together church and state that a man [could not] obtain justice in any of its courts."[22] A nine-day convention, presided over by Colonel John J. Musser, voted to secede from Utah Territory, produced a territorial constitution modeled upon that of the state of California, and adopted the name Nevada. A ratifying election was held on September 7 concurrent with elections for a governor and territorial legislature.

Support for the 1859 constitution was substantial. The election returns were not preserved, but "there is evidence that the majority for the constitution was about four hundred, . . . although the board of canvassers failed to meet to canvass the votes, and the certificate of the president of the board, J. J. Musser, alone testified to the result."[23] Musser's certificate of election did not issue until December, three months after the election, leading to doubts about the veracity of the reported results. In any event, Isaac Roop was elected territorial governor and the legislature was to meet on December 15. The legislature did meet on that date but was unable to act for lack of a quorum; only four members attended. After an address by "Governor" Roop, the group adjourned, never to meet again. Roop, however, did continue to act as governor for some time.

Undeterred by the unauthorized actions of the settlers, U.S. District Court Judge John Cradlebaugh arrived in Genoa in the summer of 1859. Although not a Mormon, Cradlebaugh was a representative of the Utah territorial government, and Carson County residents refused to work with him. In yet one more attempt to establish control over the western settlers, Probate Judge Child attempted unsuccessfully to hold court in September and also called for new elections on October 8. In protest, only three of the county's ten precincts opened for the election. Under those rather disconcerting and unsupportive circumstances, the winning candidates refused to take office. Child could finally enjoy some sense of achievement in August 1860 when elections were successfully held to select various officeholders, including a representative to the Utah Territorial Assembly.

Attempts by the western settlers to achieve separate territorial status and some measure of law and order were exacerbated by three significant, contemporaneous events. In September 1859 James M. Crane, the settlers' delegate to Washington, D.C., died in Gold Hill of a heart attack. He was replaced by the aforementioned John J. Musser, who was unable to persuade Congress during its 1859–1860 session to establish an independent territory in Carson County. Complicating matters further was President Buchanan's appointment of R. P. Flenniken as the new judge of the Second U.S. Judicial District to replace Judge Cradlebaugh—and Cradlebaugh's refusal to leave his position. Thus was created the unworkable situation of two federal judges attempting to enforce the law. Conflict between the two only increased the judiciary's impotence in the face of escalating lawlessness. The ineffectiveness of any government authority to maintain law and order was further exacerbated by a third event: the discovery of gold and silver in what became known as the Comstock Lode. The Comstock Lode brought with it a huge tide of humanity, including miners and the tradespeople who sought to supply them. New towns sprang up overnight, and thousands of people rushed to make their fortunes. In addition to dealing with the general lawlessness to be expected with the sudden, unplanned influx of so many fortune seekers, the western territory now had a new problem with which to cope: conflict between various parties over ownership of lucrative mining claims.

Thus, the years 1857 to 1861 were marked by anarchy and confusion, without any strong authority to establish law and order and without an effective government. Confusion was at an all-time high, with at least three governments in operation: the provisional government of Isaac Roop, the Utah territorial government of Probate Judge John S. Child, and the divided federal court authority exercised by warring U.S. District Judges John Cradlebaugh and R. P. Flenniken. A San Francisco newspaper of the time noted that

> There is no government. Nominally the Mormon government bears sway over that portion of the territory as well as over Salt Lake City. But practically Mormon laws are a nullity, they are not enforced, nor could they be. Should a Mormon judge or justice of the peace attempt to hold his court at Carson City or Virginia City, he would not only find that he possessed no power to execute the mandates of his court, but also that all attempts to do so would endanger his personal safety. . . . Politically, the people are in a chaotic state, without law and without a Constitutional [*sic*] government. . . . The present position of the people is deplorable. The evils to which they are exposed are terrible to contemplate and the coming season it is to be feared, will witness scenes of anarchy and bloodshed, fearful to behold, as the rich silver mines

will attract thither a large crowd of desperate and abandoned men, who, in the absence of law and a well established government will give full scope to their vicious inclinations.[24]

Chapter Two

Nevada

Territory and Statehood

In 1861, the settlers' representative, John J. Musser, finally persuaded Congress to establish a separate territory in western Utah. Musser was aided by the election of Abraham Lincoln as president and the resulting secession from the Union of the southern states. With the pro-slavery states no longer represented in Congress and unable to block the territory bill, passage was virtually guaranteed. And it certainly did not hurt the settlers' cause that the influx of population and the increase in lawlessness in Carson County as a result of the discovery of the Comstock Lode had shown that the non-Mormon territorial government of Governor Cumming was no more effective than Brigham Young had been in assuring law and order and in quelling the desire for separate territorial status among the western Utah residents. On February 26, 1861, the U.S. Senate passed legislation entitled An Act to Organize the Territory of Nevada; the House of Representatives followed suit on March 2, and President Buchanan signed it into law later that day. Thus, after ten years of uninterrupted pleas and petitions, the western Utah settlers achieved their goal: the establishment of Nevada Territory.

Two days after Buchanan signed the act establishing Nevada Territory, Abraham Lincoln was sworn in as president of the United States. The responsibility to name the territory's first officers, therefore, devolved upon him. On March 22 he announced the appointment of James W. Nye of New York as territorial governor and Orion Clemens (brother of Samuel, better known as Mark Twain) as territorial secretary. Both were patronage appointments: Nye was a good friend of Lincoln's secretary of state, William H. Seward, and the two had campaigned in the West for Lincoln during the 1860 election; Clemens had studied law in the St. Louis law offices of Edward Bates, Lincoln's attorney general.

Governor Nye arrived in Nevada on July 7, 1861. He chose Carson City as his site of operation and later instructed the first territorial legislature to meet there, indicating the town's ascendance in the territory over the previously dominant Genoa. During the month of July, Nye issued three proclamations: the first named his appointees to various territorial offices (July 12); the second announced the creation of a judiciary (July 17); and the third called for elections to be held on

August 31 for the purpose of selecting a delegate to Congress and members of the territorial legislature (July 24).

Nye's July 17 proclamation establishing a judiciary was one of the most important actions he took in this early organizational period. The lawlessness that characterized Nevada demanded the creation of courts to enforce law and order; indeed, aside from the Mormon question, the absence of legal authority was the major reason the settlers had lobbied for separate territorial status. Following the dictates of Section 9 of the Territorial Act of 1861, Nye established a supreme court, three district courts, probate courts, and justices of the peace. Three Lincoln-appointed territorial judges each heard cases on original jurisdiction in one of the district courts, and all three sat *en banc* as the supreme court to hear appeals. The lower-court judges were appointed by Nye until such time as elections could be held. In a letter to Secretary of State Seward, Nye confirmed the importance of establishing a judiciary in the territory when he noted that there was "no such thing as law or order existing in the Territory" and that there was, in particular, a great need for a court system to establish mining rights.[1]

In the August election, Judge Cradlebaugh was chosen to serve as the territory's first delegate to Congress. Also elected were nine members to serve in the Council and fifteen to serve in the House of Representatives, the upper and lower houses, respectively, of the territorial legislature. The legislature met only three times: in 1861, 1862, and 1864. The first session convened on October 1, 1861, at Abe Curry's Warm Springs Hotel two miles outside of Carson City, a site purchased later by the territorial government for $75,000 that now serves as the Nevada State Prison. During this first session the legislature passed 107 pieces of legislation organizing the territory. Some of the more noteworthy acts were those adopting the common law of England, forming nine counties in the territory to be governed by three-member boards of commissioners, and establishing a system of common schools. And in marked contrast to what Nevada's future would hold, some of this early legislation made divorce difficult except under the most extreme circumstances and prohibited gambling, which Governor Nye had referred to in his address to the legislature as "the worst" of "all the seductive vices," which "captivates and ensnares the young, blunts all the moral sensibilities and ends in utter ruin."[2]

Two of the most controversial issues facing this first legislative session were the permanent location of the capital and the generation of revenue for supporting the territorial government. The question of where to locate the territorial capital was, apparently, a difficult and emotional one, resulting in charges of underhanded dealing and a barroom brawl in the Ormsby House Hotel between a Virginia City councilman and a Carson City representative. By a vote of 15 to 9, it was decided that Carson City, and not Virginia City, would be the capital. The issue of how best to raise revenue in the territory was a precursor of the events that would disrupt and derail later attempts to write a state constitution. Governor Nye proposed a tax on the gross proceeds of mines, at that time the major source of the territory's wealth. The mining-dominated legislature vehemently objected and eventually passed a general property tax measure of forty cents per one hundred dollars valuation on property in the territory. Counties could, in addition, adopt a levy of up to sixty cents more per one hundred dollars valuation on all property within their jurisdictions. The mines and their products would be untaxed. This battle over the taxation of mining property was only the first of many to come, leading one Nevada observer to note, "The background of Nevada politics for thirty years was a fight of mine operators against paying taxes."[3]

Statehood

Although Nevada had been a territory for little more than a year when the second session of the legislature met in 1862, an election was called for September 1863 to determine support for statehood and, assuming support, the selection of thirty-nine delegates to a convention to draft a constitution for the State of Washoe. Support for statehood in the fledgling territory was overwhelming, with a vote of 6,600 in favor and 1,502 opposed.[4] Even though Congress had authorized neither the election nor statehood for the territory, a convention met in Carson City for thirty-two days in November and December of 1863 to draft a constitution for the state they chose to name Nevada rather than Washoe, as the 1862 legislature had wished, or Esmeralda or Humboldt, as some of the delegates had proposed.

The 1863 Constitution

The delegates to this unauthorized convention were optimistic not only that Congress would grant statehood but also that their handiwork would be as overwhelmingly supported by the citizens as the question of statehood had been in the September election. In that, they were sadly mistaken. Except for an unprecedented clause in which the state's citizens pledged "paramount allegiance" to the federal government, the constitution coming out of this body was itself rather unremarkable, based as it was on California's and New York's constitutions. This constitution's lack of originality is not surprising when one considers that of the thirty-nine delegates, "all but 5 had come from California, all but 5 were under 50 years of age, and all but 2 had been in the territory less than 5 years."[5] In addition, a plurality of the delegates listed New York as their place of birth. Although many issues divided the delegates during the course of their deliberations, two of the most controversial spelled overwhelming defeat at the polls for the constitution they had so carefully and painstakingly crafted.

Just as mine taxation had led to a dispute between Governor Nye and the 1861 legislature, so it disrupted the 1863 convention. The move from territorial to state status would eliminate the federal government's subsidy of the Nevada government, creating a need for additional revenue to support it. Indeed, the additional cost to be borne by a state government, as opposed to a territorial one, was a common concern among some members of various antistatehood movements in the West during the later nineteenth century.[6] One faction, led by convention president John W. North, proposed that mines should be taxed the same as other property, arguing that "all property should bear alike the burdens of society."[7] A second faction, led by the powerful mining lawyer William M. Stewart, objected that such a tax would "mean the death of the mining industry" by "impos[ing] a burden upon the miners which would be heavier than they could bear. It would mean a tax on the shafts, drifts, and bed-rock tunnels of the mines whether they were productive or not."[8] Stewart noted ominously that taxing unproductive mines, ninety-nine out of one hundred by his calculation, would stop the mining industry dead in its tracks and lead to economic disaster for the state. Instead, the Stewart faction favored taxing only the net proceeds of the mines. The North faction prevailed, however, and the convention adopted a provision requiring the legislature to "provide by law for a uniform and equal rate of assessment and taxation and [to] prescribe such regulations as shall secure a just valuation for taxation of all property, both real and personal including mines, and mining property."[9]

The second issue responsible for the 1863 constitution's defeat at the polls involved the election of officeholders to serve in the new state government. Convention delegates decided to offer a single slate of officeholders on the ballot with the constitution; thus, in voting for the constitution, one would also vote for a particular slate of candidates. This proved deadly. Even though the mining-tax issue created a serious rift in the territory, it is possible that the constitution, voted on by itself, could have been ratified. Indeed, Stewart, defeated as he was in the convention on the tax issue, supported the constitution's adoption and fought mightily for ratification. But the slate of candidates, to the chagrin of many, had been handpicked by Stewart in a pair of rather nasty Union Party conventions, first in Storey County and later at the territorial convention in Carson City.[10] Stewart's domination of the Union Party proceedings led to a split in the party and the defeat of territorial supreme court justice John North, his nemesis from the constitutional convention, in his bid for the party's gubernatorial nomination. Much of Stewart's vigorous support for the 1863 constitution, including as it did the mining-tax provision he opposed, was a result of his desire to be rid of the territorial judges, including North, whom he hated as much as, if not more than, the mining tax, and his belief that his chosen candidates for "the First State Legislature would amend the new Constitution to provide taxation only of the net proceeds of productive mines."[11]

The split in the Union Party had a twofold, negative impact on the quest for ratification. First, North and his followers, who supported the constitution itself, were in no mood to vote for its ratification if that meant, as it did, the concurrent election of Stewart's slate of candidates. North and other disappointed office seekers, "and their names were legion, became hostile to [the constitution's] adoption."[12] Second, small mining companies were unwilling to take a gamble that the legislature would, in fact, repeal the mine tax, especially if that meant turning control of the state government over to Stewart and the large San Francisco mining companies he represented. As historian David A. Johnson has noted, much of the opposition to the 1863 constitution was "based upon a widespread conviction that Stewart intended to control the new state government as a means to further his own interests and those of the mining corporation officials he represented."[13]

The unlikely combination of disappointed Union Party office seekers, small miners, merchants, farmers, and a few Democrats residing in the territory—who supported the Confederacy and wished, therefore, not to become a Union state— was large enough to ensure the overwhelming defeat of the constitution in the January 1864 election. The 4 to 1 vote against the constitution, 8,851 to 2,157, was ironically similar to that which had favored statehood earlier. In a letter later that year to his old friend Secretary of State Seward, Governor Nye noted that the chief reason for the constitution's defeat was a "dissatisfaction with some of the State ticket, and the proceedings of some of the county conventions [that] caused its opponents to act in concert, and all combined they were strong enough to defeat it."[14] A delegate to the second constitutional convention in 1864, John A. Collins, shared Nye's belief and laid blame for the constitution's defeat on "efforts to introduce a certain set of delegates into the State Convention."[15] Yet there were those who disagreed, including Charles E. DeLong, also a delegate to the 1864 convention, who noted colorfully that the mining-tax provision, which had "stunk in the nostrils of the people," was the true cause for the failure of the 1863 constitution to be ratified.[16]

The defeat of the 1863 constitution, however, did not entirely quell Nevadans' desire for statehood; the 4 to 1 vote in favor of statehood in the September 1863 special election was evidence enough of its force in the territory. But for the mining-tax provision and the Union Party split engendered by Stewart's political legerdemain, the 1863 constitution might well have been ratified. Nonetheless, as will be discussed later, the mining depression that gripped Nevada Territory in mid-1864 reduced statehood desires within the territory itself. What ultimately provided the impetus for Nevada's statehood came quite outside the young territory's borders; national issues were quickly coming to a confluence that would give Nevada its cherished prize. Within twenty days after the defeat of the 1863 constitution, a bill was introduced into Congress allowing the territories of Nevada, Colorado, and Nebraska to hold constitutional conventions and establish state governments. The bill, introduced on February 8, 1864, by Senator James R. Doolittle (R-Wisconsin), easily passed both houses of Congress and was signed by President Lincoln on March 21.

The driving force behind Doolittle's bill had four components. First, Lincoln desired additional votes in Congress to assure the two-thirds vote he needed in both houses for passage of the Thirteenth Amendment, which would abolish slavery and thereby place a constitutional imprimatur on his Emancipation Proclamation. Second, Lincoln expected that he would need Nevada's three electoral votes to win the 1864 presidential election. Third, the Radical Republicans, already at odds with their own party's president over the coming reconstruction of the southern states, had their own reasons for supporting Nevada statehood: they sought additional Republican votes in Congress to support congressional, rather than presidential, policies on such matters. Finally, with the third-party candidacy of John C. Frémont, it was thought (until his withdrawal in September) that the 1864 presidential election might be so close that no candidate would win a majority in the electoral college and the decision would thus be thrown into the House of Representatives; an additional Republican vote from Nevada in that body would help to assure selection of the Republican nominee.

The 1864 Constitution

Acting quickly, Governor Nye called on May 2 for an election to be held on June 6 for the purpose of choosing thirty-nine delegates to attend a second constitutional convention. Unlike the gathering in 1863, this convention was legally authorized by Congress and, ultimately, successful.

The convention, presided over by J. Neely Johnson, former governor of California, met in Carson City on July 4 and concluded its work on July 27; thirty-five of the thirty-nine elected delegates attended. The demographic makeup of the convention was similar to that of its predecessor: ten members had served in the 1863 convention; most were from California; lawyers and mining interests dominated; and all but one, Francis Proctor, a Democrat from Nye County, were Union Party members. Unlike the 1863 convention, antagonists John W. North and William M. Stewart were not delegates.

The Nevada Enabling Act established a number of limitations on the type of constitution the convention delegates could draft. Those restrictions, to which the delegates faithfully adhered, included the following:

(1) The new State Constitution must be republican in nature and not repugnant to the Federal Constitution or the Declaration of Independence; (2) there shall be no slavery or involuntary servitude other than for punishment of crimes, without the consent of the United States and the people of Nevada; (3) the Constitutional Convention must disclaim all rights to unappropriated lands in Nevada; (4) land owned by U.S. Citizens outside Nevada must not be discriminated against in taxation; and (5) there must be no taxation of federal property in the state.[17]

There were a great many areas of dispute among the delegates at the 1864 convention; some of the more interesting and significant included the naming of the state and the ever-present issue of mine taxation.[18] The convention as a whole supported the move to statehood but debated vigorously the state's name. Among the suggested appellations were Washoe, Humboldt, and Esmeralda, all of which had also been proposed at the 1863 convention, and Bullion, Oro Plata, and Sierra Plata. Because the territory's name was Nevada and the area was, therefore, known throughout the nation by that designation, and because the congressional Enabling Act had used that name, the convention agreed to call the new state Nevada. The delegates also agreed early in their proceedings to use the failed 1863 constitution as the basis for its new draft. Although some of the members had urged abandoning the rejected document and starting anew, utilizing the California Constitution as a base, it was agreed that the 1863 constitution "owed much of its substance to the California Constitution, [so] there was no point in starting all over again."[19] In addition, by using the 1863 document as a starting point the convention saved considerable time and expense, since several hundred copies of it were already in print.

A statistical analysis of twenty-eight significant issues voted upon in the 1864 convention has shown that, to no one's surprise, the delegates' voting behavior was much the same as it had been in the 1863 convention. The chief division among them came along "economic and geographical lines," particularly in regard to variations in voting between mining and agricultural/ranching interests. Given that all except Francis Proctor were members of the Union Party, party affiliation was "largely meaningless" in explaining any of the divisions among the delegates.[20]

The 1864 constitution differed in two major respects from its failed 1863 predecessor. On the divisive issue of mine taxation, the delegates had apparently learned their lesson. Delegates from the nonmining "cow counties" continued to support the language of the 1863 constitution that allowed for the taxation of mines at the same rate as other property. Their strong feelings on the question were generated by at least two complementary issues: equity and colonization. In regard to equity, the cow-county delegates thought it unfair that mines be taxed only on the basis of their net proceeds, as some had suggested, while all other types of property were taxed on their assessed value. George A. Nourse, an attorney from Washoe County, argued that if mines were to be taxed solely on their net proceeds, then the constitution should also provide that "farms, and saw-mills, and other property shall be taxed only on their net proceeds"; only then would there be "some degree of fairness."[21] In pursuing an exemption from taxation, the mining interests were clearly exhibiting one of history's oldest political axioms: additional costs are fine (in this case, the higher expenses of statehood)—as long as someone else picks up the check.

On the issue of colonization, resentment had festered for some time in Nevada over the fact that large, wealthy mining companies from California controlled most of the area's mineral wealth. The *Virginia City Territorial Enterprise*, for example, had editorialized in 1862 that "the interests of no parent country and colony could possibly be more closely united than are those of California and Nevada. The colony has untold wealth of gold and silver, and the mother country manages . . . to get it all as fast as it is dug out."[22] This resentment was echoed at the 1864 convention by A. J. Lockwood, a mechanic from Ormsby County, who noted, "I am in favor of taxing the mines, because I want to make those gentlemen who are rolling in wealth in San Francisco, pay something for the support of our government, for the support of our common schools, and for the support of our courts."[23] Indeed, even now, San Francisco is still referred to by some as the "city Nevada built."

At the other end of the spectrum were those who did not want the mines taxed at all. E. F. Dunne, a lawyer from mining-dominated Humboldt County, warned that a tax on mines would "encumber the mining interest, which shall destroy it, or thwart its development, and . . . strike a ruinous blow" to the state's other economic interests.[24] More explicitly, delegate Charles E. DeLong from Storey County threatened that "but for the mines, all your stores would be removed, your farms would dry up, and be abandoned, and your wagons would stop in the streets or be turned elsewhere."[25] In addition to their superior numbers at the convention and the ghost of the 1863 constitution's failure, the miners held one other important card: the legality of taxing mining property. As noted above, the Enabling Act passed by Congress prohibited the state's taxation of unappropriated public lands within Nevada. Convention president Johnson, a lawyer from Ormsby County, concluded that this provision of the Enabling Act rendered the state powerless to tax the mines, which were situated on unappropriated federal lands.

The mining-tax debate was a long, divisive one in the convention; several proposals were offered and rejected by both sides. The unlikely alliance of small miners, farmers, and disappointed office seekers who had defeated the 1863 constitution now fell apart, victim of its own internal disagreements.[26] Eventually, however, in order to prevent the total collapse of the convention, the delegates agreed by a vote of 23 to 10 to a compromise proposal stating that "the legislature shall provide by law for a uniform and equal rate of assessment and taxation, . . . excepting mines and mining claims, the proceeds of which alone shall be taxed."[27] It was left to the legislature to determine whether these taxable "proceeds" would be net or gross. The compromise was not without cost, however. The mining exemption from taxes marked a turning point in the convention; thereafter, the small miners, who had previously supported positions taken by the cow-county delegates, began voting uniformly on the side of the large mining interests.[28] At the end of the convention, the "odious and unjust discrimination between different kinds of property" led George A. Nourse and Israel Crawford, an editor from Ormsby County, to vote against the constitution.[29]

The second significant distinction between the 1864 constitution and its 1863 predecessor was in the election of the state's first officers. This time the constitutional ratification vote and the election for state officials would take place separately, the former on September 7 and the latter on November 8. Thus, in the 1864 ratification election the voters would be free to support statehood and the constitution without necessarily voting for a particular slate of candidates they might find unacceptable.

Support for the 1864 constitution was overwhelming. At the convention it received a positive vote of 19 to 2, and in the September 7 election it was decisively supported by a popular vote of 10,375 to 1,284, a margin of more than 8 to 1.[30] In its haste to admit Nevada as a state before the 1864 national elections, Congress, in the Enabling Act, waived the right to inspect and approve the constitution and allowed Nevada Territory to become a state upon acceptance of the constitution by President Lincoln. On October 17 the territorial government wired the entire text of the state constitution to the nation's capital at a cost of $3,416.77, making it the "longest and most expensive telegram ever dispatched in the United States up to that time."[31] Finding the constitution acceptable, on October 31, 1864, President Lincoln issued the proclamation making Nevada the thirty-sixth state in the Union.

Thus, in the course of approximately one year the residents of Nevada had made a complete turnaround from rejecting to accepting a state constitution. Clearly the 1864 convention's decisions to tax only the proceeds of the mines and to separate the ratification ballot from that for state officers are critical in explaining this reversal. Two other issues, however, bear brief mention here. The first of these was a mining depression that hit the territory hard in 1864. The 1864 mining depression had two effects on the acceptance of the 1864 constitution. The depression's impact upon the region's economy was so immense that six of the eight delegates at the convention who had also served in the 1863 convention and who had previously voted against the tax exemption for mining property supported it in 1864. With the mining economy now fallen upon hard times, the tax exemption compromise was more acceptable to them, since "concern over economic survival supplanted [their] fear of domination by outside interests."[32] In short, Nevadans had come to believe, accurately, that the day of the solitary miner was over and that mining could survive only with the infusion of capital from other places and the "corporatization" of what had previously been an individual labor. The California capital they had so feared and distrusted in 1863 had come to be seen as crucial to the mining industry's, and thus the state's, survival.[33] The depression also had the effect of strengthening statehood desires

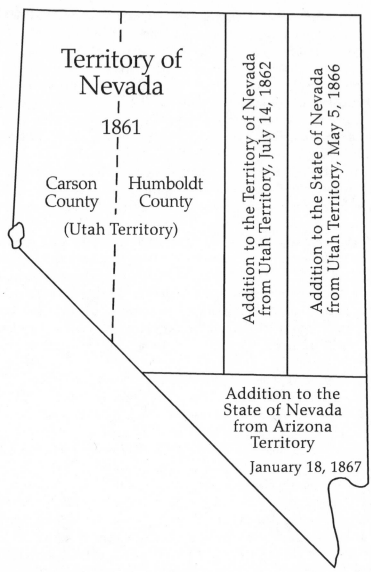

Map 2.1

Territory of Nevada formed in 1861 from Carson and Humboldt Counties of Utah Territory. In 1862 Nevada Territory enlarged by extension eastward one degree into Utah Territory. Enlarged Territory, and State as created in 1864, coextensive in size. Additional extension eastward one degree into Utah Territory in 1866 by State of Nevada. Extension south into Arizona Territory to the Colorado River by State of Nevada in 1867. Nevada Territory existed in two different sizes; Nevada as a state in three different sizes. *Source:* Frankie Sue Del Papa, *Political History of Nevada, 1990,* 9th ed. Reprinted with permission.

among the general populace. This sentiment was evidenced by an editorial in the *Territorial Enterprise:* "The only hope we have of effecting a speedy and absolute cure of our crushing ills is in the adoption of a state government. . . . Better to pay even double taxes, if by doing so we can make our property ten times more productively valuable, than to pay even less and let property continue to depreciate. . . . If we should have flush times again, we must vote for the State Constitution."[34]

The second issue, to be noted again in chapter 8, was the sad and disreputable state of the territorial judiciary. The residents of Nevada Territory were now as resolute in ridding themselves of the federally appointed territorial judiciary as they had been in 1858 in ridding themselves of the Mormon-dominated judiciary emanating from Utah. Indeed, DeLong noted at the 1864 convention that "many are going to vote for the Constitution in order that we may be released from the present judiciary system."[35] The territorial judges were accused of being corrupt and of worsening the mining depression by failing to move mining cases along quickly enough. Although the judges had behaved in a sometimes unprofessional manner, much of the opposition to them was politically motivated and engineered by William M. Stewart. As historian Hubert Howe Bancroft has noted:

> Probably the first federal judges would have been able to hold their own against the criminal element in Nevada; but opposed to the combined capital and legal talent of California and Nevada, as they sometimes were, in important mining suits, they were powerless. Statutes regarding the points at issue did not exist, and the questions involved were largely determined by the rules and regulations of mining districts, and the application of common law. Immense fees were paid to able and oftentimes unprincipled lawyers, and money lavished on suborned witnesses.[36]

Stewart could certainly be counted among the "unprincipled" lawyers to whom Bancroft referred. At a time when "cases were to be won through the bribing and browbeating of witnesses, juries, and justices," it has been observed, "Stewart had no equal on the [Comstock] lode."[37]

Stewart's attacks on the alleged corruption of the territorial judges disguised in a cloak of good government his continuing desire to control the state government and to remove from the bench his old enemy, John North. Stewart's dispute with North, which had begun over the mining-tax provision in the 1863 convention, had now reached a boiling point with Judge North's decisions in several mining cases that were adverse to the financial interests of Stewart's California clients.

On August 22, 1864, North and the other two territorial judges, Powhatan B. Locke and Chief Justice George Turner, resigned, giving (unwarranted) credence to Stewart's claims of corruption and bribe taking. That they did so was in no small part due to attacks upon them and a petition signed by more than 3,500 voters in Virginia City and Gold Hill demanding their resignations.[38] Stewart and his supporters took the opportunity to push for ratification of the constitution on the grounds that statehood would be the only remedy to ensure justice in the region. The *Nevada Transcript* editorialized, for instance, that "[Nevada] can never prosper while the judiciary is suspected. Capital will refuse to go there for investment unless at heavy premium for risk, and men of families will decline to make a spot for their homes where vice instead of virtue reigns."[39] Although there is no proof the three judges were corrupt, it is hard to imagine that the intense campaign impugning their integrity had no effect on those voting on the constitution slightly more than two weeks after their mass resignation. As Robert M. Clarke, Nevada's second attorney general, later observed, "Nevada became a state to escape the dead-fall of her Territorial courts. Her Temple of Justice had been transformed into a den of iniquity."[40]

After their territory became a state on October 31, Nevadans' first duty was to hold elections for state officials and for their representative to the U.S. House of Representatives (at that time, prior to the Seventeenth Amendment, U.S. senators were selected by the state legislatures). "Battle Born" and loyal to Lincoln and the Republicans who had given them the statehood they had desired, Nevada voters lived up to congressional expectations. Republicans won the presidential ballot, all executive and judicial seats, and all but two of the legislative contests. Republican H. G. Worthington was elected to the House, and when the legislature met in December, Republicans William Stewart and James Nye were selected as the state's first U.S. senators. All three federal representatives from Nevada voted in favor of the Thirteenth Amendment, and the state ratified it in 1865. They were not needed, however, to ensure Lincoln's reelection; the 1864 presidential and vice-presidential elections were not, as had been widely expected, thrown into the House and Senate, respectively. Thus, the state's first elections not only put Nevada firmly in the Republican fold but also began the domination of the state's politics for years to come by the victorious William M. Stewart.

The Nevada State Constitution

The State of Nevada continues to function under its 1864 constitution, although that document has been amended approximately 110 times since. Its contents are not particularly remarkable or unique, based as they are on the constitutions of California and New York. What does distinguish it most of all, perhaps, is that it is the culmination of a series of five "constitutions" proposed, sometimes ratified and sometimes rejected, that sought to govern the area. From the 1851 squatters' compact to the Cornwall Constitution of 1854, the ineffective constitution of 1859, and the rejected 1863 state constitution, Nevadans have shown an abiding interest in and respect for constitutional government. The 1864 constitution must, then, be seen as the successful product of those other attempts at constitution making and as the ultimate will of the state's people.

The Constitution of the State of Nevada consists of nineteen articles that perform the functions of all such documents: creation of an organized government, distribution of government power among its divisions, and the protection of individual rights from government infringement. Because the Tenth Amendment of the U.S. Constitution reserves to the states all powers not delegated to the federal government or prohibited by it to the states, state constitutions do not grant powers but seek to structure and limit those powers reserved to the states. Therefore, like the constitutions of the other forty-nine states, the Nevada Constitution tends to be longer and more specific than the federal Constitution, particularly in regard to express limitations on the power of the state. Daniel J. Elazar, the nation's most prominent scholar of federalism, cites Nevada's constitution as an example of the "Frame of Government" type of constitution, a type that is "found exclusively among the less populated states of the Far West" and characterized as a "business-like" document of moderate length reflecting "the relative homogeneity of the states themselves."[41]

In the chapters that follow, we shall examine various provisions of the state's constitution in more detail as they relate to particular topics in Nevada's post-1864 political history.

Chapter Three

Civil Rights and Liberties in Nevada

Civil rights are generally defined as those "positive acts of government designed to protect persons against arbitrary or discriminatory treatment by government or individuals."[1] Civil rights include those we deem necessary for equality to prevail among and between citizens: the right to vote, for example, and the right to equal employment and housing regardless of gender, race, color, creed, or religion. Civil liberties, on the other hand, refer to "negative restraints" upon the government in its exercise of power.[2] Included here would be those rights normally found in a bill of rights, such as the freedoms of speech, press, and religion. In this chapter we shall examine the past and present of Nevada's record on civil rights and liberties, a record that is at times sad and at other times cause for jubilation.

Civil Rights

Nevada, like most states, has a mixed and sometimes pitiful historical record in protecting the civil rights of its citizens. Indeed, for many years, the state was referred to as "the Mississippi of the West." Although that sobriquet was neither entirely justified nor entirely wrong, the state's treatment of minorities does not, unfortunately, always suggest the actions of an enlightened populace or government.

The roots of discrimination against ethnic, religious, and other minorities run deep in Nevada history. The Declaration of Rights that forms the first article of the Nevada Constitution states that "all men are by Nature free and equal and have certain inalienable rights." Yet even the men who wrote those words did not necessarily believe that they applied to *all* men, and most assuredly not to women. For example, delegates to the 1864 constitutional convention, the very convention at which those awe-inspiring words were written and adopted, also agreed upon Article II, which gave the right to vote to white males only. Indeed, Nelson E. Murdock, one of these delegates, noted during the convention's deliberations over the issue of voting rights that "I think the Anglo-Saxon, the Celtic, or any other of the White or Caucasian races, is a far superior race of men to the Indian, the Negro, or any of the colored races. . . . Why should we condescend to make any of the inferior races our equals?"[3] The irony of the convention's actions on the issue of voting rights in the face of both its previous high-sounding rhetoric and the fact that Nevada was born in the midst of a civil war over the issue of slavery apparently never occurred to the delegates.

Although politically incorrect by today's standards, Murdock's speech before the convention delegates represented nothing more than a continuation of the attitudes that had existed in the territory for some time. In one of its first acts, the Nevada Territorial Legislature, meeting in 1861, provided that "no black person, or mulatto, or Indian, or Chinese" would be allowed to give evidence in court either in favor of or against any white person, presumably because they were considered untrustworthy. Similarly, the legislature prohibited cohabitation with "Indians, Chinese, or negroes [sic]" and made a breach of that law punishable by either a fine or a jail term. Things were little better after the granting of statehood, when the state legislature amended the law to allow blacks, but not Indians or Chinese, to testify against a white person.

Native Americans

Although virtually all minorities in the United States have been discriminated against at one time or another, Native Americans have arguably been the only group targeted for genocide. As noted in chapter 1, prehistoric peoples entered the Great Basin as early as 12,000 years ago via a land bridge between Asia and North America at the present site of the Bering Strait near Alaska. Those who settled in present-day Nevada eventually came to be known as the Northern Paiutes (in northern and western Nevada), Southern Paiutes (in southern Nevada), Shoshones (in northern and eastern Nevada), and the Washos (in a small area of western Nevada).

One of the first encounters between these Native Americans and whites, as noted earlier, came in 1833, when at least thirty of them were killed by members of Joseph Walker's trapping party; unfortunately for the Indians, it would not be the last hostile meeting between the natives and the new immigrants. The influx of new settlers and treasure seekers to the Great Basin led to numerous conflicts with the various tribes. One of the most noteworthy was the Pyramid Lake War of 1860. That episode involved Bannock Indians who were temporarily staying at Pyramid Lake after leaving their homes farther north for the winter. The Bannocks killed either three or five whites (accounts differ) at Williams' Station after two Indian women had been kidnapped by the men and reportedly held in a cave near the station. In retaliation, more than one hundred white settlers moved, mistakenly, against the Northern Paiutes, who had, in fact, refused the Bannocks' invitation to join their raid on Williams' Station. Prepared for the assault they knew would come, the Paiutes, led by Chief Sequinata, also known as Chiquito ("Little") Winnemucca, killed seventy-nine whites and wounded another twenty-six before the defeated settlers-turned-militiamen returned to Carson City. More battles ensued, with the now-outnumbered Paiutes receiving the worst of it. The U.S. Army was called in to build a garrison at Fort Churchill, and thirteen military outposts were eventually established in Nevada to "control" the Native American population. The influx of troops and the coming of the railroad eventually made it clear to all that the Native Americans could not stop the increasing tide of white settlers and miners. Ultimately most of their land was taken and treaties with the federal government were routinely broken. In the 1870s, reservations were created to house these, Nevada's first inhabitants: the Pyramid Lake Reservation and the Walker River Reservation in 1874 for the Northern Paiutes, the Moapa Reservation in 1875 for the Southern Paiutes, and the Duck Valley Reservation in 1877 for the Shoshones.

During the period after white settlement in Nevada, Native Americans quickly became foreigners in their own land, the object of both social and legal discrimination. Through various laws, first the territory and then the state of Nevada prohibited the sale of alcohol, firearms, and ammunition to the Indians, prohibited intermarriage between the tribes and whites, controlled fishing on the Walker River Reservation, sought to diminish the size of reservations in order to secure prime timber property, and prohibited Indians from attending public schools. During this early period of Nevada's history, the Native Americans were exiled to live on the fringes of white society, performing unskilled labor. At one point, legislators went so far as to suggest that any Indians who could not be "subjugated" should be "exterminated."[4]

In the 1920s, Indian children were allowed to attend public schools, and in the 1940s Native Americans began to see somewhat better legislation as the state recognized the validity of Indian marriages, repealed laws prohibiting the sale of alcohol to Indians, and allowed the use of peyote in Native American religious ceremonies. In 1965 an Indian Affairs Commission was created by the legislature to study and make recommendations to the state government on issues relating to Nevada's Native American population.[5] At the federal level, Congress established the Indian Claims Commission in 1946 to place a monetary value on, and pay compensation to the tribes for, the lands taken. Although the amounts to be paid were in the millions of dollars, some tribes, most notably the Western Shoshone, refused the money; to this day, the Shoshone continue to press legal claims to approximately one-third of the land in Nevada.

The Chinese

Chinese immigrants began arriving in Nevada after 1849 for the same reason their white counterparts had come: to find wealth in the area's mines. Discrimination against them began almost immediately, and what the law could not accomplish, physical violence often did. Apparently not satisfied that the Chinese were prohibited by state statute from owning property, whites singled out Chinese miners as the subjects of frequent attack, and they were soon driven out of the industry and relegated to service occupations such as laundering and cooking.

The greatest increase in the Chinese population occurred from 1867 to 1869, during the construction of the Central Pacific Railroad across the state. Because they were willing to work hard in dangerous situations for little pay, the Chinese were prized workers for the railroads. However, in spite, or perhaps because, of this, they were despised by the local inhabitants, who saw them as a threat to their own livelihoods. Mining unions saw them as threats "to the union against the bosses" and "as tools of corporate monopolists."[6] They were excluded from union membership and thus were denied employment in the mines, which at that time were closed union shops. Discrimination against the Chinese was so intense that most left the state after the railroad's completion. Various federal acts in 1882, 1907, 1921, and 1924 established strict immigration quotas and regulations, slowing to a trickle any further Chinese emigration to the United States.

Although the Chinese were allowed after 1881 to give testimony in court against whites, jurors often disregarded that testimony. In a case tried in 1903, more than twenty Chinese witnesses testified to the guilt of five white men who had beaten and killed two elderly Chinese laundrymen in Tonopah's Chinatown. All five were acquitted.[7] Various anti-Chinese organizations were created in the state, including one in Virginia City that passed a resolution stating that "the presence of the Chinese in Nevada 'was injurious to the welfare of the State and a danger to the Republic.'"[8] And in one of the most blatant and egregious acts of violence against the Chinese, most of Reno's Chinatown, including private homes, was burned to the ground in 1908 by a mob acting upon the instructions of local officials.

Beginning in the 1940s, the federal government relaxed its laws limiting Chinese immigration to the United States. Employment prohibitions against the Chinese were repealed by the state legislature in 1959. In addition, as we shall see later, various antidiscrimination laws enacted by the federal and state governments in the 1960s and 1970s worked to free the Chinese, as well as other minorities, from much of the discrimination that had impeded their progress over the years.

African Americans

The existence of a sizable community of African Americans in Nevada is a relatively recent phenomenon. Even though African Americans lived in the state in the latter nineteenth and early twentieth centuries, their numbers were small. Fewer than 40 blacks lived in Las Vegas at the time of the 1910 census, and only 134 lived in the entire state at the turn of the century. African Americans in Nevada were discriminated against in various ways and never treated as full equals, but the worst discrimination against them did not begin in earnest until Nevada's black population began to rise in the 1930s and 1940s. In the early period of statehood, Nevadans, like the inhabitants of other western states, expressed a "paternalistic—if condescending—interest in the few blacks who migrated to [the] state."[9] Indeed, Nevada, as a Republican-dominated state, easily and eagerly ratified the Thirteenth and Fourteenth Amendments and was the first state to ratify the Fifteenth Amendment to the U.S. Constitution, which prohibited denial of the right to vote on the basis of race.

Discrimination against African Americans certainly existed from the beginning, with prohibitions on their testimony against whites and their exclusion from public schools. A significant number of African Americans came to the Las Vegas area in the 1930s and 1940s as a result of the federal government's construction of Hoover Dam and the creation of war-related industries and military bases. Perhaps because of the growing African-American population in the state at that time, discrimination against blacks began to increase in 1931 when the companies constructing the Hoover Dam near Las Vegas refused to hire them.

Unlike the southern states, where statutes existed mandating separate and unequal treatment for blacks, Nevada had no laws requiring segregation; nonetheless, African Americans found themselves increasingly discriminated against by private segregation in housing and employment. In addition to their relegation to only menial jobs, they were not allowed to gamble, eat, drink, or attend shows in casinos and restaurants; the state's business owners did not want to offend their white clientele, many of whom were Californians who had migrated west from the southern states. Indeed, African-American entertainers such as Sammy Davis Jr. and Lena Horne were not even allowed to stay in the hotels in which they played.

With the looming threat by NAACP leader Dr. James McMillan of massive demonstrations and sit-ins such as those that had occurred in the South, Las Vegas mayor Oran Gragson announced in March 1960 that segregation in public accommodations in the city would end; the businesses on the Strip, outside city limits, soon followed suit. The state's crisis in race relations, however, did not end there. A sit-in at Reno's Overland Hotel and demonstrations at various Reno casinos and the state capitol building in Carson City occurred in 1961 to protest unequal treatment and to support creation of a state Equal Rights Commission. In 1969 and 1970, several riots occurred at Las Vegas schools over the race issue.

Even though discrimination against and segregation of African Americans in Nevada was the result of private actions, the federal and state governments were forced to come to grips with the issue, just as they had in the states of the former Confederacy. The U.S. Congress responded by passing the Civil Rights Act of 1964, the Voting Rights Act of 1965, and the Fair Housing Act of 1968. In Nevada, the state legislature moved more slowly. At the urging of Governor Grant Sawyer, who had supported civil rights legislation since at least his election in 1958, the state legislature in 1965 passed a civil rights bill outlawing discrimination in public accommodations and employment on the basis of race, creed, national origin, or color (a prohibition on sex discrimination was not added to the law until 1971). Discrimination in employment did not end with the passage of civil rights legislation, however. Hotels and casinos continued to discriminate until 1971, when a consent decree was signed in Las Vegas in which the hotels and unions, without admitting that any discrimination had occurred, agreed not to engage in discriminatory practices.[10] Also in 1971, under the threat of federal court action and with the support of Governor Mike O'Callaghan, the state legislature finally passed a fair housing act ending residential segregation.

Much more recently, attention has focused on lending practices of the state's major banking institutions. A 1992 survey by the Las Vegas Alliance for Fair Banking found that only 59 of almost 11,000 loans for home purchases, refinancing, or improvements in the Las Vegas area went to the predominantly African-American Westside. Black families were denied loans 50 percent more often than white families with the same income. Even more significant was the study's finding that black families earning $41,000 per year were more likely to be rejected for home loans than were white families with incomes as low as $27,000. At this point, it is too soon to know whether or not the visibility and attention given to the issue will result in changes in the banks' lending practices.

Hispanics

To speak of Hispanics as a single group can be somewhat misleading; in fact, Hispanics trace their roots to any number of Spanish-speaking countries and territories, including Mexico, Puerto Rico, Cuba, and the various nations of Central and South America. It is important to bear in mind that these different groups often have disparate cultures, backgrounds, and political and social ideologies. Similarly, although some are new immigrants to the United States, others are native-born citizens whose families have lived in this country for many years. Some of the immigrants, such as the Cubans, have come to escape political oppression, while others, such as the Mexicans, have fled poverty and poor economies in their native homelands. Nonetheless, for purposes of simplicity, in this section we shall speak of Hispanics generally while observing those areas in which the various groups differ.

As noted in chapter 1, the Spanish and, later, Mexicans were the first nonnative explorers of the area now known as Nevada, although they did not settle here in large numbers. During the pre-statehood period of gold and silver mining, however, Hispanics were represented in large and important numbers; indeed, the Comstock mine was first discovered by Ignacio Paredes of Sonora, Mexico, who abandoned it prematurely. Miners from northern Mexico not only were responsible for the discovery of many of Nevada's ore sources but also taught Anglos the methods of panning, placer mining, dry digging, and ore reduction.[11] As was the case with other minorities on the western frontier, however, Hispanics were frequently treated as second-class citizens, receiving less pay than did their Anglo counterparts.

Hispanics began migrating to the state in large numbers in the 1860s for the same reasons that other groups did: opportunity. They worked in the mines, in service occupations, and as sheep and cattle ranchers. In this early period, most of Nevada's Hispanic population resided in the north. Hispanic migration into southern Nevada began in the early twentieth century with the construction of a railroad line between Los Angeles and Salt Lake City that passed through the Las Vegas Valley. Along with the Chinese, Mexican laborers performed much of the work on this and other railroads in the state. In the American Southwest as a whole, including Nevada, Mexicans made up 70 percent of the section crews and 90 percent of the extra gangs on the principal railroad lines.[12]

The most significant migration of Hispanics to the state began after World War II. Federal investment in the state in the form of capital and military expenditures brought Hispanics to Nevada in large numbers as construction workers and soldiers and to fill a number of other occupations. As had been the case with other minorities, however, these new residents frequently found themselves the victims of discrimination. In Las Vegas, for example, Hispanics, like African Americans, were concentrated on the Westside or in North Las Vegas as a result of restrictive covenants by white homeowners prohibiting the sale of property in most parts of Las Vegas to anyone other than whites.

Virtually all Hispanics residing in Nevada prior to the 1960s were of Mexican descent; that pattern changed somewhat with the communist revolution of Fidel Castro in Cuba. With casino experience derived from the gaming halls of Havana, many of these exiles settled in Nevada to continue the occupations they had known in their homeland. Many Hispanics from the East Coast, primarily Puerto Ricans, also began to migrate to the state during this period.[13] As had African Americans, Hispanics in the 1960s began to demand equality in housing, employment, and education. The changes noted above in the discussion of African Americans in Nevada apply equally to Hispanics in the state. Civil rights laws passed during the 1960s did much to make Nevada a more egalitarian state for all minorities.

Unlike African Americans, however, Hispanics have often been at odds with one another over even the most basic issues. As sociologist Jim Frey has noted,

> Cubans were class conscious and tended to look condescendingly at lower-class Mexicans and Chicanos, while some Chicanos viewed the Cubans as aggressive, arrogant, materialistic, overly rational, and motivated totally by self-interest and greed. These personality traits, combined with prior experience in Cuba's pre-Castro gaming and tourism, helped them to gain employment in highly paid positions in gaming and tourism. Mexicans and

Chicanos, on the other hand, continued to be relegated to low-paying jobs in the service industry, some blue collar positions, and general laborers.[14]

Although the 1980s and 1990s have seen unity among Hispanic groups on some issues, the community frequently remains divided. This division and the small percentages of Hispanics who register and vote have had the effect of marginalizing their political power even though they constitute the state's largest minority. By 1996, few public officeholders were of Hispanic origin.

Continued growth in the Hispanic population of Nevada, as well as the United States in general, is likely to continue for some time. As anthropologist Tony Miranda has noted, Hispanics are on average younger than most of the state's other residents, which means that they are approaching or have reached child-bearing age. Thus, as a natural consequence of birthrates, there will be more Hispanics in the state in the years to come. Also, Hispanic immigration is likely to continue as many Hispanics flee from California's faltering economy to Nevada's more robust one. Additionally, many Hispanics outside the United States who speak little English find Nevada's gaming and tourist economy one in which they can thrive in unskilled but relatively well paying jobs. Those who are bilingual can find higher paying jobs and are much in demand as Nevada markets itself to an increasingly international community.[15]

It should come as no surprise, therefore, to discover that while Hispanics made up 6.8 percent of the state's population in 1980 (54,130 out of 800,493), by 1990 their population was estimated at 10.4 percent (124,419 out of 1,201,833). That this trend will continue is undoubted; what remains to be seen, however, is whether these numbers will translate into increased economic and political power for Hispanics as they have in California, Arizona, and other southwestern states.

Other Minorities

As in most other states, discrimination was applied in Nevada to virtually all minorities, in addition to those already discussed. It was noted earlier that women were not allowed to vote under the 1864 constitution. Unlike the state's lag in guaranteeing equal rights for racial minorities, however, Nevada was among the first to grant women the right of suffrage. Whereas the Nineteenth Amendment to the U.S. Constitution granting women the right to vote was not added until 1920, women in Nevada had had suffrage rights since 1914. Women's success in Nevada, at least on this issue, was due in no small part to the efforts of the untiring Anne Martin, president of the Equal Franchise Society in Nevada.

Economically, however, the struggle for equal rights for women was a different matter. Although women were sometimes employed in the lucrative fields of dealing and bartending in northern Nevada casinos, that was not true in southern Nevada. Indeed, the Las Vegas City Commission recommended as late as 1958 that women not be hired as dealers for fear that their lower salaries would undercut the men; only one of the city's many dealers' schools would even permit women to enroll. In 1959 the North Las Vegas City Council prohibited women from being hired as bartenders. Instead, women were more often to be found in the lower paying jobs of waitress, cashier, and keno runner. Only a few southern Nevada casinos would hire women as dealers and bartenders. It was not until 1981 that Las Vegas's casinos and unions signed an agreement to end discrimination against women in employment-related matters.[16]

Nevada is also noteworthy as one of only 15 states that failed to ratify the proposed Equal Rights Amendment to the federal Constitution. Proposals to ratify the ERA were defeated in the state senate in 1973 and 1975 and in the state assembly in 1977. Wishing to avoid the heat and controversy created by the ERA issue, the legislature washed its hands of the affair and submitted the ratification issue to the voters. After heavy lobbying against the proposal by conservative women, some business interests, and the Mormon Church, the measure failed in a 1978 election by a 2 to 1 margin.

The changes wrought by the state's 1965 civil rights legislation worked to the benefit of all minorities in the state, not only African Americans. Asians, Native Americans, and Hispanics likewise have benefited from its liberalization of employment, public accommodations, and housing. One group, however, that remains excluded from state civil rights legislation is Nevada's estimated 100,000 homosexuals. These individuals are not covered by federal or Nevada law and are often discriminated against for the sole reason of their sexual orientation; they may be, and are, fired from their jobs and refused rental and service simply on that basis. However, in 1989 and 1993, respectively, the state legislature added sexual orientation to the state's hate crimes statute and repealed Nevada's antisodomy law, a law aimed specifically at the state's homosexual minority.

Civil Liberties

As noted at the beginning of this chapter, civil liberties are those "negative restraints" upon government that define what it cannot do to its citizens. In general, these liberties are of the type found in the U.S. Constitution's Bill of Rights: freedom of speech, freedom of the press, freedom of assembly, the rights to counsel and a jury trial, and so on. In 1833, however, the U.S. Supreme Court held in the landmark case *Barron v. Baltimore* that none of the twenty-three provisions in the Bill of Rights applied to the states.[17] That is, although the Bill of Rights prohibited the federal government from engaging in any of these violations of civil liberties, the state governments were not bound in any way by these provisions. Thus, the only protections that an individual had from the state government were those in his or her own state constitution's bill of rights.

In light of that, the framers of Nevada's 1864 constitution included as the document's first article a Declaration of Rights to protect the state's citizens from an overzealous state government. Included within Article I are the standard civil liberties protections we have come to know in the United States: freedom of speech, press, and assembly; trial by jury; religious freedom; *habeas corpus;* a prohibition on excessive fines and bails, cruel and unusual punishment, bills of attainder, ex post facto laws, unreasonable searches and seizures, and double jeopardy; and the right to just compensation for property taken by the government through its power of eminent domain.

The Nevada Constitution's Declaration of Rights was far more significant in 1864 than it is today. At that time, it constituted the sole protection the state's citizens had against intrusions into civil liberties by the state government. However, in a series of cases from the 1920s through 1969, the U.S. Supreme Court, in a process known as incorporation, held that virtually all of the provisions in the U.S. Bill of Rights apply to the states via the due process clause of the Fourteenth Amendment. Thus, today the state governments are held to the same federal constitutional standards as the federal government has always been; even if Nevada's Declaration of Rights did not exist, Nevadans would now be protected in their civil liberties from both federal and state intrusion by the U.S. Constitution's Bill of Rights.

The process of incorporation, however, does not render state bills of rights obsolete. In some states (California, Oregon, Washington, and Hawaii), state courts have held that their state bills of rights grant civil liberties protections to their citizens even greater than those in the U.S. Constitution. The Nevada courts, however, have not followed the lead of their western counterparts and have traditionally interpreted civil liberties protections in the state's Declaration of Rights to be parallel to similar clauses in the federal Bill of Rights. For that reason, any student familiar with the rights embodied in the Bill of Rights will also be knowledgeable about the rights protected by Nevada's Declaration of Rights. Nonetheless, there are a few areas in which the Declaration of Rights differs from the Bill of Rights, and they are worth discussing.

Although juries in both civil and criminal trials at the federal level must be unanimous, that is not the case in Nevada. Article I, Section 3, of the Nevada Constitution allows a jury in civil cases to reach a decision by a three-fourths vote of its members (nine of twelve jurors). The rationale for what at the time was a departure from tradition and practice in the country can be found in Nevada's unfortunate history with juries during the territorial period. During that period many a jury was unable to reach a unanimous verdict, and civil cases often ended in a mistrial with a split vote (a hung jury)—the result of the bribing of at least one juror by the mining companies that stood to win or lose fortunes, depending upon the verdict. Apparently believing that it was more difficult to bribe four jurors than one, the framers of the constitution, over the objections of the cow-county delegates, agreed upon the three-fourths requirement. Like their federal counterparts, however, juries in criminal cases in Nevada have always been required to reach unanimous verdicts.

A second distinction in the Declaration of Rights can be found in the guarantee, in Article I, Section 11, of the right to keep and bear arms. The U.S. Constitution's Second Amendment guaranteeing the right to keep and bear arms is one of the few provisions in the Bill of Rights that has not been incorporated and applied to the states. Consequently, although the federal government may not infringe upon this right, the states are free to do so. Thus, in the face of increased calls for gun control across the country, Nevada's voters added a provision to the state constitution in 1982 guaranteeing the right to keep and bear arms.

One last distinction between the two constitutions is in the area of eminent domain. The Nevada Constitution, like the federal Constitution, allows the government to take private property for government use if it provides "just compensation" to the property owner. Unlike the U.S. Constitution, however, the Nevada Constitution requires that the compensation be made *prior* to the taking unless the property owner waives that right.

Chapter Four

Political Parties and Elections

Nevada has traditionally been a competitive, two-party state in which elections are fought more on the basis of personalities and issues than parties. Nevadans are notorious ticket-splitters who take pride in the fact that they vote for the "person" and not the "party." Nonetheless, it is possible to divide Nevada's political history into five distinct periods of voting patterns.[1]

From the granting of statehood in 1864 until 1890, the Republicans dominated the state's elections. That they did so is chiefly explained by the support of the national Republican Party for Nevada statehood and the lingering effects of the Civil War, which had been fought against the Democratic-dominated, pro-slavery states of the South. As noted in chapter 2, all of Nevada's state and federal officers selected in 1864, with the exception of two legislators, were Republicans. Of the elections held during the twenty-six years of this period, Republicans won six of seven presidential races, eight of ten for the U.S. Senate, ten of thirteen for the House, four of seven for governor and lieutenant governor, seven of seven for secretary of state, five of seven for state treasurer, seven of seven for state controller, and five of seven for attorney general.

During the second period, 1892 to 1906, the state's voters turned to the Silver Party for leadership. During that time, the national issue of free coinage of silver dominated the politics of Nevada and the other western mining states. In the first two elections of this period, the Silver Party won all but two statewide positions.[2] In 1896 the Silver Party joined with the Democrats to become the Silver-Democrats and dominated the state's political landscape until 1908.

Between 1908 and 1930, electoral victories in the state were roughly equal between the Democrats and Republicans, with the Democrats winning more positions but the Republicans winning the top spots at the presidential, congressional, and gubernatorial levels. The fourth period of electoral dominance began in 1932 with the election of Franklin D. Roosevelt to the presidency. From 1932 until the mid-1980s, Democrats tended to dominate state politics with an overwhelming number of registrants and control of the legislature and most of the six executive offices.

In the 1980s the Republican Party began a resurgence in the state that has lasted into the 1990s. During this fifth period, no one party has dominated the state's elections. As of 1996, for instance, elective positions in the state were fairly evenly divided; two of the six executive officers were Democrats, both members

Table 4.1

Voter Registration in Nevada by Party in Presidential Election Years, 1960–1995

Year	Democrats	Republicans	Other*	Total	Percent Democrats
1960	81,682	41,357	5,858	128,897	63.4
1964	104,630	50,462	8,383	163,475	64.0
1968	111,390	65,302	12,119	188,811	58.9
1972	133,278	80,199	17,568	231,045	57.6
1976	149,397	83,374	18,182	250,953	59.5
1980	158,617	115,182	23,519	297,318	53.3
1984	184,199	146,553	25,632	356,384	51.7
1988	209,048	188,571	47,314	444,933	47.0
1992	295,111	255,897	98,905	649,913	45.4
1995**	270,861	271,716	98,151	640,728	42.3

Source: Secretary of State's Office.
*The "Other" category includes independent (nonpartisan) voters and those registered in minority parties (e.g., Libertarian, American Independent).
**1995 figures are from October 1995.

of the U.S. House were Republicans, both U.S. Senators were Democrats, the 1995 state senate was majority Republican, and the state assembly was evenly split between the two parties. The resurrection of the Republicans in the state to the point that they have become competitive with the previously dominant Democrats is due to several factors: increased voter registration activity by the Republicans, the popularity of Ronald Reagan, and the recent pattern of migration by upper-middle- and upper-class retirees to the state. By the end of 1995, Republican registrants had overtaken Democrats for the first time since 1930: 42.4 percent of the voters were registered as Republicans (up from 33 percent in 1976), 42.3 percent were registered Democrats (down from 60 percent in 1976), and the remaining 15.3 percent were either nonpartisan (independent) or members of a minority party such as the Libertarians (see Table 4.1).

One of the most interesting facets of Nevadans' voting patterns is their almost unerring ability to vote for the winner in presidential elections. Of the thirty-three presidential elections in which Nevadans have participated between 1864 and 1992, the state voted for the winning candidate twenty-seven times; of the six instances in which Nevadans voted for the losing candidate, they had supported the free-silver crusader William Jennings Bryan three times (1896, 1900, 1908) and had one time (1892) voted for the candidate of the People's Party, who had been endorsed by the Silver Party. Since 1908 the state has voted for the eventual winner in all presidential elections except in 1976, when Nevadans voted for the Republican ticket of Gerald Ford and Robert Dole instead of Democrats Jimmy Carter and Walter Mondale. Thus, in the twenty-one presidential elections between 1912 and 1992, Nevadans have gone with the winner in twenty instances. Perhaps those figures indicate that Nevada is much more like the rest of the country than we have traditionally wanted to believe.

Political Parties

Political parties in the United States have traditionally been much weaker than those in other parts of the world. That is particularly true in Nevada, where political-party labels have little meaning. Democrats and Republicans in the state tend to be rather conservative, and there exist few in either party who would describe themselves as liberal, much less radical. Nonetheless, it is possible to say that, *as a general rule,* Democrats are more supportive of education and labor issues, while Republicans support business and the conservative social agenda to a greater degree.

European political parties are "responsible" parties. That is, members of the party, once elected to office, are expected to support the party platform, defer from publicly criticizing party leaders, and vote with their party on each issue that may come forward. Failure to do so could lead to drastic consequences, including the loss of one's position. In Nevada, and in the United States generally, elected officials win or lose based on their own personalities and stands on the issues, regardless of party affiliation. The parties have few measures available to discipline errant members and have little ability to keep them off the ballot. Candidates raise their own campaign funds, run their own campaigns, and owe little to the party with which they are nominally affiliated.

The chief function of political parties in Nevada and elsewhere is to select candidates to run in a general election against an opponent from the other party. Prior to the election of 1910, the method of selecting candidates was a generally close-knit affair. Members of the party would gather in precinct meetings to select delegates to county party conventions that in turn would select a smaller number of delegates to a state party convention. Party nominees would then be chosen by the state convention of each party. Typically, only a few party activists would participate in such meetings, leaving the vast number of voters out of the process. In 1909, the state legislature adopted a direct primary law mandating that parties select their candidates in primary elections held in September of each year in which a general election is to be held. Primary elections give the average party member more control over who his or her party's nominees will be than did the old system. At the same time, however, primaries have reduced whatever hold the party's leadership may have once exercised on its party's slate of nominees; candidates now rely upon the voters, not the party elite who attend the precinct meetings and party conventions, for their place on the general election ballot.

Elections in Nevada

Eligibility to Vote

As it was originally ratified in 1864, the state constitution allowed only white males of the age of twenty-one or older to vote. Even though Nevada was the first state to ratify the Fifteenth Amendment to the U.S. Constitution (1870) prohibiting the denial of the right to vote on account of race, the word *white* was not removed from this part of the state constitution until 1880. In 1914, six years before the Nineteenth Amendment to the U.S. Constitution gave women the right to vote, Nevadans amended their state constitution to extend the right of suffrage to them; nonetheless, Nevada was one of the last western states to do so. In 1971, the state's voters barely approved a referendum to ratify the Twenty-sixth Amendment to reduce the voting age across the nation to eighteen.

Today, the chief requirements one must meet in order to vote in the state are age, residency, and registration. In addition to the minimum age of eighteen, one must be a U.S. citizen and have resided in the state for at least thirty days. Actually, the state constitution requires a six-month residency period, but when the U.S. Supreme Court declared such lengthy residency requirements unconstitutional in 1972, that provision became unenforceable. The state legislature subsequently adopted the thirty-day requirement; but for reasons unexplainable, the voters refused in 1976 to amend the constitution with parallel language. The state legislature has also adopted registration provisions requiring one to register in order to vote. One may register as a member of a political party or as an independent, or nonpartisan.

Specifically excluded by the constitution from voting are those who have been judged "idiot" or "insane" and those who have been found guilty of treason or a felony, unless they have had their civil rights restored. The 1864 constitution also prohibited anyone who had borne arms against the United States or who had served in an office of the Confederacy from voting. That the framers included this provision is not surprising, given the state's entrance into the Union during the Civil War. This prohibition was removed by constitutional amendment in 1914 at the same time that suffrage was extended to women.

The 1864 constitution also provided for payment of a poll tax in order to vote. All males between the ages of twenty-one and sixty, "uncivilized American Indians excepted," were required to pay the tax. White males had to pay the tax in order to vote; minorities were also required to pay the tax even though they were not allowed to vote. In 1910 that section of Article II was amended to remove the connection between paying the tax and voting, and the proceeds of the poll tax were earmarked for public roads. In 1966, the entire poll tax provision was eliminated by an amendment to the state constitution.

Today anyone may vote who is at least eighteen years of age, a U.S. citizen, a resident of the state for at least thirty days, registered to vote, and neither insane nor a felon.

Primary Elections

The Direct Primary Law of 1909, as noted earlier, opened the process of candidate selection to the average party member, who could now simply show up at the ballot booth and cast a vote within a few minutes rather than attend a lengthy precinct meeting or party convention. The law also provided, four years before ratification of the Seventeenth Amendment to the U.S. Constitution, that party nominees for U.S. Senate seats would also be selected in the primary.

State primary elections in Nevada occur on the Tuesday following the second Monday in September of even-numbered years. It is here that each party will select its nominees to run in the November general election. Nevada primaries are "closed," which means that only those who are registered to vote in a particular party may vote in that party's primary election. Republicans and Democrats cannot cross over to vote in the other party's primary election, and independent voters cannot vote in party primaries at all, although they can vote in primary elections for nonpartisan seats such as the supreme court.

Prior to 1993, the two candidates winning the most votes in a nonpartisan primary election would go on to run against one another in the general election regardless of the number of votes each received. A law passed by the 1993 legislature now mandates that in such primaries, should any single candidate win a majority of the vote, he or she would be declared the winner of the seat with no further need to run in the general election.

In the November general election, the candidate who wins the most votes (a plurality) is declared the winner, regardless of whether he or she actually receives a majority. Thus, unlike some other states, particularly those in the South, Nevada does not have run-off elections when no one receives a majority of the vote in the general election.

Prior to the presidential election of 1976, Nevada's delegates to the national parties' presidential conventions were selected in the traditional manner of precinct meeting, county convention, and state convention, as discussed earlier. However, in 1973 the legislature approved a law allowing the parties to hold presidential primaries for the purpose of choosing each party's delegation to the national conventions. That process was followed in the 1976 and 1980 elections for president. In 1981, however, the legislature rescinded that legislation, and national party convention delegates in 1984, 1988, and 1992 were once again selected by state party conventions. The 1995 legislature approved a compromise proposal allowing each party to decide whether it would use presidential primaries or state conventions to choose delegates to represent the state at future national conventions. Should a party choose the presidential primary option, it may also determine whether to allow only party members to vote or to open the election to independent voters. Unlike the 1973 statute, the 1995 version attempts to cut costs by mandating the use of mail-in ballots in presidential primaries rather than opening the polls. Most observers predict that the experience of 1996 will become the pattern: parties with an incumbent president will adhere to the state convention method, while the challenging party will use the mail-in primary method.

One of the unique aspects of Nevada elections is the availability of the "none of these candidates" option. In both primary and general elections for statewide offices (e.g., governor, U.S. Senate) the voter may choose to vote for one of the candidates or for none of them. Thus, rather than simply not voting in a particular race, voters can now show their dissatisfaction with the slate by voting for "none of these candidates." Even if the "none" option receives the most votes, as occurred in the 1976 Republican primary for Congress, the actual candidate who receives more votes than his or her opponent(s) is declared the winner.

Campaign Finance

In 1974, Congress passed the Federal Election Campaign Act, which limits individual donations to no more than $1,000 per year to any candidate for federal office; all donations of $100 or more must be reported to the Federal Election Commission. These regulations apply to all candidates running in U.S. Senate or House elections in Nevada.

In 1975, the Nevada Legislature followed suit and passed limitations on spending in state races and required candidates to disclose the sources of contributions. Following the lead of the U.S. Supreme Court,[3] the Nevada Supreme Court upheld the disclosure requirement but declared the spending limitations to be unconstitutional as a violation of freedom of speech.[4] The 1977 and 1991 legislatures amended the statute, and state law today requires the disclosure of the source of any contribution of $500 or more. Individuals may contribute up to $10,000 to a candidate for statewide office and up to $2,000 to a candidate for local office. Groups are limited to $20,000 and $10,000, respectively.

Although the state's campaign finance laws are designed to inform the voters of the source of a candidate's campaign funds and to prohibit any single person or individual from having too much influence in the election process, they have been criticized by proponents of more openness in government. Under current law, contributors of $499 or less to individual candidates do not have to be identified. Further, political parties and their caucuses are not required to disclose the source of any donation, no matter how large. These groups are then able to "bundle" these contributions and give an unlimited amount to their party's candidates without disclosing to whom it was given. The secretary of state has estimated that the sources of only $2 million out of more than $5 million donated to candidates and parties in the 1994 legislative campaigns were required to be disclosed. The Senate Republican Leadership Conference, for example, received almost $400,000 in donations from individuals and groups; neither the donors' names nor the names of the candidates receiving funds from the SRLC were required to be made public. To no one's surprise, the parties and caucuses are seen by many individuals and corporations as an effective method for hiding the source and amount of their contributions to candidates. For example, in the 1994 legislative elections, four of the top five contributors were the Senate Republican Leadership Conference (#1), the Senate Democratic Caucus (#2), the Republican Assembly Caucus (#3), and the Assembly Democratic Caucus (#5). The fourth-ranked contributor was BizPAC, the political action committee of the Las Vegas Chamber of Commerce.[5]

Campaign finance was a major issue in the 1995 legislature when Secretary of State Dean Heller's proposals for reform were defeated by his Republican brethren in the state senate. Heller's proposals, which died in the final hours of the session, would have reduced a candidate's disclosure threshold to $100, required political parties and their caucuses to identify the sources of contributions of $100 or more, and limited parties and their caucuses to the same $20,000 and $10,000 donation limits that currently apply to other groups.

Direct Democracy Elections

In the late nineteenth and early twentieth centuries, the United States, especially the western states, was swept up in a wave of reform and a move toward greater democratic participation by the individual in government. The Progressive Era, as this period was known, resulted in the direct primary and civil service reform. It also led to the creation in Nevada and elsewhere of three special types of elections: initiative, referendum, and recall. The three are generally referred to as "direct democracy" elections. They allow the voters to bypass the legislature and directly initiate and approve laws and constitutional amendments, approve or reject laws passed by the legislature, and remove elected officials prior to the expiration of their terms.

Initiative

The state constitution's provisions on initiative were added in 1912 and have been amended seven times over the intervening years. Prior to that time, only the legislature could enact laws and propose constitutional amendments. The initiative allows the citizens of the state to propose and enact constitutional amendments and legislation, independent of the legislature.

In order to propose a statute or constitutional amendment through the initiative process, a petition must be signed by 10 percent of the number of those who voted in the previous general election, and the signatures must be gathered in 75 percent or more of the state's counties. Since Nevada now has seventeen counties, a petition must receive the signatures of 10 percent of the voters from at least thirteen counties who voted in the previous general election. This requirement prohibits the state's two most populous counties (Clark and Washoe) from putting an initiative on the ballot without the support of at least eleven other counties. The total number of signatures on the petition must also be equal to at least 10 percent of those in the entire state who voted in the previous general election.

If the initiative petition proposes a *statute*, the proposed legislation goes to the next session of the legislature, which then has forty days to act. If the legislature approves and the governor signs, the proposed statute becomes law. If the legislature or governor disapproves or does nothing, the proposal goes on the next general election ballot for approval or disapproval by the voters. If the voters approve, the measure becomes law and cannot be changed by the legislature for at least three years. Should the legislature wish, it has authority to propose an alternative measure that would go on the same general election ballot as the initiative proposal. Should both measures pass, the one winning the most affirmative votes would become law.

If the initiative petition proposes a *constitutional amendment,* the proposal does not go to the legislature. Instead it must be put directly on the ballot and must be approved by a simple majority at the next two general elections. Should the measure fail to pass either election, it is defeated.

Referendum

The referendum process was added to the state constitution in the election of 1904 and has been amended twice since then. The referendum allows voters to approve or disapprove any law passed by the legislature. A law may be referred to the voters by the legislature itself, or the voters may demand a referendum election by petition. A referendum petition requires the signatures of at least 10 percent of the number of voters who participated in the state's last general election. Unlike the initiative petition, these signatories are not required to be dispersed among several counties.

Should the appropriate number of signatures be acquired, the law in question is put on the ballot for a vote by the people. If the law is supported by a simple majority, it remains on the statute books; if it is not, the law is repealed and no longer in effect. A law that is approved by a referendum initiated by the voters cannot be repealed or amended by the legislature; it can be changed or repealed only through another direct vote of the people. This fact led pro-choice forces in Nevada to refer the state's abortion statutes to a vote of the people in 1990. These statutes, generally along the guidelines approved by the U.S. Supreme Court in *Roe v. Wade,*[6] were approved. Therefore, even if the Supreme Court were to some-day overturn *Roe,* pro-life forces could not repeal or change the state's abortion laws without another time-consuming and costly referendum election. This im-munity from legislative change, however, applies only in those cases where the referendum has been called by petition; laws approved through legislatively man-dated referendum elections can be amended or repealed by the legislature at its discretion.

Recall

State constitutional provisions on recall were added in 1912. Recall allows the voters to remove any state or local, but not federal, official from office prior to the expiration of his or her term. No statewide official has ever been recalled in Ne-vada, and the process has generally been unsuccessful at the local level as well. Only seven local officials have been successfully recalled in the state, most re-cently in 1984, when the voters of Storey County removed their district attorney. In 1995, Lincoln County commissioner Eve Culverwell survived a recall vote that had been called to protest her vote in favor of a resolution supporting the location of a nuclear waste dump near the town of Elgin.

Recall elections can be held only after a petition seeking recall has been signed by 25 percent of the number of voters who voted in the last general election in that unit of government (e.g., state, county, district, township, city). If, for ex-ample, the governor or a supreme court justice is the target of the recall, the appropriate number of signatures is based on the number of voters in the previ-ous general election for the entire state; should a mayor be the target, the number of signatures necessary is based on the number of voters in the previous general election for that city or town.

Once the required number of signatures has been obtained, the official has five days to resign. If he or she refuses to do so, a recall election is held within twenty days. At that election, both sides have the opportunity to state their case on the ballot. Other candidates may run against the targeted official, and the candidate winning the most votes serves the remainder of the term. Should no other candi-dates file, the voters simply vote to recall or not to recall. If the official is recalled, the seat is declared vacant and is filled as for any other midterm vacancy.

Officeholders are protected by the constitution from harassment by their losing campaign opponents and their opponents' supporters in two ways. First, the official must have been in office for at least six months before being subject to a recall. The sole exception is for members of the legislature, who may be recalled after ten days from taking office. Second, those wishing to promote a second recall effort against an official must first pay the costs of the first recall election.

Constitutional Amendment and Revision

There are two ways to amend the state constitution: initiative and legislative proposal. The initiative process, discussed previously, has been available for amending the constitution only since 1912. Prior to 1912, the sole method for amending the constitution was by legislative proposal; that process still exists today. The legislative proposal method of amending the constitution is a multi-step process requiring (1) the approval of a proposed constitutional amendment by two consecutive sessions of the legislature and (2) ratification by the voters at an election. Just as is the case with other legislation, the proposal must be passed by a majority of the total membership of each house and not simply a majority of those present. In the ratifying election, a simple majority of those voting on the amendment is needed to formally add the amendment to the constitution.

There is also a provision in the state constitution (Article XVI) allowing for its revision, that is, for writing an entirely new constitution rather than simply adding amendments. There have been four attempts, all occurring in the late nineteenth century, to revise the constitution; none were successful. Not surprisingly, the process of revision is more difficult than that for mere amendment. A convention to revise the constitution can be called only with the approval of two-thirds of the total membership of each house of the legislature and a majority of the voters at a general election. If the voters give their approval, the convention must occur within six months of the election. The number of delegates to the convention cannot be less than the total number of legislators in both houses of the legislature (currently sixty-three). There is no provision in the state constitution for selecting these convention delegates; presumably those details would be included in the legislature's proposal to call a convention.

Also not included in the revision provisions of the state constitution is a requirement that the proposed constitution coming out of the convention be ratified by the voters. The issue was not discussed at the 1864 constitutional convention. However, since the Enabling Act allowing Nevada to form a state required a ratification vote on the 1864 constitution, it is probable that the revised constitution would have to be approved by the state's voters if, as required by the U.S. Constitution, the state is to have a "republican" form of government. Furthermore, it would be strange indeed for a constitutional amendment to require voter ratification, while an entirely new constitution would not.

Chapter Five

Interest Groups and Lobbying

Introduction

While political parties are concerned with ensuring that their members are elected to various governmental positions, interest groups are more interested in seeing that the policies they favor are enacted into law, regardless of which party controls the government. Thus, parties tend to be more personnel oriented, while interest groups are more issue oriented. Of course, those lines are often blurred by the fact that some interest groups are more likely to support one party over another, since that party and its members are, in turn, more likely to favor a group's interests than is the other party (e.g., mining and ranching interests are likely to find that working with Republicans is easier for them than attempting to persuade Democrats, who are more often sympathetic to environmental causes). The decline in the importance of political parties in the United States that was noted in chapter 4 has been accompanied by a rise in the power of interest groups. A study of Nevada politics and history, therefore, would not be complete without an examination of the interest groups that have affected the state since its inception.

Political scientist Don W. Driggs has argued that the dominance of various interest groups in the state has changed over time.[1] Not unexpectedly, the first fifty years of statehood found railroad and mining interests dominating the political landscape. Chief among the lobbyists for those groups were Charles "Black" Wallace of the Central Pacific Railroad and various agents of the big California banks (the "Bank Crowd") that owned the most lucrative mines in the state. In addition to using the usual forms of political activity, Wallace and his counterpart with the Virginia and Truckee (V & T) Railroad, H. M. Yerington, ensured their success through bribery, vote buying, and intimidation (see chapter 11).

For the next fifty years, from roughly 1908 to 1958, the chief forces in the state were those representing Nevada's powerful political machines. From 1908 until he lost most of his wealth in the depression, George Wingfield controlled the state's politics through a bipartisan, but predominantly Republican, machine. He was replaced by the machine of Senator Pat McCarran, a Democrat, and his allies, John Mueller and Norman Biltz. The McCarran-Mueller-Biltz machine was dominant until McCarran's death in 1954, when he was replaced by E. L. Cord, inventor of the Cord automobile. The Cord-Mueller-Biltz machine, however, suffered a staggering blow in 1958 when Grant Sawyer defeated the machine's candidate for governor. Driggs notes that Sawyer's 1958 victory spelled the end of machine politics in the state.

Since that time, no one group has dominated the state's politics in the way that the railroads and the Bank Crowd had done. That is not to say, however, that some groups and individuals are not more successful than others. Since 1958, three groups in particular, two organized and one not, have been highly successful in influencing state politics. Not surprisingly, gaming interests have been extremely powerful in the state. As the state's chief industry and primary campaign contributor, gaming has been extraordinarily successful in getting its preferred candidates elected to office in large numbers. Although they do not have the financial resources of the gaming industry, the various state teachers' organizations have also been successful in obtaining their goals in Nevada. The teachers' unions are unable to contribute monetarily to campaigns to the same degree as gaming; however, they have thousands of volunteers at their disposal to walk districts, stuff envelopes, and engage in other forms of campaigning that candidates depend upon to win elections.

Unorganized but still highly effective have been the media power brokers in the state. Through their endorsements and decisions over what stories to run in their newspapers and on their television and radio stations, these individuals have shaped the state's politics in significant ways. Jack McCloskey of the *Mineral County Independent,* Walter Cox of the *Mason County News,* Hank Greenspun and Mike O'Callaghan of the *Las Vegas Sun,* and Donald Reynolds of the *Las Vegas Review-Journal* have certainly had a great influence on the state. Indeed, O'Callaghan's columns on the 300 percent pension increase that legislators gave themselves in 1989 and the public outcry that resulted are partly responsible, along with television editorials by Las Vegas newsman George Knapp and the actions of Common Cause of Nevada, for the legislature's repeal of the provision in a special session later that year. Whether the media will continue to have the same degree of influence since the deaths of media giants Greenspun and Reynolds remains to be seen. However, it is likely that as the state grows and voters become more removed from direct contact with state government officials in the years to come, the influence of the media will become even more significant. This would seem to be particularly likely in the area of the electronic media, which most citizens rely upon for news and information.

Lobbying in Nevada

Interest groups and the lobbyists who work for them have a wide array of tools at their disposal with which to affect governmental policy. They may provide campaign contributions to candidates they favor, testify for or against bills at the legislature, seek to persuade executive-branch officials to adopt or reject certain rules and regulations, encourage writing campaigns to officeholders, organize protest marches, endorse candidates, or attempt to influence the appointment of judges and other officials who are outside the electoral arena. The appropriateness of a particular method in a given situation will depend upon the goals to be achieved, the interest group's available resources, and the venue in which the lobbying takes place.

Interest groups attempt to influence officials at all levels and in all branches of state government. At the executive level they will, for instance, contribute to and campaign for favored candidates and lobby executive branch officials, both elected and appointed, to enact regulations and rules that they favor. In the judiciary, interest groups will attempt to influence the selection of judges either by lobbying the governor to appoint a particular judge or by contributing to the campaigns of judicial candidates they support. In addition, they may bring test cases, that is, lawsuits challenging the constitutionality or application of state laws with which they disagree. Or they may file *amicus curiae* (friend of the court) briefs in cases brought by others in an attempt to convince a judge to rule in a particular way that is favorable to the group's interests.

By far the most visible lobbying activities of interest groups, however, occur at the biennial sessions of the state legislature. During these sessions, Carson City becomes a beehive of lobbyists intent on persuading the legislators to pass laws favorable to them or to defeat laws they find unpalatable. That the actions of the legislature are of growing importance to the state's organized interests can be seen in the fact that about 350 lobbyists registered for the 1975 session, 519 registered in 1985, and 642 were registered in 1995. A study in 1991 concluded that the Nevada legislature was the sixth "most lobbied" legislature in the country, with 9 lobbyists for every legislator;[2] the 1995 session surpassed that mark with an average of more than 10 lobbyists per legislator.

Because the Nevada State Legislature is a part-time body, legislators are especially reliant upon lobbyists for information regarding bills that are pending before them. Although, as we shall see in chapter 6, they have the expertise of professional lawyers, auditors, and researchers in the Legislative Counsel Bureau available to them, the legislators are, by virtue of their part-time status and the press of time, dependent upon lobbyists for information regarding the potential effects of legislation. A survey of legislators and lobbyists at the 1971 session found general agreement between the two groups that a major purpose of lobbyists is to provide information to the legislators.[3]

That same survey indicated that lobbyists and legislators agreed on the five most effective lobbying techniques in the state legislature: personally presenting arguments; presenting research results; testifying at hearings; initiating contacts by constituents; and contributing or withholding a contribution to a candidate.[4] It is doubtful that those conclusions have changed in the years since the survey was taken. Indeed, an examination of the 1995 session indicates the continuing prominence of these techniques. Gaming lobbyists testified in favor of a bill limiting the legal liability of hotels and casinos in some cases, teachers' union officials testified against a bill that would allow unlicensed professionals to teach, and the Greater Nevada School Counselor Association lobbied the governor through a telephone campaign to veto a bill that would open school counseling records to parents. In each of these cases, the lobbying campaign was successful.

Regulation of lobbyists in Nevada only began in 1973. Prior to that time, lobbyists were not required to register, they did not have to identify the group or groups for whom they were lobbying, and in some cases they were actually permitted to sit on the floor with legislators. As one observer has noted, "Nevada legislators have been traditionally very friendly toward lobbyists."[5]

In 1973, when it appeared that a more stringent initiative supported by Common Cause of Nevada might qualify for the ballot, the legislature reluctantly passed a bill requiring lobbyists to register with the secretary of state. Spurred by the same fears in 1975, the legislature required lobbyists to report monthly on their expenditures during the session for entertainment, gifts, and loans to legislators. In 1979, lobbyists were further required to wear identification badges while in the halls of the legislature, and the registration site was moved from the secretary of state's office to the Legislative Counsel Bureau.

One of the most important pieces of legislation to regulate lobbyists was enacted during the 1993 session. The legislators passed a law requiring not only that lobbyists list their expenditures for the session, as they had done since 1975, but that beginning with the 1995 session they specify the individual legislators on whom the expenditure was made and the amount of that expenditure. The law has had a significant effect on lobbyist spending on legislators. Not wanting to find themselves on a list of those frequently wined and dined by lobbyists, a distinction that election opponents would surely use against them, many legislators simply avoided the gifts and free meals they had willingly accepted in past sessions. To no one's surprise, spending by lobbyists on legislators dropped by more than 90 percent between the 1993 and 1995 sessions.

Winners and Losers

Interest groups and their lobbyists have always been controversial in the United States. On the one hand are those who argue that they serve an important function in a democratic system by allowing people to band together and make their wishes known to their elected representatives; interest groups simply serve to communicate to officials what their constituents want. On the other hand are those who abhor the increased importance of interest groups and their money in the governmental process and who note that what is in the best interests of these organized groups is often not in the best interests of either the state or its citizens.

As noted earlier, some groups are more successful in obtaining their wishes than others. As with any aspect of politics, there are winners and losers. The winners, not unexpectedly, are often those with the greatest resources: money, organization, effective leadership, and a cadre of dedicated members who campaign for and against candidates. The losers, not infrequently, are those without such resources.

By far the most frequent winner in Nevada politics is the gaming industry. Although it has not dominated the issues to quite the same degree as banking and railroad interests did in the nineteenth century, the gaming industry is clearly the biggest winner in the state. That it finds itself in this position is the result of several factors.

First, gaming is the single most important industry in the state. Nevada has typically been a one-industry state, first with mining and now gaming. As a result, the economic health of the industry is of vital concern to the state's officials, who must protect jobs and encourage economic growth if they are to remain in office. Proposals that affect gaming are sure to result in close inspection by the state's officials. With the "corporatization" of casinos in the 1960s and the declining influence of organized crime in the industry, gaming has succeeded in establishing for itself a clean reputation and a legitimacy that, with its economic dominance, gives it influence beyond that of other groups.

Second, gaming is a significant contributor to election campaigns in Nevada. A 1993 study by the Western States Center, comparing seven western states, found that gaming gives more to political candidates in Nevada than the primary industries of the six other states give to their preferred candidates. The study also found that of disclosed contributions in the 1990 state and legislative elections, gaming provided 18 percent, mining 2 percent, organized labor 3.7 percent, and resource development industries 2.8 percent. Although gaming and other contributors frequently give to both candidates (just in case), the industry has a knack for choosing winners: "winning candidates got 41.5 percent of their traceable funds from gambling, while losers got just 13.5 percent."[6] It is, of course, a matter of conjecture whether gaming is simply good at backing winners or whether candidates in Nevada are unlikely to win without gaming support.

Third, gaming has been successful as a result of its high-quality, well-connected lobbyists. For many years, gaming interests were represented by the powerful and hugely talented Jim Joyce. A survey of the 1983 legislature indicated that the three most effective lobbyists were all from the gaming industry: Jim Joyce, Harvey Whittemore, and Sam McMullen.[7] Joyce died in 1993, but the influence of gaming has been continued by Whittemore, Richard Bunker, and other lobbyists, including Joyce's son, Robin. It has also been the case that the gaming industry has achieved an amazing degree of access to government officials through its hiring of lobbyists who also run the election campaigns of state and legislative officials. In 1995, for example, Billy Vassiliadis, who had managed Governor Bob Miller's 1994 reelection campaign, was hired by gaming to represent its interests in Carson City.

In the 1995 legislature, the gaming industry continued its string of successes. On nine major bills before legislators, gaming won victories in five, partial victories in three, and was defeated on only one.[8]

For different reasons, the Nevada State Education Association has also been a frequent winner in state politics. The association does not have the economic clout and deep pockets of the gaming industry, but the tremendous growth in the state's population has vastly increased the number of schoolteachers, giving NSEA thousands of volunteers willing to walk precincts to campaign for or against electoral hopefuls. The loss of the group's executive director prior to the 1995 session left it weakened but not ineffectual. The group was also hobbled by the fact that it had overwhelmingly endorsed Democrats in the November 1994 elections, an unfortunate move for the NSEA, since the 1995 state senate was controlled by the Republicans and the assembly was split evenly between the two parties. On fourteen issues important to the NSEA, it claimed victories on nine.[9]

Other groups have also had success in lobbying state government. Organized labor and the State of Nevada Employees Association, as a result of their cadres of volunteer campaign workers, have been successful on occasion, particularly with Democrats. The Chamber of Commerce and the Nevada Taxpayers Association have been more influential with Republicans.

Some of the "losers" in Nevada politics tend to vary over time, finding themselves victorious in one era but not in another. Yet others seem to find themselves chronically defeated and disappointed. Mothers Against Drunk Driving (MADD) had some successes in the 1980s and early 1990s but was soundly defeated by the gaming industry in 1995 when it worked for legislation to lower the legal intoxication level from .10 to .08 and to make bars and casinos legally liable for accidents caused by drivers who had been drinking at their establishments.

Welfare recipients and their advocates have regularly found themselves among the state's lobbying underdogs. As far back as 1955, a study of social welfare policies found Nevada's services for the poor were in such dreadful condition that they fell "below those of many of the poorest states" and the state consistently "turn[ed] a cold poormaster's eye to its poor, its sick, and its socially misshapen."[10] In the four decades since, services have gotten better, but the state continues to rank near the bottom of any national list assessing state-provided social services. An attempt in the 1995 legislative session to increase welfare payments was as unsuccessful as previous efforts had been. Because the poor tend to vote less often than others, because they are unorganized, and because they are often seen by the public and officials as architects of their own condition, they simply do not achieve the victories that gaming, teachers, the Chamber of Commerce, and any number of other groups in the state do.

Chapter Six

The Nevada Legislature

Introduction

Like the federal government, the state government of Nevada consists of three branches that oversee one another through a series of checks and balances. The state legislature is the first of these. Unlike the federal Constitution, which merely implies the separation of powers, the state constitution establishes this separation explicitly in Article III. That separation of power is maintained by the constitution through a separation of duties and a separation of personnel. In terms of the former, Article III specifically prohibits any branch from exercising the powers of another. And in terms of the latter, no person may serve in more than one branch simultaneously.[1]

As noted in chapter 2, the Tenth Amendment to the U.S. Constitution reserves to the states all powers not delegated to the federal government or prohibited to the states. Consequently, the framers of the 1864 constitution sought to incorporate into that document limitations and exclusions on the legislature's vast reserve of power. The Declaration of Rights, discussed in chapter 3, is one example of that effort, as are the various provisions in the constitution limiting the power of the legislature in areas such as taxation, borrowing, and spending. The constitutional convention delegates of 1864 feared the possibility of an all-powerful legislature run amok. During the convention's debates, E. F. Dunne of Humboldt County noted, "The fact is, that whenever the Legislature is in session, the people wait with fear and trembling for it to adjourn, and then they thank God that it is over."[2]

Apportionment

Nevada's legislature, like that of all other states except Nebraska, is bicameral; the lower house is called the Nevada State Assembly and the upper house is the Nevada State Senate. Currently there are forty-two members in the assembly and twenty-one in the senate. Although those numbers are not constitutionally mandated and have been altered over the years, Article XV does limit the total number of legislators to seventy-five and Article IV requires that the number of senators be no more than one-half or less than one-third the number of members of the assembly.

For fifty years the senate was wildly malapportioned, with representation not commensurate with population. From 1915 to 1965 the state senate was apportioned on the basis of one senator per county. In addition, each county, no matter how sparsely populated, was given at least one assembly member. This scheme had the effect of overrepresenting the rural counties while underrepresenting the urban areas of the state. For instance, prior to 1966, the districts representing the state's most populous areas, Reno and Las Vegas, contained 75 percent of the population but had only twenty-one of thirty-seven seats in the assembly (57 percent) and two of seventeen seats in the senate (12 percent). The fourteen least populous counties, on the other hand, had only 21 percent of the population but controlled 37 percent of the assembly seats and 82 percent of the senate seats. The remaining population and representatives were to be found in Elko County, which was slightly overrepresented in the legislature.[3]

From the beginning, this arrangement was of dubious constitutionality, since Articles I and XV of the state constitution require that legislative apportionment in both houses be based on population. Nonetheless, it was not until 1964, in *Reynolds v. Sims*,[4] that the U.S. Supreme Court interpreted the federal Constitution to require that both houses of all state legislatures be apportioned on the basis of population. The failure of the 1965 legislature to fairly apportion legislative seats led Flora Dungan, a member of the assembly from Las Vegas, to file suit in federal court. A three-judge federal court held that Nevada's apportionment scheme was unconstitutional, and they ordered the governor to call a special session of the legislature for the purpose of reapportionment.[5] The governor called the session in 1966, and the legislature, dominated by the rural counties, grudgingly reapportioned its seats on the basis of population. The effect of that reapportionment, and the succeeding ones that occur after the census every decade, has been to shift legislative power from the rural counties to the populous urban counties, especially Clark County, which now has a majority in both houses.

Structure and Function of the Legislature

Qualifications, Sessions, Salary

Article IV of the state constitution requires only that members of the legislature be "duly qualified electors in the respective counties and districts which they represent." Under the constitution, an "elector" is not necessarily the same as a "registered voter." Any U.S. citizen who is eighteen years of age or older, who has not been convicted of a felony, and who has resided in the state for thirty days is considered a qualified elector, regardless of whether he or she is registered to vote. However, the legislature has also required by statute that a legislator be at least twenty-one years old at the time of election and have resided in the state for at least one year prior to the election. And the courts have held that although candidates running in a nonpartisan election do not have to be registered to vote, political parties can require that candidates in party primaries be registered to vote in that party.

Members of the state senate serve four-year, staggered terms; members of the assembly serve terms of two years. Thus, every two years all seats in the assembly and approximately half of those in the senate are up for election. This structure parallels that in the U.S. Congress and guarantees some continuity, at least in the senate, at each legislative session. Although originally the constitution required that vacancies occurring between sessions be filled by election, amendments adopted in 1922 and 1944 now allow county commissioners to fill them. In doing so, however, the commissioners must select an individual who is of the same party as the legislator vacating the seat and who lives in the district to be represented. These interim appointments may be made only if there is to be no regular election prior to the next legislative session and are valid only until such time as a regular election does occur, at which time the remaining term, if any, is up for election.

The sixty-three members of the state legislature meet in regular session biennially, that is, every other year, for a period of approximately six months. These sessions begin on the third Monday of January in odd-numbered years. The 1864 constitution originally placed a limit of sixty days on regular sessions and twenty days on special sessions; that limit was removed by constitutional amendment in 1958 when it became clear that the state's business could no longer be conducted within that time frame. The tremendous growth in both the population and complexity of the state has meant that over the past several years the length of sessions has progressively increased. Whereas the 1973 session lasted 102 days at a cost of slightly more than $1 million, the 1995 session, the longest in state history, went for 169 days at a cost of slightly more than $9 million.

The length and cost of these sessions has resulted in calls by some to adopt annual sessions, or at least to establish a limited session in even-numbered years to deal with budget issues. In 1958 the voters approved an amendment to the constitution allowing for annual sessions but promptly repealed it in 1960. Although biennial sessions have created significant problems for the legislature, particularly in its attempts to accurately predict revenues and then budget for a two-year cycle, further proposals to adopt annual sessions, including one in 1995, have died in the legislature. The single post-1960 proposal that did manage to get through the legislature died at the hands of the voters by an almost 2 to 1 margin in the 1970 elections. To date, Nevada is one of only seven states continuing to mandate biennial sessions.

In addition to these regular biennial sessions, the legislature may meet in special session when called by the governor. Unlike some other states, Nevada does not allow its legislature to call itself into special session; only the governor may do so, and the legislature is prohibited by the constitution from conducting any business other than that for which the governor has called it. Like regular sessions, special sessions since 1958 have had no limit placed on their length. To date there have been sixteen special sessions, the most recent in 1989, when Governor Bob Miller called on the legislators to repeal a controversial and unpopular 300 percent pension increase they had voted themselves during the 1989 regular session. The 1989 special session is also noteworthy for its brevity: it lasted only about two hours and is the shortest on record. Because most special sessions have been called by the governor for the purpose of dealing with revenue and appropriations shortfalls between sessions, the creation of the Interim Finance Committee in 1969 has decreased the need for special sessions. That committee, made up of the members of the Senate Finance Committee and the Assembly Ways and Means Committee, has authority between regular sessions to appropriate additional funds to agencies experiencing a shortfall.

Since 1985, legislators have received $130 per day for salary and $66 per day for living expenses plus telephone and travel expenses. As part of the compromise to remove the limit on the length of legislative sessions, the constitution provides that the salary figure may be paid only for the first sixty days of a regular session and the first twenty days of a special session. The per diem for expenses, however, is paid for the entirety of the session. Attempts since 1985 to increase the salary of legislators have, not unexpectedly, run into opposition from the public.

Organization of the State Legislature

The presiding officer of the senate, the president of the senate, is the lieutenant governor, one of the few instances in which the constitution allows an individual to serve in two branches simultaneously. In that sense, the lieutenant governor is like the vice-president of the United States, who serves as president of the U.S. Senate. In this capacity, the lieutenant governor has the authority to interpret rules and has the power to exercise a "casting vote" in case of a tie. In the absence of the lieutenant governor, the senate is presided over by the president pro-tempore, an elected position held by a member of the majority party.

The real power of the senate, however, is held by the majority leader and, to a lesser extent, the minority leader. These individuals are chosen by their party caucuses at the beginning of each session. Each is considered the leader of his or her party in the senate and in that capacity makes committee assignments for his or her party's members; in addition, the majority leader chooses the chairs of each senate committee and controls floor debate. The power of the majority leader is tremendous, and no better example of that can be found than Republican senator William Raggio of Reno, who has served in that position for four of the past five sessions. As majority leader, Raggio has managed to advance Republican issues

Table 6.1

Party Control of the Nevada Legislature, 1961–1995

Year of Session	Majority Party, Senate	Majority Party, Assembly
1961	R	D
1963	R	D
1965	D	D
1967	D	D
1969	D	R
1971	D	R
1973	D	D
1975	D	D
1977	D	D
1979	D	D
1981	D	D
1983	D	D
1985	D	R
1987	R	D
1989	R	D
1991	D	D
1993	R	D
1995	R	Split*

Source: Compiled by the author from data on legislative membership.
*1995 assembly split evenly (21–21) between Democrats and Republicans.
D = Democrat   R = Republican

and protect the interests of northern Nevada by delaying, forcing compromises, and killing bills in the senate in spite of Clark County's majority in that body. Near the end of the 1995 session, for example, Raggio demanded and received a vote in the assembly on a Republican-sponsored welfare bill before he would allow a vote in the senate on an unrelated Democratic-sponsored jobs bill.

In the assembly, the presiding officer is the speaker of the assembly. The speaker, who is selected by the majority party caucus, not only presides over the assembly but also serves as his party's leader. In that capacity, he appoints his party's members to the various committees and selects the majority leader, the speaker pro-tempore, and the committee chairs. Unlike the senate majority leader, who typically serves for many sessions, assuming his or her party controls the upper house, only four speakers of the assembly have served two or more consecutive terms.

The record is held by Democrat Joe Dini of Yerington, who held the speaker's position in 1987, 1989, 1991, 1993, and was co-speaker in 1995. The assembly minority leader makes committee assignments for his or her party members.

No one party has dominated Nevada politics, and that is true also for the legislature. In the senate, the Republicans have been the majority party forty-one times; the Democrats, twenty-one. In the assembly, Democrats have reversed that trend and been the majority party thirty-seven times, compared to twenty-five for the Republicans.[6] In an odd turn of events in 1994, the Democrats and Republicans each won twenty-one seats in the 1995 assembly. After substantial maneuvering, legal and political, it was determined that co-speakers and committee co-chairs would be appointed and would alternate their service on a daily basis. That is, the Republican co-chair would preside over a given committee on Monday, the Democratic co-chair on Tuesday, and so on (see Table 6.1).

Lawmaking in the Legislature

The process of making laws in the Nevada legislature is quite similar to the process in the U.S. Congress, but with some important distinctions. Unlike the U.S. Constitution, which leaves such matters up to congressional discretion, the Nevada Constitution quite specifically lays out the procedures that must be utilized by the state legislature in passing a bill into law.

Although the importance of committees in Congress cannot be overstated, their importance in the state legislature is even more significant. Because the members of the legislature are part-time legislators and meet for only six months every other year, the level of expertise developed in various policy areas may often be less than that of members of Congress who serve as full-time legislators in a full-time legislature. Consequently, members of the state legislature are more dependent upon the specialization developed by committee members and more compelled by the press of time to complete their business before the new fiscal year begins on July 1. It is, therefore, relatively rare that a committee recommendation on a bill is rejected by the full house.

A second difference from the U.S. Congress comes in the types of bills that may be introduced. The U.S. Constitution, for example, mandates that all revenue (i.e., taxation) bills originate in the House of Representatives. The Nevada Constitution makes no similar distinctions, so a bill of any type may originate in either house.

Yet a third difference arises in the time-honored practice of attaching nongermane amendments to legislative proposals. In Congress it is common practice to attach an unrelated amendment (or "rider") to a popular bill in order to ensure the amendment's passage. For example, a controversial welfare proposal might be attached to a popular crime-control bill that members of Congress would have a hard time voting against. Nongermane amendments in the Nevada legislature are prohibited by Article IV of the state constitution, which requires that all bills "embrace but one subject."

The majority necessary to approve a bill in the state legislature also differs from that at the federal level. The framers of the 1864 constitution were fearful that a handful of legislators, in the absence of others, would pass obnoxious legislation. Consequently, whereas in the U.S. Congress a bill needs only a positive vote by a majority of those present to pass, the Nevada Constitution requires a majority of the *elected* members of each house to vote for passage of a bill. Thus, for a bill to pass it must have eleven votes in the senate and twenty-two in the assembly, regardless of how many legislators are actually present and voting on the proposal.

Two final differences in the lawmaking process occur once a bill has been passed by both houses and is transmitted to the governor. In order for a bill to become a law, it must be signed by the governor or his veto must be overridden. Once a bill is transmitted to the governor, he has five days (Sundays excepted) to consider the bill if the legislature is in session and ten days (Sundays excepted) if the legislature has adjourned. By the end of that period the governor must sign or veto the entire bill (in Nevada, unlike some other states, the governor does not have the power of line-item veto and thus cannot pick and choose parts of the bill to sign or veto). If the governor does nothing, the bill automatically becomes law. Unlike the president, then, the governor of Nevada does not have a pocket veto, whereby a bill may be vetoed by inaction.

To override a gubernatorial veto, the legislature must obtain a two-thirds majority of the *elected* membership of each house (fourteen in the senate, twenty-eight in the assembly) and not, as in the Congress, simply two-thirds of those present and voting. Bills that are vetoed by the governor after the session has adjourned are returned to the legislature for any override action at the beginning of the next regular session two years later.

Modernization

Over the past several decades, concomitant to the state's tremendous population growth, the legislature has attempted to modernize its proceedings in order to deal with the ever-increasing complexity of state government. As noted above, the Interim Finance Committee was established in 1969 to deal with appropriations issues between regular sessions and reduce the need for additional special sessions. With the opening of a new legislative building in 1971, each legislator got an office, something that had not happened during previous sessions when legislators met in the cramped confines of the State Capitol Building. In 1995 the legislature appropriated funding to build an additional wing so that assembly

Table 6.2

The Nevada Legislature, Famous Firsts

First Nevada-born assembly member	Frank P. Langan (1889)
First Nevada-born state senator	George D. Pyne (1889)
First woman to serve in the assembly	Sadie D. Hurst (1919)
First woman to serve in the state senate	Helen Herr (1967)
First African American to serve in the assembly	Woodrow Wilson (1967)
First African American to serve in the state senate	Joe Neal (1973)
First Hispanic to serve in the assembly	Arthur Espinoza (1967)
First Hispanic to serve in the state senate	Bob Coffin (1987)
First Basque to serve in the state senate	Peter Echeverria (1959)
First woman to lead a party in the state senate	Dina Titus (1993)

Source: Secretary of State's Office and the Nevada State Library and Archives.

members would have office space commensurate in size to that of their senate counterparts in time for the 1997 session.

Perhaps the most important step toward modernization, however, has been the creation and expansion of the Legislative Counsel Bureau. The LCB was established in 1945 and has been essential to the success of Nevada's citizen legislature. The bureau is overseen by the Legislative Commission, which is made up of six members from each house and which meets monthly between sessions. The Legislative Commission has the authority to appoint the director of the Legislative Counsel Bureau. The director in turn is responsible for hiring the LCB's staff, including its four division heads.

The Legal Division of the LCB is of primary importance. It provides legal advice to the legislature and drafts bills requested by legislators. As citizen legislators, members of the assembly and senate rarely possess the knowledge and skills necessary to draft complex legislation without the assistance of the professionals in the Legal Division. The Legal Division also possesses the authority to issue advisory legal opinions, although like those of the attorney general they are not binding upon the courts in any later litigation.

Not as well known or as visible as the Legal Division, but equally important, are the three other divisions of the LCB: Audit, Fiscal Analysis, and Research. The Audit Division performs legislative audits on the various agencies of the executive branch in order to provide the legislature with the information it needs to ensure that appropriated funds have been expended properly and efficiently. The Fiscal Analysis Division is responsible for providing the legislature with information on the fiscal effects of various spending and revenue proposals by the executive branch. In that sense, then, they too assist the legislature in its ability to check and balance the governor and other members of the executive branch. The Research Division provides necessary research and background information to the legislature on a multitude of issues confronting it. For example, with the even party split in the assembly in 1995, the Research Division was assigned the task of determining what legislatures in other states had done when faced with the same dilemma.

Chapter Seven

The Nevada Executive

Introduction

In general, the executive power can be defined as one that enforces and implements the laws passed by the legislature as interpreted by the courts. The area now known as Nevada has been governed by an executive throughout its recorded history. During the period of Spanish colonialism the area was governed by a provincial governor. After the Mexicans overthrew their Spanish conquerors, parts of what is now Nevada were governed by the Mexican governor of the Province of Alta California (headquartered in Monterey) and the governor of the Province of New Mexico (located in Santa Fe). From the time of the Compromise of 1850 until Nevada became a separate territory in 1861, the northern 90 percent of the Great Basin was under the formal authority of the Utah territorial governor, while the southern 10 percent was controlled by the governor of the vast New Mexico Territory. James W. Nye served as the only territorial governor of Nevada Territory from its inception in 1861 until statehood was granted in 1864.

Since 1864, when Republican Henry G. Blasdel was elected the state's first governor, Nevada's chief executive has continued to be its governor. As in all other states, the governor may be considered the "chief" executive, but in Nevada he or she is not the only member of the executive branch to be elected by the voters. Nevada has what is called a "plural executive." Under this system, voters elect six executive-branch officers: the governor, lieutenant governor, attorney general, secretary of state, treasurer, and controller. Under the 1864 constitution the surveyor general and the superintendent of public instruction were also elected executive officers; the former was eliminated entirely and the latter was made an appointive office through constitutional amendments approved by the voters in 1954 and 1956, respectively.

In some states, these five other executive branch officers are appointed by the governor and are responsible solely to him or her. The framers of the Nevada constitution, although on good relations with territorial Governor Nye, were generally distrustful of concentrating too much power in the hands of any single officer or branch. The incorporation of a plural executive in the constitution was, therefore, a purposeful effort on their part to diffuse the executive power among the six officers. Because these five other officers are all elected by the voters, they owe their allegiance to them and not the governor; the governor cannot command them to do anything nor can he or she remove them. This provides for a system of multiple constitutional checks upon the executive branch: the governor is prevented from absolutely controlling the entire executive branch, the other five executive officers are held accountable to the voters and not to the governor, and executive power is made less dangerous by its diffusion into the hands of six officers instead of one.

Eligibility, Election, and Removal

All six elected members of the executive branch must meet the same eligibility requirements for office. They must be at least twenty-five years of age, qualified electors (see chapter 6), and residents of the state for the previous two years. Each serves a term of four years and all are chosen at the same general election; that is, their terms are not staggered like those in the state senate.

The failed 1863 constitution had included a term of only two years for the governor. For reasons not indicated in the published debates, the framers of the 1864 constitution increased it to four years. Under the original 1864 constitution, all six officers could serve an unlimited number of four-year terms. However, in 1970 the voters approved a constitutional amendment, similar to the Twenty-second Amendment to the U.S. Constitution, limiting the governor, but not the other five officers, to no more than two full terms and up to two years of his or her predecessor's unexpired term. Even before passage of the 1970 amendment, however, no governor had ever been elected to a third term and none of the three who had attempted to do so (Lewis R. Bradley, Charles H. Russell, and Grant Sawyer) were successful. At the end of his term in January 1999, Governor Bob Miller will become the longest-serving governor in Nevada history, having served two full terms and the last two years of Governor Richard Bryan's term, which became vacant upon Bryan's move to the U.S. Senate in January 1989.

The six elected officers of the executive branch are all subject to removal through recall by the voters (discussed in chapter 4) or impeachment by the legislature. Article VII of the state constitution provides for the sanction of impeachment for reasons of misdemeanor or malfeasance in office. The process of impeachment is similar to that at the federal level: the lower house, the assembly, votes on articles of impeachment, which require a simple majority to be approved, and the upper house, the senate, conducts the trial. A two-thirds majority in the senate is needed for conviction and removal from office. One important difference between the federal and state procedures for impeachment, however, is the state constitution's provision that these majorities be based on the number of *elected* members of each body and not, as in Congress, on the number of those present and voting. Thus, impeachment in Nevada would require at least twenty-two votes in the assembly, and conviction would require at least fourteen votes in the senate, regardless of how many legislators actually vote.

As noted in chapter 6, the lieutenant governor serves as the president of the senate. Consequently, he or she would preside in an impeachment trial. However, in the case of an impeachment trial involving the governor, the chief justice of the Nevada Supreme Court has been designated by Article VII as the presiding officer. The framers of the constitution thought it inappropriate for the lieutenant governor to preside over the impeachment trial of the governor, since the lieutenant governor would become acting governor if the governor were to be convicted and removed from office. To have the lieutenant governor preside over the governor's impeachment trial would constitute a clear conflict of interest, and every decision that he or she made in that capacity would be questioned. The difficulties that an acting governor would have in establishing his or her own legitimacy to the office after having presided over the preceding governor's removal led the framers to follow the federal constitutional model, which provides that the chief justice of the United States preside over an impeachment trial of the president.

Should an officeholder be impeached and convicted, the legislature has authority only to remove him or her from office and to disqualify that person from other state office in the future. If the removed officeholder has committed any crimes, he or she could also be subject to a trial in the courts and any appropriate penalties that might ensue; this does not constitute double jeopardy. To date, no executive official in Nevada has ever been impeached.

The Governor

Between 1864 and 1998, the state of Nevada will have had twenty-six governors: eleven have been Republicans, eleven have been Democrats, and the remaining four were members of either the Silver Party or the Silver-Democrat Party. These four governors served from 1895 to 1911, when the issue of free coinage of silver was an important one in Nevada and other western mining states. Although those figures indicate that no one party has dominated the governorship, the Democrats have held the office for all but sixteen years since 1935 (see Table 7.1).

Other patterns can also be found among the men, and they have all been men, holding the office. During the first twenty-four years of statehood, when mining and ranching were the state's chief industries, all ten of the state's governors had backgrounds in mining, cattle ranching, or both. Since 1959, five of the six have been attorneys and four of those have previously served as county district attorney. Four have been graduates of the University of Nevada, Reno (Emmet D. Boyle, Charles H. Russell, Grant Sawyer, and Richard Bryan), none have been graduated from the University of Nevada, Las Vegas, and only seven have been native-born Nevadans (the most recent being Paul Laxalt, who served from 1967 to 1971). Six

Table 7.1

Governors of Nevada, 1864–1999

Name	Party	Years
James W. Nye, acting governor	R	Oct. 31–Dec. 5, 1864
Henry Goode Blasdel	R	1864–1871
Lewis Rice Bradley	D	1871–1879
John H. Kinkead	R	1879–1883
Jewett W. Adams	D	1883–1887
Charles C. Stevenson*	R	1887–1890
Frank Bell, acting governor	R	Sept. 1, 1890–1891
Roswell K. Colcord	R	1891–1895
John E. Jones*	S	1895–1896
Reinhold Sadler, acting governor	S	Apr. 10, 1896–1899
Reinhold Sadler	S	1899–1903
John Sparks*	SD	1903–1908
Denver S. Dickerson, acting governor	SD	May 22, 1908–1911
Tasker L. Oddie	R	1911–1915
Emmet D. Boyle	D	1915–1923
James G. Scrugham	D	1923–1927
Fred B. Balzar*	R	1927–1934
Morley Griswold, acting governor	R	March 21, 1934–1935
Richard Kirman, Sr.	D	1935–1939
Edward P. Carville**	D	1939–1945
Vail M. Pittman, acting governor	D	July 24, 1945–1947
Vail M. Pittman	D	1947–1951
Charles H. Russell	R	1951–1959
F. G. "Grant" Sawyer	D	1959–1967
Paul Laxalt	R	1967–1971
D. N. "Mike" O'Callaghan	D	1971–1979
Robert List	R	1979–1983
Richard H. Bryan**	D	1983–1989
Robert J. "Bob" Miller, acting governor	D	Jan. 3, 1989–1991
Robert J. "Bob" Miller	D	1991–1999

Source: Frankie Sue Del Papa, *Political History of Nevada, 1990,* 9th ed., 128. Reprinted with permission.

*Disabled and/or died in office and succeeded by lieutenant governor.

**Resigned governorship to take a seat in the U.S. Senate; succeeded by lieutenant governor.　　D = Democrat　R = Republican　S = Silver　SD = Silver-Democrat had served in the legislature prior to becoming governor, two (Richard Bryan and Robert List) had served as attorney general, and other than those six who became acting governor upon the vacation of the office by their predecessors, only one (Laxalt) had previously served as lieutenant governor.[1]

Should the office of governor become vacant, Article V of the constitution provides that the lieutenant governor become acting governor. Should both offices be vacant, that section provides for the president pro-tempore of the senate to exercise gubernatorial powers. In the rare chance that all three offices are vacant, the legislature has provided by statute that the line of succession be continued with the speaker of the assembly and the secretary of state. Succession to the office of governor by the lieutenant governor has occurred six times in Nevada. One of those instances involved the disability (and later death) of the governor, three were cases in which the governor died in office, and two involved resignations by the governor to serve in the U.S. Senate.

Chief Executive

Although one of only six elected executive officers, the governor is considered the chief executive of the state. In this capacity it is his or her duty to see that the laws of the state are faithfully executed. In order to achieve that goal, he is imbued with the power to appoint a substantial number of executive-branch officials. Currently the governor appoints about 80 heads and deputy heads of cabinet-level departments and the members of 134 boards, commissions, and committees. In addition, he is a member of several state boards and commissions.[2] Among the most important appointments the governor makes are the heads of the departments of Motor Vehicles and Public Safety, Human Resources, and Employment Security, and the members of the Gaming Control Board, the Gaming Commission, the Public Works Board, and the Parole Commission.

In making these appointments, the governor is more powerful than the president of the United States and the governors of many other states because he or she is not required to solicit the approval of the state legislature. Although, as we have noted earlier, the framers were distrustful of a strong executive and sought to limit its power, the irony of their giving the governor sole power to appoint these officials was no doubt related to the fact that they were also realists who knew that the legislature would be in session for only a few months every other year and thus in no position to approve or disapprove the governor's appointments.

Even though it would be unwieldy for legislators to attempt to approve gubernatorial appointments, they have unsuccessfully attempted to assert power over the governor's appointees by granting themselves the authority to overturn regulations adopted by agencies of the executive branch. A ballot question giving the legislature this power was defeated by the voters in 1988, and a similar bill passed by both houses of the state legislature in 1995 died when the assembly failed to override Governor Miller's veto. The legislature may yet get its way, however, given that a constitutional amendment on the 1996 ballot, if passed by the voters, would grant them this authority.

That the governor is more powerful in his discretion to select executive-branch appointees than are his counterparts in many other states is an anomaly in a system in which his power is generally quite limited. For example, as noted above, he is one of only six members of Nevada's elected plural executive. Not only is he without power over the actions of these other officers, they may be, indeed are likely to be, members of other political parties and may use their positions to actively oppose him and his policies at every turn. This often has the effect of reducing his ability to see that the laws are duly enforced. The governor's power over these other five constitutional officers is, as political scientist Richard Neustadt once noted concerning the power of the president of the United States, ultimately nothing more than the power to persuade them to do what he thinks is right. In only thirteen out of thirty-four elections for state officers has a single party controlled all six executive positions; the last time was 1946 (see Table 7.2).[3]

Consistent with their thoughts on limiting the power of the governor, the framers of the 1864 constitution also denied to him the sole power to issue pardons, a power held by the president and many state chief executives. In its debates on the issue, the convention's delegates stated that the power to issue a pardon for crimes against the state's citizens "should not rest upon one man alone."[4] Apparently, modern Nevadans agree: a constitutional amendment to grant the governor that power was defeated by the voters in 1960 by a 59–41 majority. Instead, the governor serves as one member of a seven-member state Board of Pardons Commissioners; the other members are the attorney general and the five justices of the state supreme court. A majority of the board must vote to grant a pardon. However, even here the governor has some leverage, albeit negative. According to Article V, he exercises a veto in that he must be one of those in the majority to grant a pardon; therefore, even if all six of the board's other members were to vote in favor of a pardon and the governor did not, a pardon would not be granted.

As chief executive the governor exercises other constitutional powers as well. He has the power to appoint officials to serve in some offices should a vacancy occur between elections, he may suspend a fine or forfeiture and grant a reprieve for up to sixty days from the time of judgment, and he must sign all grants and commissions from the state. In addition to his membership on the Board of Pardons Commissioners, the governor also serves on the Board of State Prison Commissioners, which oversees the state prison system, and the Board of Examiners, which reviews all claims against the state for money or property; no money can be appropriated by the legislature to pay a claim against the state unless it has first been submitted to the Board of Examiners, although the board's recommendation is merely an advisory one.

Chief of State

Like the president of the United States, the governor serves as chief of state. This is a ceremonial and symbolic function but an important one nonetheless. The governor serves as the state's chief goodwill ambassador, attending various state functions and representing the state to the world outside of Nevada. In this role, he or she will meet with the president and other governors and engage in more low-profile activities such as ribbon cuttings at new casinos and groundbreakings for important construction projects. In performing these noncontroversial functions the governor not only is able to meet with the people and hear their concerns but also is guaranteed generally positive media attention that will aid him in his reelection or in bringing his pet issues to the state's attention.

Chief Legislator

Although not a member of the legislature, the governor is deeply involved in its biennial sessions in a number of ways. The state constitution requires the governor to give a State of the State address to the legislature at every regular session. Through this address the governor is able, in part, to set the legislative agenda by proposing bills he would like to see adopted, supporting those proposed by others that he favors, and indicating those that he would be unwilling to sign into law should they be passed. The constitution requires a State of the State message only at each biennial session of the legislature; some modern governors, however, have seized upon the media's attention to this address and have sometimes given one in even-numbered years, when the legislature is not meeting.

The governor's chief method for shaping the legislative agenda, however, has not been with the State of the State address but through his budget proposals. The executive branch uses a system of "central clearance," which means that all budget requests by state agencies must be submitted to the governor prior to transmission to the legislature. The governor and his budget director may reduce or add to these requests before submitting them to the legislature. Woe be unto the agency head who attempts to subvert the governor by asking for more at the legislature than the governor has recommended, for his or her time in office may be short. Although the money committees in the legislature often consist of legislators who are seasoned in budget matters and who are aided by budget professionals in the Fiscal Analysis Division of the Legislative Counsel Bureau, the brevity of legislative sessions means that the governor's budget is usually adopted with only a few modifications by the legislature.

That the legislature generally adopts the governor's budget with few changes is probably to the good, as far as the governor is concerned, for he is held responsible by the voters for the state's economy despite the fact that it is often buffeted or bolstered by factors over which he has no control. For example, the recession that hit California in the early 1990s reduced the number of tourists from that state to Nevada and created a decline in revenue to the state's coffers. Unfortunately, there was little the governor could do other than reduce state spending, which he did.

As chief legislator, the governor has some limited power over the legislature's commencement and adjournment. As noted in chapter 6, he may call special sessions of the legislature, which are restricted to conducting only the business for which he has called them. Also, should the two houses of the legislature find themselves unable to agree upon a time of adjournment, Article V gives the governor authority to adjourn them at "such time as he may think proper."

As discussed in chapter 6, the governor also exercises the power of the veto. All bills passed by the two houses of the legislature in the same form go to the governor for his action. In order for these legislatively approved bills to become law, the governor must sign them, do nothing, or have his veto overridden. In this respect, governors of Nevada have not fared as well as those nationally; whereas the national average is only 1 percent of gubernatorial vetoes overridden, Nevada's governors have been overridden 12 percent of the time.[5]

Other Duties

Chief executive, chief of state, and chief legislator duties take up most of a governor's time and efforts, but he also engages in a number of other functions given to him by the constitution, statutes, or custom. Articles V and XII of the state constitution make the governor commander-in-chief of the Nevada National Guard. As commander-in-chief, he has authority to call the guard into service during emergency situations such as riots or catastrophes of nature, and he appoints the functional head of the guard, the adjutant general.

By custom the governor is seen as the chief of his party in the state. It is considered his responsibility to ensure that members of his party are elected to various positions, especially in the legislature. Success in this area, of course, works to the governor's advantage, since he would prefer to see an executive branch and legislature dominated by his party rather than by the opposition. As chief of his party the governor is also expected to use his patronage power to reward members of his party by appointing them to important posts in the state government.

Lieutenant Governor

Unlike the situation at the federal level where the president and vice-president run on a ticket and are, therefore, of the same party, the lieutenant governor in Nevada runs for office independently and may be of a different party from the governor. This has occurred only nine times out of a total of thirty-four elections.[6] When it does occur, a problem could develop when the governor is out of state.

Table 7.2

Party Control of the Executive Branch, State of Nevada, 1864–1994

Election Year	Governor	Lieutenant Governor	Attorney General	Secretary of State	Treasurer	Controller
1864	R	R	R	R	R	R
1866	R	R	R	R	R	R
1870	D	D	D	R	D	R
1874	D	D	D	R	D	R
1878	R	D	R	R	R	R
1882	D	R	R	R	R	R
1886	R	R	R	R	R	R
1890	R	R	R	R	R	R
1894	S	S	S	S	S	S
1898	S	S	S	S	SD	SD
1902	SD	SD	SD	R	SD	SD
1906	SD	SD	SD	R	SD	R
1910	R	D	D	D	R	R
1914	D	D	D	D	D	D
1918	D	D	D	D	D	D
1922	D	D	D	D	D	D
1926	R	R	D	D	D	R
1930	R	R	D	D	R	R
1934	D	D	D	D	D	D
1938	D	D	D	D	D	D
1942	D	D	D	D	D	D
1946	D	D	D	D	D	D
1950	R	D	D	D	D	R
1954	R	R	D	D	D	R
1958	D	R	D	D	D	D
1962	D	R	D	D	D	D
1966	R	R	D	D	D	R
1970	D	D	R	D	D	R
1974	D	D	R	D	D	R
1978	R	D	D	D	D	R
1982	D	D*	R	D	R	R
1986	D	D	R	D	R	R
1990	D	R	D	R	R	R
1994	D	R	D	R	R	R

Source: Compiled by the author from general election returns.

*Lt. Governor Robert Cashell was elected as a Democrat but changed his affiliation to Republican during his term.

D = Democrat   R = Republican   S = Silver   SD = Silver-Democrat

Under Article V of the state constitution, the lieutenant governor becomes acting governor not only through a vacancy but also in case of the governor's "absence from the state" for any reason. Exactly what *absent* means became a matter
of some importance in 1965 during the governorship of Grant Sawyer, a Democrat, who was serving with a Republican lieutenant governor, Paul Laxalt. While
Sawyer was out of the state for five hours, Laxalt requested that a state judge
impanel a grand jury to investigate the Highway Department. When Sawyer returned, he rescinded the order.

The case eventually landed in the Nevada Supreme Court, where the
justices voted to construe the constitutional language narrowly. In *Sawyer v.
District Court,* the state's highest court held that in order for the lieutenant governor to serve as acting governor in the governor's absence, there must be an "effective absence" and a critical, emergency need for action; the governor's absence
must be "measured by the state's *need* at a given moment for a particular act."
Given that the grand jury impanelment was not critically needed during the
governor's absence, the court held Laxalt's request for a grand jury constitutionally invalid.[7]

Constitutionally, the lieutenant governor has few powers, and the position is
considered a part-time one. He or she serves as president of the senate with a
"casting vote" in case of ties and serves as acting governor when the governorship is vacant through death, disability, impeachment, or recall or when the governor is "effectively absent" from the state and emergency action must be taken.
Should the lieutenant governor become acting governor, he or she holds both
offices until the next general election, at which time a successor is chosen. Most
recently this occurred between January 1989 and January 1991, when Lieutenant
Governor Bob Miller also served as acting governor.

By statute, the legislature has given the lieutenant governor the chairship of
two state commissions important to Nevada's livelihood: Economic Development
and Tourism. The lieutenant governor may also serve as the governor's confidant
and adviser when the two are close; but when they are not, the lieutenant governor is frequently left out of the executive "loop." Such was the case after the 1994
election with Governor Bob Miller, a Democrat, and Lieutenant Governor Lonnie
Hammargren, a Republican. However, in Miller's first term he had been on rea-
sonably close relations with Nevada's first woman lieutenant governor, Sue Wagner,
also a Republican.

Attorney General

Next to the governor, the attorney general is probably the most visible member of
the executive branch. Although chief legal adviser to the state, the attorney gen-

eral is not legally required to be an attorney; it would, nonetheless, be improbable that a layperson could now be elected to the position. Constitutionally, the attorney general has few powers. He or she serves with the governor and secretary of state as a member of the Board of Prison Commissioners and the Board of Examiners and with the governor and justices of the supreme court on the Board of State Pardons Commissioners.

Other duties have been given to the attorney general by statute, including the obligation to provide legal advice to the various agencies of state government through advisory legal opinions. These advisory opinions serve only as guidelines to the agencies and are not binding upon the courts in any subsequent legal action that may arise. The attorney general is also responsible for defending the state or prosecuting cases at the Nevada Supreme Court and the U.S. Supreme Court. Technically, the attorney general also has authority to oversee the district attorneys in Nevada's seventeen counties. Since these district attorneys are popularly elected by the voters of their individual counties, however, the attorney general rarely involves his or her office in their affairs. He or she will do so, however, if a district attorney has a conflict of interest in a case or if it appears that out of favoritism or a lack of fortitude a district attorney has failed to pursue a case. Finally, the attorney general is required by statute to submit a biennial report to the governor on the condition of law enforcement in the state.

Secretary of State

The secretary of state is primarily a custodian of the state's records. Constitutionally, he or she is prescribed only three duties. First, the secretary of state, along with the governor, must sign all state grants and commissions. Second, with the governor and attorney general, he or she serves on the Board of State Prison Commissioners and the Board of Examiners. Third, the secretary of state is required by Article V to "keep a true record of the Official Acts of the Legislative and Executive Departments," which includes printing the official acts of government departments and the journals of the legislature and returning to the legislature at the beginning of each regular session any bills that may have been vetoed by the governor after the adjournment of the previous session.

In the furtherance of these duties, the secretary of state is responsible for managing the state's archives, issuing certificates of incorporation to Nevada businesses, and regulating securities issued by these state-based entities. Statutorily, the secretary of state commissions notaries public in Nevada. Although Article V makes the Nevada Supreme Court the official canvasser of votes in the state, the secretary of state is responsible for preparing the official ballot, publishing official election results, and issuing certificates of election to the winners.

Table 7.3

The Nevada Executive, Famous Firsts

First woman to serve as lieutenant governor	Maude Frazier (1962–1963)*
First woman elected lieutenant governor	Sue Wagner (1991)
First woman elected attorney general	Frankie Sue Del Papa (1991)
First woman elected secretary of state	Frankie Sue Del Papa (1987)
First woman elected state treasurer	Patricia D."Patty" Cafferata (1983)
First Asian American elected secretary of state	Cheryl Lau (1991)

Source: Secretary of State's Office.

*Frazier was appointed on July 13, 1962, to fill the unexpired term of Rex Bell and served until January 1963.

Controller and Treasurer

The offices of controller and treasurer are created by the state constitution, but that document assigns them no particular responsibilities. Consequently, whatever functions they do perform are prescribed in state statutes. A move in the 1995 legislature by Treasurer Bob Seale to propose a constitutional amendment combining the two offices and allowing the treasurer to appoint the controller led to frosty relations between Seale and Controller Darrel Daines.

The deterioration in relations between these two officers is unfortunate, since they must work closely together. The treasurer receives all moneys paid to the state and disburses them upon receipt of a warrant from the controller. It is the responsibility of the treasurer to deposit all state funds and to ensure not only that they are not lost, as happened in Orange County, California, in the mid-1990s, but that they build the state's treasury by accumulating interest at the highest rate safely possible.

In addition to issuing warrants to the treasurer, the controller serves as the state's chief bookkeeper, making an annual report of state expenditures to the governor and serving as the chief auditor in any claims against the state. In this latter capacity, the controller, along with the Board of Examiners, makes advisory recommendations to the legislature on appropriations to pay such claims.

Chapter Eight

The Nevada Judiciary

Introduction

In interpreting the meaning of various statutes and constitutional provisions, the judges of Nevada's courts engage in a form of policy making that affects not only the lives of the litigants in each case but also the lives and fortunes of all the state's citizens. It should come as little surprise, then, that the state's judges, especially the justices of the Nevada Supreme Court, have come under intense scrutiny and, on occasion, criticism for the decisions they have made. Two periods of Nevada history in particular illustrate the vigor of the courts' critics.

The early years of the judiciary in the Great Basin were not good ones. As noted in chapter 1, early settlers in the Carson Valley were eager to gain separate territorial status as early as 1851. This desire was based in part on their wish to rid themselves of the Utah territorial judiciary, Mormon judges who were accused by the settlers of "so [mixing] together church and state that a man [could not] obtain justice in any of its courts."[1] Even after separate territorial status was granted in 1861, however, the courts were not spared criticism of their actions. President Lincoln's three appointed territorial judges (Chief Justice George Turner, Associate Justice Horatio N. Jones, and Associate Justice Gordon N. Mott) and their successors were subjected to at least as much criticism as their Mormon predecessors, albeit for different reasons.

Although, as we will discuss, the Nevada territorial judges did behave in unprofessional and inappropriate ways, the primary factors undermining them were the overwhelming number of disputed mining claims they were forced to handle and the unbridled desire of William M. Stewart to control the territorial and state governments. The Nevada territorial courts were inundated with mining claims and did not have the staff to deal with them in a timely fashion. As one historian of the period has noted, "The first result of the opening of the Comstock mines was wild speculation, and the second almost endless litigation."[2] Chief among the reasons for this litigation was the question whether various lucrative ore veins were part of a single ledge and therefore the property of one company or whether they were separate ledges that would allow ownership by a number of individuals or companies.

A decision by the judges on behalf of either theory meant the gain or loss of tremendous fortunes to those involved. With such high stakes at issue, the judges were in a no-win situation and could not escape severe criticism regardless of how they decided. To make matters worse, there were virtually no statutes governing the issues at hand and the judges were forced to apply obscure mining district regulations and common law, when those were available. As though the deck were not stacked enough against the judges, witnesses and jurors in these cases were often bribed by the mining companies, which stood to win or lose millions of dollars.

It is perhaps possible that the first territorial judges could have survived the controversy over mining claims, had it not been for the actions of William M. Stewart. As explained in chapter 2, Stewart was partly responsible for the failure of the 1863 constitution because he maneuvered control over the Union Party convention in Storey County and ensured that individuals allied with him were listed on the ballot for the state's first officers. The unwillingness of many in Nevada Territory to allow Stewart and his minions to control the new state government led them to defeat the proposed constitution and Stewart's handpicked slate of candidates by a 4 to 1 margin. Stewart, however, was not to be stopped.

Politically and economically, Stewart had much to gain by destroying the territorial judges' legitimacy. As a well-paid attorney for wealthy California mining companies, he and his clients stood to win (or lose) vast riches depending upon the judges' decisions in these mining-claim cases. Politically, Stewart could achieve two goals important to him by undermining the territorial judiciary. He could, on the one hand, increase support for statehood and rid the area of its appointed territorial judges, replacing them with elected state judges, whom he believed would be more controllable. On the other hand, he could wreak revenge against his old nemesis, John North, who had replaced Justice Mott on the territorial bench.

Stewart's conflict with Justice North had begun at the 1863 constitutional convention over the issue of mine taxation; North had also opposed Stewart's stacking of the 1863 ballot with his allies. The relationship further deteriorated between 1863 and 1864 when North, serving in his capacity as a district court judge, ruled against several of Stewart's clients, including the Chollar Mining Company. Stewart appealed his Chollar loss to the territorial supreme court, where North and Justice Powhatan B. Locke, who had replaced Justice Jones, upheld the earlier decision against Stewart's client and in favor of the Potosi Mining Company. Politically and economically, then, North had stood in Stewart's way, and the latter was not a man to be denied.

On August 22, 1864, Stewart had his revenge when he and his allies forced all three territorial judges to resign. That they did resign was due in no small part to their own unprofessional conduct. North himself had ascended to the bench under dubious circumstances. A newspaper of the time reported that the Potosi Company had paid Justice Mott a $25,000 bribe to resign so that he could be replaced by North, whom the company knew to favor their cause. North muddied the waters further when he accepted a loan from the Potosi Company to build a mill in Washoe City, even though he knew he might be assigned the Potosi-Chollar litigation. Chief Justice Turner was threatened by Stewart with an arrest warrant charging that Turner had accepted a $5,000 bribe in a previous mining case. Justice Locke, after deciding with North in favor of the Potosi Company, issued an addendum to the file, reopening the hearing of evidence. Besieged by that company, he then withdrew it, causing him to gain enemies from both sides. Thus, from August 22 until December 1864, when the state's first officials took office, Nevada Territory was without a judiciary. That fact certainly led many, as Stewart had surely hoped, to support statehood.

From 1864 until 1984 the Nevada courts enjoyed a period of relative calm, although there were various problems over the years. In the decades of the 1980s and 1990s, however, the Nevada Supreme Court was once again the subject of much criticism and debate. And like their territorial predecessors, the justices of that court are in no small part responsible for their own difficulties.

In 1984 two particularly nasty judicial elections dominated the state's attention. The race for district court judge in Clark County between Charles Thompson and Joe Bonaventure and the supreme court race between incumbent Noel Manoukian and challenger Cliff Young were rampant with charges of conflict of interest and unethical behavior on the part of the candidates and their supporters. Unfortunately, that pattern continued in the distasteful and expensive (more than $1 million) contest for an open supreme court seat between Thompson and Miriam Shearing in 1992. Eighteen percent of those voting in the Thompson-Shearing race were apparently so disgusted that they cast their votes for "none of these candidates."

It is perhaps to be expected that election campaigns, even for judgeships, will sometimes be too vigorously contested. However, the troubles of the supreme court have not ended there. In late 1991, three justices of the supreme court publicly attacked glaucoma-afflicted Chief Justice John Mowbray's proposed bid for reelection, claiming that he was unable to perform his duties and should step down. With charges and countercharges flying between the parties over competency, conspiracy, and inappropriate telephone use, Mowbray eventually decided not to run, thus setting up the open seat that resulted in the Thompson-Shearing free-for-all.

In 1993 the supreme court involved itself in proceedings of the Commission on Judicial Discipline into the actions of Washoe County district judge Jerry Carr Whitehead. Whitehead had been accused of attempting to intimidate attorneys who sought to have their cases removed from his court. The court's proceedings were held in secret and two of its members recused themselves from the case, one voluntarily (Cliff Young) and one by force (Robert Rose). In a series of decisions between 1993 and 1995 the supreme court removed the attorney general as the commission's legal adviser and dismissed the charges against Whitehead. Only

Justice Shearing, the first woman to serve on the high court, dissented from these orders. Whitehead, in a bargain with federal authorities, eventually resigned from the bench in order to avoid prosecution for unspecified federal charges.

Whether it was true or not, many believed that the court was merely acting to protect one of the state's "good ol' boys," and the justices' standing among the public and the legal community declined even more. In a 1994 poll of three hundred attorneys conducted by the state's largest newspaper, the *Las Vegas Review-Journal,* 75 percent indicated that they had only "some" or "not much" confidence in the supreme court.

Recently the state's high court has attempted to salvage its image in various ways. The court has opened to the public its meetings to discuss administrative rules changes that affect how the courts operate. In addition, it has determined that disciplinary proceedings against attorneys by the State Bar of Nevada are to be open once probable cause has been established. And in an addition to the Whitehead case, the justices unanimously agreed in 1995 to open to the public the proceedings of the Commission on Judicial Discipline once a complaint is judged to have merit. Any sanctions against a judge by the commission must also be made public.

Structure and Functions

The state court system of Nevada operates separately and independently of the federal court system. Its chief function is to interpret state statutes and state constitutional provisions and impose sanctions on those who violate them. State court decisions based entirely on state law cannot be appealed to the federal courts; however, should a state case also involve issues of federal law (e.g., a state drug case in which the defendant invokes the Fourth Amendment protection from unreasonable searches and seizures), it could be appealed to the U.S. Supreme Court.

The state court system is divided into three levels: appellate court (Nevada Supreme Court), courts of general jurisdiction (Nevada district courts), and courts of limited jurisdiction (justice courts and municipal courts). Nevada is one of only eleven states not to have an intermediate court of appeals between its supreme court and trial courts. Proposed constitutional amendments to reduce the supreme court's increasing workload by adding an intermediate court to the state judicial system have been defeated by the voters three times: 1972, 1980, and 1992.

Nevada Supreme Court

The Nevada Supreme Court is the court of last resort in the state judicial system. Except when a federal issue is involved, its decisions are final. Justices on the court are elected for six-year, staggered terms. Between 1864 and 1915, these elections were partisan; since 1915, however, candidates for the high court run in nonpartisan elections. Constitutionally, any "qualified elector" (see chapter 6) is eligible to run for election. By statute, however, one must also be at least twenty-five years of age, an attorney licensed to practice law in Nevada, and a two-year resident of the state.

The 1864 constitution established a three-member supreme court. Given the perceived corruption of the territorial judiciary, there was great debate among the convention delegates on the issue. Some of the delegates favored a five-member court, believing that five justices would be harder to bribe than three, while others, including James A. Banks of Humboldt County, thought it impossible to find more than three "pure" and "able" justices to sit on the bench.[3] A compromise adopted in the convention established the number of justices at three and included the proviso that the legislature could increase the number to five without constitutional amendment. In 1967 the legislature exercised that option. In 1976 the voters approved a constitutional amendment removing the cap on the number of justices and leaving the matter solely to the discretion of the legislature. Should the legislature increase the size of the supreme court beyond five, it must continue to provide for staggered terms and may provide for the court to hear cases in panels of three or more justices, as is done in the U.S. Courts of Appeal. A proposal supported by some of the court's justices to increase supreme court membership to seven failed in the 1995 legislature.

The expansion of the court's membership in 1967 from three to five also created a difficulty in selection of the chief justice. The chief justiceship is a rotating position held by the most senior justice, that is, the justice in his or her last two years of a term. When there were only three justices on the court, their staggered terms of office made the question of who would serve as chief justice an easy one. However, now that there are five justices, it is often the case that there will be two justices serving the last two years of their terms at the same time. In those cases, the constitution provides for the selection of the chief justice by lot, typically a coin toss. In some instances the two justices have cooperated, with one of them serving as chief justice in the first year and the other in the second. The other would serve as vice–chief justice during the year in which he or she was not chief justice. In 1992 the voters rejected a constitutional amendment that would have allowed the court to select its own chief justice.

The supreme court exercises both original and appellate jurisdiction. However, few original jurisdiction cases are decided by the court; its appellate docket constitutes the vast majority of the court's workload. On original jurisdiction, the court has authority to issue various writs, including writs of mandamus, certiorari, prohibition, quo warranto, and habeas corpus. The legislature is prohibited from increasing or decreasing the court's original jurisdiction, without a constitutional amendment.

The court hears appeals coming from the state's district courts but is restricted to hearing questions of law only (e.g., was a confession illegally obtained) and not questions of fact (e.g., is the defendant innocent or guilty). Like the U.S. Supreme Court, the court cannot give advisory opinions or hear cases involving moot issues. Its appellate jurisdiction includes power to issue the writs noted above and any other writs that may be necessary or proper in the exercise of its appellate duties.

The state's booming population has led to an increase in the court's workload. From 1955 to 1990, the number of cases filed increased by an astounding 2,000 percent.[4] In 1993, 1,256 new cases were filed with the supreme court; 900 had been held over from its previous term. The court disposed of a record 1,131 cases in 1993, but 1,025 cases remained unresolved and held over until 1994. The court's increasing backlog means that unless something happens soon, Nevadans will be waiting longer than ever in the future for final disposition of their cases.

As is true in other appellate courts in the United States, the supreme court justices do not hear evidence, witnesses, or testimony. Instead, the attorneys for both sides submit written briefs to justices, indicating why they believe the proceeding in the district court was proper or improper. In some of these cases, the attorneys are allowed to present oral arguments to the justices in open court as well. The justices then meet in secret conference to discuss and vote on the case and write a majority opinion. In some cases, justices will also write concurring opinions (agreeing with the decision but for different reasons than the majority opinion) or dissenting opinions (disagreeing with the majority's decision).

Should a justice be disabled or disqualified from hearing a case, as were two justices in the Whitehead matter noted above, the governor is empowered to appoint a district court judge to sit in his or her place. In practice, however, the court itself, typically the chief justice, will suggest a judge to the governor, who will then make the appointment.

Nevada District Courts

District court judges are, like supreme court justices, chosen in nonpartisan elections for six-year terms. They must meet the same eligibility requirements as members of the high court. Unlike supreme court justices, however, they do not serve staggered terms; the state constitution mandates that all district court judges stand for election at the same time.

Although the number has varied over the years, since 1973 there have been nine judicial districts in Nevada (see Table 8.1). It is the prerogative of the legislature to determine the number and boundaries of these districts and the number of judges serving in them. Some districts may have only one judge; others will have several. The Eighth Judicial District, comprising only Clark County, is the

Table 8.1

Judicial Districts in Nevada, 1996

District	Area Encompassed	Number of Judges
First	Carson City and Storey County	2
Second	Washoe County	11*
Third	Churchill and Lyon Counties	2
Fourth	Elko County	2
Fifth	Mineral, Esmeralda, and Nye Counties	1
Sixth	Lander, Pershing, and Humboldt Counties	2
Seventh	Eureka, White Pine, and Lincoln Counties	2
Eighth	Clark County	22**
Ninth	Douglas County	2

Source: Nevada Revised Statutes (n.r.s.) Section 3.010 et seq.

*One of these judges is statutorily required to serve in family court.

**Six of these judges are statutorily required to serve in family court. A law passed during the 1995 legislature increases the number of judges in the Eighth Judicial District to twenty-four (eight of whom will serve in family court), effective January 1997.

state's most populous and, consequently, has the largest number of judges; in 1997, it will have twenty-four, eight of whom serve in the family court division. Regardless of the number of judges in a judicial district, however, district courts are single-judge courts, meaning that cases are heard by a single judge and not by a panel as in the supreme court. In some civil cases and in all "serious" criminal cases, defined as those in which the defendant may receive a penalty of a fine of more than $500 or incarceration of more than six months, the defendant is entitled to a jury trial. It is always within the discretion of the defendant, however, to waive a jury trial and be tried solely by the judge. As noted in chapter 3, criminal-trial juries must be unanimous to reach a verdict, while civil juries may do so with only a three-fourths decision.

The district courts exercise both appellate and original jurisdiction. Their original jurisdiction is broad and includes all cases in which the legislature has not granted jurisdiction to the courts of limited jurisdiction. These cases involve more serious criminal offenses and civil cases over $5,000. However, under a law passed by the state legislature in 1991 to reduce the district courts' workload, all civil cases of less than $25,000 must first be submitted to nonbinding arbitration. If no agreement is reached, the case proceeds to district court for a hearing. Original jurisdiction of the district courts also includes the authority to hear appeals from the final orders of state administrative agencies such as the Gaming Control Board.

In addition, the district courts have power to issue the same writs as the supreme court. Decisions made by the district courts in any cases that are part of their original jurisdiction are appealable to the state supreme court.

The appellate jurisdiction of the district courts is found in their authority to hear appeals from the decisions of the municipal and justice courts. At one time, justice and municipal courts were not required to record their proceedings. Since they were not courts of record, all appeals from them to the district courts were given a trial *de novo*, that is, an entirely new trial. The large number of appeals from the courts of limited jurisdiction led, by the late 1970s, to a tremendous workload on the district courts. In 1979, the state legislature mandated that all justice courts tape-record their proceedings, thereby transforming them into courts of record. To reduce the district courts' workload further, a 1991 statute allows municipal courts to record their proceedings as well. Appeals from the justice courts and the municipal courts that have chosen to tape trials are no longer mandatory upon the district courts, and the appellants must show that they did not receive a fair trial.

In 1990, the voters approved a constitutional amendment allowing the legislature to establish family court divisions within the district courts. The legislature exercised that authority in 1991 and created family courts to hear cases involving issues such as child support and custody and other civil, domestic-law matters.

Municipal and Justice Courts

The lowest tier in Nevada's judicial system, the courts of limited jurisdiction, consists of the justice and municipal courts. They have original jurisdiction only and hear minor criminal and civil matters, most notably traffic violations.

Judges in the justice courts are referred to as justices of the peace and are selected by the voters of the state's fifty-five townships in nonpartisan elections for six-year, staggered terms. The only constitutional requirement for office is that they be qualified electors; the constitution does not require them to be attorneys. However, by statute the legislature has mandated that all justices of the peace serving in townships with populations of 250,000 or more be licensed to practice law in the state. Justice courts have three major duties: to hear cases involving minor criminal offenses, to hear civil cases of $5,000 or less, and to hold preliminary hearings in felony cases to determine if there is probable cause to hold the defendant over for trial in a district court.

Incorporated cities in Nevada must also have a municipal court. The chief function of these courts is to hear traffic cases and cases involving violations of city ordinances. The method of selection and term of office for municipal court judges varies from city to city and is outlined in each city's charter. For example, Sparks and Las Vegas elect their municipal judges, while Boulder City's is appointed by the city council.

Judicial Discipline, Removal, and Vacancies

Nevada Commission on Judicial Discipline

In 1976 the voters of Nevada approved a constitutional amendment establishing a state Commission on Judicial Discipline. The commission consists of seven members: two judges or justices appointed by the supreme court, two members of the State Bar of Nevada selected by the bar's board of governors, and three laypeople appointed by the governor. The 1976 amendment gave the commission authority only to censure, retire, or remove supreme court and district court judges and retire or remove, but not censure, municipal and justice court judges.

In 1994, however, the voters amended the constitutional provisions regulating the commission to allow the supreme court to establish other sanctions against misbehaving judges. In 1995 the supreme court adopted new rules that allow the commission to fine judges, prohibit them from running again, require them to issue public apologies, and force them to enter counseling or training programs. In addition, the commission was authorized by the court to issue public reprimands, something less than censure, against wayward judges. Any discipline imposed by the commission can be appealed to the state supreme court.

At least partly in response to the Whitehead proceedings noted above, the court also directed that once the commission has decided that a complaint against a judge has merit, all further proceedings must be open to the public. Furthermore, any sanctions issued against a judge must be made public. Previously some judges avoided public knowledge of their misdeeds by agreeing to private sanctions from the commission. The supreme court clearly hopes that making such matters public not only will make judges more obedient to the code of judicial conduct but also will help the public regain its confidence in the state's judicial system. It is too soon to know, but such disclosures may also have the unintended consequence of increasing the supreme court's workload, since judges might feel compelled to appeal all sanctions, no matter how small, in order to clear their names.

Judicial Removal

Although voters always have the option of not returning a judge to the bench at election time, judges in Nevada may also be removed from office prior to the expiration of their terms in four ways. They may be recalled (see chapter 4), they may be retired or removed from the bench by the commission on judicial discipline, and, in the case of supreme court justices and district court judges but not justices of the peace, they may be impeached (see chapter 7) or otherwise removed by the legislature.

Legislative removal provides a method short of impeachment whereby the state legislature may remove a supreme court or district court judge for "any reasonable cause." The majority necessary to do so (a two-thirds majority of the elected members in both houses) is more stringent than that required for impeachment, but this procedure dispenses with the need to bring formal charges and to conduct a trial in the senate. Many at the constitutional convention feared that such a process would undermine the independence of the judiciary. Others, however, believed that some sort of process was necessary for removing judges in an emergency situation or for dealing with a judge who was behaving badly but had not engaged in any misdemeanor or malfeasance sufficient to invoke impeachment.

The legislative removal provision was widely supported by the mining interests at the convention. Given, as noted above, the tremendous financial stakes involved in mining litigation, they wished to have at their disposal a less formal method than impeachment to remove "unfavorable judicial opinion."[5]

Judicial Vacancies

Prior to 1976, a vacancy on the supreme court or district courts was filled by gubernatorial appointment. In 1976, however, the voters chose to limit the governor's sole power to fill vacancies by approving a constitutional amendment creating the Nevada Commission on Judicial Selection. Under this system, when a vacancy occurs the commission takes applications from interested parties and recommends three names to the governor. The governor then selects one of these three individuals to fill the vacancy; he or she cannot go off the list and must make a selection within thirty days or be prohibited from making any other appointments until such time as he has filled the judicial vacancy. Judges selected in this way serve only until the next general election, when they must run in a nonpartisan election for the remainder, if any, of the term.

Those who support the election of judges on the basis that the electoral process is more likely to hold judges accountable will, no doubt, be unpleasantly surprised to find that since 1939, 67 percent of the justices who served on the supreme court were initially appointed to their positions to fill midterm vacancies. It has also been the case in Nevada that incumbent judges, even those appointed to fill vacancies, are rarely if ever defeated at the polls. Since the state adopted nonpartisan elections in 1915, 93 percent of incumbents running for reelection to the supreme court have won; 71 percent of these winners failed to even draw an opponent.[6]

Should a vacancy occur at the supreme court level, the so-called "permanent commission" determines the three names to be submitted to the governor. The "permanent commission" consists of the chief justice of the supreme court or an associate justice designated by him, three members of the state bar appointed by the bar's board of governors, and three laypeople named by the governor. Should the vacancy be at the district court level, the list of nominees is developed by a "temporary commission" made up of the permanent commission plus one other member of the state bar and one other layperson residing in the district in which

Table 8.2

The Nevada Judiciary, Famous Firsts

First woman to serve on the state supreme court	Miriam Shearing (1995)
First woman to serve on the district court	Miriam Shearing (1983)
First African American to serve on the district court	Dell Guy (1975)
First Hispanic to serve on the district court	John Mendoza (1967)

Source: Secretary of State's Office and the Nevada State Library and Archives.

the vacancy has occurred. The members of the permanent commission serve four-year, staggered terms of office, and the terms of the two additional members of a temporary commission expire once the list has been submitted to the governor.

Vacancies in the justice courts are filled by the county commission with jurisdiction over the particular township in which the vacancy occurs. Municipal court vacancies are filled according to the rules and regulations embodied in the city charter.

Chapter Nine

City and County Governments

It is generally true that most citizens pay far more attention to the actions of the national and state governments than they do to local governments such as counties and cities. This is due in part to the nature of the issues dealt with by those larger entities, such as war and peace and economic policies; in part it is due to the microscopic attention paid by the mass media to their every move. Yet, the policies and concerns of local governments affect citizens' lives in significant ways: taxes, streets, sewage and garbage services, law enforcement, zoning, liquor licenses, schools, and a host of others. Indeed, on a daily basis, these governments may have a more profound effect on citizens than those at the national and state levels.

It is worth noting, however, that the powers exercised by local governments are highly circumscribed by the state. Under the U.S. Constitution, states are autonomous and independent of the federal government in many ways. The Tenth Amendment reserves to the states all powers not delegated to the federal government or prohibited to the states. Thus, states are generally free to exercise these reserved powers as they see fit, so long as they do not infringe upon federal power or the civil liberties of their citizens.

The same is not true for local governments. They are considered creatures of the state and have no independent power; as subdivisions of the state they may exercise only those powers given to them by the state constitution and statutes. In 1911, John F. Dillon defined the powers of local governments:

> It is a general and undisputed proposition of law that a municipal corporation possesses and can exercise the following powers, and no others: first, those granted in express words; second, those necessarily or fairly implied in or incident to the powers expressly granted; third, those essential to the accomplishment of the declared objects and purposes of the corporation—not simply convenient, but indispensable. Any fair, reasonable, substantial doubt concerning the existence of power is resolved by the courts against a corporation, and the power is denied.[1]

Dillon's rule, as this formulation is called, continues to hold sway in Nevada in the later twentieth century. One other point of interest that will become clearer below is that local governing boards (e.g., county commissions and city councils) are not required to abide by the separation of powers that characterizes the national and state governments. These boards exercise executive, legislative, and, on occasion, quasi-judicial powers.

Counties and Townships

When Nevada's first territorial legislature met in 1861, it established nine counties. Between 1861 and 1864, two additional counties were created so that, at the time of statehood, Nevada had eleven. During its first decade of statehood, four more were created and one of the original nine, Roop County, was folded into Washoe County. Today, the state has seventeen counties; the most recently established is Pershing County (1919), although in 1969 the legislature consolidated Carson City and Ormsby County into a single city-county. Given that the state constitution requires a majority of a county's voters to approve the abolition of their county, it is doubtful that further changes will take place.

Article IV of the state constitution requires the legislature to establish a "uniform" system of county and township governments. This language means that the legislature may not arbitrarily single out a certain county for special treatment; all must be treated uniformly. However, the state may distinguish between counties based on reasonable and neutral criteria. For example, the state supreme court has upheld a statute allowing consolidation of city and county law enforcement agencies in county seats with populations of more than 200,000, even though at the time the law was passed few cities and counties in the state would qualify. This distinction was permissible because it was "prospectively applicable to all counties which might grow into it."[2]

The governing board of each county is the Board of County Commissioners. The state constitution requires the legislature to establish these boards as elective positions, although the number and salary of commissioners is left to legislative discretion. Clark County's board, with seven commissioners, is the largest; the smallest boards, found in the least populous counties, have three. All county commissioners in the state are chosen in partisan elections for terms of four years. Midterm vacancies are filled by the governor.

As creations of the state, county boards of commissioners have only the powers given to them by the state legislature or the constitution. Their primary role is to perform the duties delegated to them by the state, such as law enforcement and administering state statutes on health, marriage, divorce, child custody, and property. Some of the more populous counties have also hired professional county managers to assist them in managing the county bureaucracies that were created to fulfill these responsibilities.

In addition to limits put upon them by the state, county commissioners and managers also find their powers over county government circumscribed by the fact that many county department heads are independently elected to their positions. Thus, these individuals are autonomous and dependent upon the voters, not the commissioners, for their continuance in office. Among these officers are the county clerk, district attorney, county recorder, county assessor, sheriff, and public administrator.

The legislature has also established fifty-five townships within the state's seventeen counties. Unlike in some eastern states, townships are not particularly important in Nevada except as legal subdivisions in which justices of the peace are elected (see chapter 8).

City Governments

Article VIII of the state constitution requires the legislature to enact laws providing for the organization of cities and towns. Cities, referred to in the constitution as "municipal corporations," may be established by general or special charters. A general charter is a "standard form of city government drawn up by the legislature that permits creation of a municipal government under its terms," while a special charter, as the name implies, is "usually drafted by a city to reflect its particular requirements," but which must still be approved by the legislature. Examples of the former are Ely and Winnemucca, while Reno and Las Vegas illustrate the latter.[3] Currently there are nineteen incorporated cities in the state: thirteen established by special charter and six by general charter.[4]

Cities perform the same general functions within their boundaries as counties do within theirs, although their powers are broader than those of the counties. They are governed by a city council chosen in nonpartisan elections. Unlike county government, which is subject to the structure imposed by the legislature, cities are free to adopt the form of government most attuned to their needs. In some cities, such as Las Vegas and Reno, the mayor is elected by the voters. In others, such as Boulder City, the city council selects the mayor from among its members.

Like the counties, some of the larger cities have hired professionals, city managers, to administer the bureaucracy. City managers, like county managers, serve at the pleasure of the council or commission, respectively. Unlike in the counties, most department heads are chosen by the manager rather than elected by the voters. Thus, the city council and manager tend to have greater control over the structure and functioning of city government than their counterparts in the county have over county government.

Other Local Governments

In 1955, the state legislature consolidated the state's 167 school districts into 17, one for each county. The Clark County School District, largest in the state, is also the tenth largest school district in the country. The governing body of each school district is an elected school board. The board, in turn, appoints a superintendent to manage the day-to-day affairs of the district. The school boards have tremendous discretion to establish district policies governing attendance, curriculum, and many other facets of their educational mission. They are, however, subject to the dictates of the elected, eleven-member state Board of Education. Higher education in the state is governed by the University and Community College System of Nevada's elected, eleven-member Board of Regents.

The state also has established more than one hundred noneducation special district governments. Indeed, nationwide such districts are the fastest growing entities at the local level. These district governments are responsible for performing a single function and include fire districts, health districts, water districts, library districts, and so on. They are governed by boards, some elected and some appointed, and some of them have the power to tax. As local government entities, they are also creations of the state and exercise only the powers given them by the state and may be altered or abolished by the state legislature.

Chapter Ten

State and Local Finance

Supreme Court Justice Oliver Wendell Holmes once noted that taxes are the price we pay for a civilized society. Although most can agree with Holmes's sentiment, questions over who will pay taxes and how those funds will be spent inevitably invite disagreement. Indeed, revenue and appropriations questions are the epitome of what we call "politics." Deciding who does and who does not pay taxes and who benefits from these moneys is the quintessential method of determining the winners and losers in the world of politics and government.

As noted in chapter 2, political conflict over taxation began early in the state's history. Territorial governor Nye had battled with the legislature at its first session in 1861 over whether mines and/or their products would be taxed. The 1863 constitution had been defeated, at least in part, because it included a provision taxing mines at the same rate as all other property. That "indiscretion" was avoided in the 1864 constitution, which taxed only mining proceeds.

Mines, however, were not the only industry in the state attempting to benefit from sympathetic constitutional provisions. The failed 1863 constitution had also included a section allowing the state to issue up to $3 million in bonds to assist in building a railroad. Noting that Nevada would be a poor state, especially since the delegates decided to limit taxes on the state's major industry, the 1864 delegates rejected a similar proposal to aid the wealthy railroad companies and included a provision in Article VIII prohibiting the state from donating or lending money or its credit to any corporation other than those considered educational or charitable.

The state constitution requires the biennial budget to be balanced. The federal government has had deficit budgets every year since 1969, but Nevada's officials must equalize revenue and appropriations with a surplus available to deal with any emergencies that may arise. That has been made difficult over the years for a number of reasons: population growth, economic downturns, a general anti-tax stance within the state, and biennial budgeting.

For several years, Nevada has been the fastest growing state in the nation. That growth has meant unpredictability in budgeting for two-year cycles. In 1995, Nevada's population hit the 1.5 million mark, almost double the state's 800,500 residents in 1980 and more than triple the 488,738 living here in 1970. Approximately 1 million people, or two-thirds of the state's population, reside in Clark County. Although these new residents pay taxes, those revenues are spread over their lifetimes, while their needs (schools, roads, hospitals, recreation) are immediate. For example, even before they have paid a penny in taxes, these newcomers require roads for their cars and schools for their children. The need for immediate services among the fastest growing population in the nation has put tremendous strain on the state's ability to meet its citizens' needs, especially when budgets must be approved for two years at a time.

Biennial budgeting is even more difficult when it is based on an unstable revenue base. More than 75 percent of Nevada's revenue is based on gaming and sales taxes. These taxes are the most unstable of all types and create a certain degree of unpredictability in estimating state income over a two-year period. In an economic downturn, such as the state faced in the early 1980s and in the 1991–1993 biennium, fewer people are likely to visit the gaming tables or purchase big-ticket items. Thus, in a recession, when residents' needs for state services such as unemployment compensation, food stamps, and welfare are at their highest, the revenues coming into the state's coffers from gaming and sales taxes will be in decline. In 1992 and 1993, Governor Miller, responding to an unexpected decline in the two tax sources, was forced to cut $173 million of previously approved appropriations in order to make the budget balance.

It was once observed that the perfect legislator is one who "votes for all appropriations, and against all taxes."[1] Indeed, most citizens want the government to offer a multitude of services; they simply do not want to pay for them. That is equally true in Nevada, which has managed to shift much of the tax burden to the state's visitors in the form of gaming and sales taxes. The state may suffer the consequences of an unstable tax base in a recession, but it seems to be a chance Nevada's residents are willing to take. Nevadans' virulent anti-tax stance is illustrated by the fact that the state is the third-lowest in the nation in its state and local tax burden, ahead of only Alaska and Wyoming.[2] Governor Miller and the 1995 legislature considered it a major success that no taxes were added or increased during the 1995–1997 biennium.

As noted in chapter 5, Nevada's low tax burden has frequently meant low levels of service for the state's poor and handicapped, who have generally been unsuccessful at the lobbying game. It is perhaps ironic to note (or perhaps not) that the state's residents, virtually obsessed with the taxes they pay, have not only the third-lowest state and local tax burden but the seventh-highest per capita income among the fifty states.[3]

Revenue

The state receives its revenue from a variety of sources: taxes, fees, fines, and the federal government (see Table 10.1). Not all of these funds can be expended at the

Table 10.1

Nevada General Fund Revenues by Source, 1977–1997 (In Percent)

Biennium	Gaming Taxes	Casino Enter. Tax	Sales & Use Taxes	Business License Tax	Insurance Prem. Tax	Cigarette Tax	Mining Tax	Liquor Tax	Slot Tax Transfer	Tobacco & Other Taxes	Nontax Revenues*
1995–1997	37.9	2.9	35.4	4.9	7.2	2.7	1.7	1.1	0.4	0.2	5.6
1993–1995	41.3	2.5	31.8	5.3	8.3	2.9	1.7	1.2	NA	0.2	4.8
1991–1993	40.1	2.3	32.6	5.7	6.5	3.6	2.1	1.3	NA	0.2	5.6
1989–1991	40.0	2.3	35.2	NA	7.2	4.4	3.3	1.5	0.6	0.3	5.2
1987–1989	41.4	3.0	35.5	NA	7.7	2.4	1.7	1.9	0.8	0.3	5.3
1985–1987	43.7	3.3	36.2	NA	5.9	1.6	NA	2.3	1.0	0.4	5.6
1983–1985	42.3	3.5	33.8	NA	7.2	1.3	NA	2.4	1.2	0.4	6.5
1981–1983	42.3	5.7	39.6	NA	3.9	NA	NA	2.6	NA	NA	5.9
1979–1981	41.5	5.8	39.9	NA	4.2	NA	NA	3.2	NA	NA	5.4
1977–1979	37.6	6.3	36.8	NA	3.3	NA	NA	4.3	NA	NA	5.5

Source: Compiled by the author from the Legislative Counsel Bureau's *Nevada Legislative Appropriations Report* for each of the biennial periods.

*Includes fees for licenses, fines, charges for services, use of money and property, and miscellaneous revenue.

Note: Rows will not always add to 100 percent, since some revenue measures have been omitted.

state's discretion. Some federal funds, for instance, are earmarked for airports, highways, or education; some taxes and fees must be spent on particular programs. In all, about 52 percent of the state's revenues are earmarked for particular purposes;[4] the remainder is disbursed at the discretion of the legislature, which must appropriate any money expended from the state treasury.

Taxes

Two forms of taxes are prohibited by the state constitution. State income taxes have long been prohibited by statute, but in the 1980s many in the state feared that the legislature might approve one in order to stabilize the state's tax base. A successful citizens' initiative in 1988 and 1990 put the issue outside legislative discretion by amending the constitution to prohibit taxes on personal income.

A constitutional amendment passed in 1942 prohibits the state from collecting inheritance taxes on the estates of deceased residents. Unfortunately, that provision also precluded the state from picking up its share of the *federal* estate tax; Nevada was the only state not to do so and its share, sometimes in the millions, reverted to the federal treasury. An attempt in 1982 to allow the state to pick up its share of the federal estate tax was defeated by the voters; apparently they thought that the proposal would create additional taxes rather than simply give the state its share of federal taxes already collected. In the 1986 election, with assurances in hand that the proposal would not create any new or increased taxes, the voters approved amending the constitution. The 1986 amendment is important because many wealthy individuals, drawn to the state by its lack of an income tax and its generally low taxes, choose to live (and die) here. Nevada may now pick up its share of what is often a substantial federal estate tax. Proceeds of the tax credit are earmarked solely for education.

Gaming taxes make up the largest share of the state's revenue, slightly more than 40 percent. There are four different types of gaming taxes in Nevada, and their distribution differs from type to type. The largest source of gaming taxes is on the gross gambling income of each casino. Proceeds from the tax go into the state's general fund to be appropriated by the legislature. The second largest source of gaming taxes is derived from an annual tax of $250 on each slot machine. Revenue from the slot machine tax is earmarked 80 percent for education and 20 percent to pay off bonds sold to construct the Thomas and Mack Center at the University of Nevada, Las Vegas, and the Lawlor Events Center at the University of Nevada, Reno. Third-largest among the gaming taxes is the casino entertainment tax, which is applied to all sales and admissions at entertainment events in the state's casinos; like the gross receipts tax, it is deposited into the general fund. Finally, the state levies a tax on each gaming table in Nevada, with the revenues being divided evenly among the seventeen counties. Without this tax, generated primarily in Clark and Washoe Counties, the less-populated counties in the state would have difficulty meeting their revenue needs.

One sort of gaming tax that will not be found is on lotteries. To the surprise of many outside the state, the Nevada Constitution prohibits lotteries. Until the constitution was amended in 1990, that provision also made it illegal to run a church raffle or other charitable lottery. Although the constitutional prohibition on charitable lotteries was frequently ignored, the voters decided that an exemption to the lottery ban was in order if for no other reason than to recognize actual practice.

Gaming taxes and sales taxes, as noted earlier, make up more than 75 percent of the state's revenue and are popular in the state, since much of these taxes are paid, at least indirectly, by tourists. Sales taxes began in Nevada in 1955 at a level of 2 percent; proceeds go into the state's general fund. The tax was brought to a referendum vote by the people in 1956 and was approved. Because the 2 percent level was approved in a popularly initiated referendum, it is immunized from legislative change, as explained in chapter 4; it can be added to only by another vote of the people. In the 1964 elections, the voters refused to raise the tax to 3 percent.

In order to meet the state's dire need for additional revenue to fund the public schools, the legislature in 1967 added a 1 percent "school support tax," to be collected at the point of all sales. Because the 1 percent was earmarked for education and was returned to the county in which it originated, the Nevada Supreme Court held that it was not a "sales" tax and, thus, did not violate the constitution.[5] In 1969, the legislature further provided for an optional one-half cent city-county relief tax to aid those counties and cities in need of additional revenues; like the school support tax, these taxes do not go into the state's general fund and are not, therefore, considered "sales" taxes. As of 1996, those making purchases in the state pay a 2 percent sales tax, 2.25 percent school support tax, and 2.25 percent city-county relief tax. Washoe and Clark Counties also have exercised their option to charge an additional 0.50 percent tax for specific purposes such as transportation and tourism.

That Nevada currently has one of the highest "sales" taxes in the country (7 percent in Washoe and Clark Counties, 6.5 percent elsewhere in the state) is the result of a deliberate decision by the state to shift the tax burden away from property owners and onto tourists. In order to stave off a proposal similar to California's Proposition 13, Governor List and the 1981 legislature approved a shift that would reduce property taxes, paid almost entirely by Nevada residents, and raise sales taxes, paid by residents and tourists alike. That List's ploy was successful can be seen in the voters' rejection of Question 6 (Nevada's version of Proposition 13) in the 1982 election.

List's "success," however, must be measured against two important facets of reliance upon sales taxes rather than property taxes for state revenue. Sales taxes are less stable and more difficult to predict than are property taxes. Thus, as noted earlier, in an economic downturn when residents' needs for social services are highest, sales taxes will be in decline. Second, sales taxes are regressive. That is, unlike an income tax, which has rates that increase as income increases, the sales tax actually takes a higher percentage of one's income the lower his or her earnings. A 1982 study concluded that a family of four living in Las Vegas with an income of $17,500 would spend 2.4 percent of their income in direct state and local taxes; direct taxes would take only 1.2 percent of the income of the same family making $100,000.[6] In order to reduce the regressivity of the tax somewhat, Nevada's voters approved a constitutional amendment in 1984 exempting food from the sales tax.

As a result of the tax shift of 1981, Nevadans pay one of the lowest property tax rates in the country. By statute, property is assessed at 35 percent of its market value. Thus, a $100,000 home is assessed at $35,000. A 1936 amendment to the state constitution limits the property tax to a maximum of 5 cents per every dollar of assessment. Thus, the maximum property tax that could be collected on a $100,000 home would be $1,750 ($35,000 x .05). In fact, the state's property tax rate comes nowhere near the maximum allowed by the constitution, and most of what is collected by the state in property taxes is returned to local governments.

In 1991 the legislature approved a business tax of $100 per employee up to a maximum of $400,000. The $400,000 cap was criticized because it worked to the benefit of the state's largest casinos, and in 1993 the legislature removed it in favor of a flat rate per employee, no matter how large the enterprise. An attempt in the 1995 legislature to repeal the tax entirely failed when it became clear that the revenue could not be made up otherwise. The business tax will provide approximately 5 percent of the state's revenues in the 1995–1997 biennium.

Excise taxes are the final type of tax used in Nevada. Like sales taxes, they are collected at the time of purchase. Unlike sales taxes, they are collected only on selected items, such as fuel, cigarettes, alcohol, and insurance. Proceeds from fuel taxes and license fees are earmarked by Article IX of the state constitution for purposes of "construction, maintenance, and repair" of public roads. Cigarette taxes are distributed to the counties and incorporated cities on the basis of population. During the 1995–1997 biennium, it is estimated, the cigarette tax will provide about 3 percent of the state's revenue and a tax on insurance premiums will make up another 7.2 percent.

In addition to taxes, state and local revenues are also derived from fines and fees. Parking and traffic fines add to the government's coffers as do fees on everything from marriage, hunting, and fishing licenses to motor vehicles. The federal government also provides various moneys to the state in the form of grants. Typically, the use of these funds is highly circumscribed and they may be used only for a designated purpose, such as education, highways, airports, and the like.

Appropriations

As noted in chapter 7, the governor's budget proposals are usually accepted, virtually intact, by the legislature. The extent to which the legislature is willing to change the governor's proposals will vary from year to year but is always constrained by the fact that the legislature has only six months or so to review, revise, and approve a budget that has taken the governor two years to develop. In the 1995–1997 biennium, the state's budget will be approximately $2.5 billion, up from $2.2 billion in 1993–1995.

In addition to using the funds it receives from the operating budget, which must be balanced, the state may finance its operations by borrowing money through bond sales. Revenue from these bonds is typically used to finance long-term construction projects such as highways and the new addition to the legislative building in Carson City. The bonds are paid off over a long period of time, thus freeing current taxpayers of the burden of paying the entire tab now for projects that will be used by future residents as well. The 1864 constitution established a bonding limit on the state of $300,000. That a specific numerical cap was injudicious quickly came to be realized when, in the early twentieth century, the state had difficulty making capital improvements out of current operating revenue. In 1916, the constitution was amended to establish a bonding capacity of 1 percent of the state's assessed valuation. After a defeat by voters in 1960, the bonding capacity was raised to 2 percent in 1989.

The state's budget is an excellent prism through which to view the needs and desires of the citizens of Nevada. By far the highest level of appropriations in the state is for education. Between 1977 and 1997, state spending on education has remained fairly stable, starting that period at 56.3 percent of the budget and falling to 53.9 percent by 1997. Alarmingly, since 1987, the education budget as a percentage of state appropriations has fallen every biennium (see Table 10.2), even though the number of students has risen dramatically in the same period.

In contrast, state spending for human services has increased slightly over the past two decades, constituting 21.9 percent of the total operating budget in 1977–1979, 23.3 percent in 1981–1983, and 25.8 percent in 1995–1997. Thus, whereas the state has responded to its burgeoning population by slightly increasing its human services expenditures, it has decreased the percentage of the budget expended on education needs.

These two items alone account for almost 80 percent of the state's operating budget for the 1995–1997 biennium. The remaining 20 percent is spent on prisons, highways, public safety, and the provision of other services in the state (see Table 10.2). That amount also includes various appropriations for special interest, or "pork barrel," projects favored by powerful legislators. For example, at the same time it failed to provide funds for a Las Vegas woman's heart transplant, the

Table 10.2

Nevada General Fund Appropriations by Type, 1977–1997 (In Percent)

Biennium	Constitutional Officers	Finance & Admin.	Education	Human Services	Commerce & Industry	Public Safety	Infra-structure	Special Purpose Agencies
1995–1997	3.0	2.6	53.9	25.8	2.3	10.9	1.4	0.1
1993–1995	2.8	1.6	55.0	25.9	2.5	10.6	1.5	0.1

Biennium	General Government	Regulatory	Education	Human Resources	Conservation	Public Safety	Motor Vehicles & Highways	Misc.
1991–1993	4.6	2.6	54.9	23.7	2.1	10.8	0.5	0.8
1989–1991	4.5	2.7	56.7	22.6	2.0	10.2	0.3	1.0
1987–1989	5.0	3.0	57.7	21.2	2.2	9.7	0.3	0.9
1985–1987	5.2	3.2	57.7	20.2	2.2	8.6	0.5	2.4
1983–1985	5.8	3.5	55.2	23.2	2.1	9.0	0.4	0.8
1981–1983	5.5	3.4	52.6	23.3	2.4	7.8	0.5	4.5
1979–1981	5.4	3.0	60.2	19.3	2.4	6.1	0.5	3.1
1977–1979	6.5	3.0	56.3	21.9	2.9	6.0	NA	3.4

Source: Compiled by the author from the Legislative Counsel Bureau's Nevada Legislative Appropriations Report for each of the biennial periods.
Note: The break between the 1991–1993 and 1993–1995 biennial periods indicates the change in categories used by the Legislative Counsel Bureau.

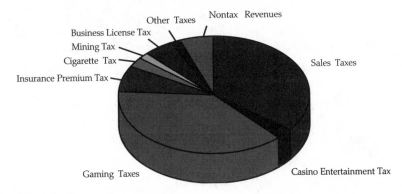

Table 10.3

Nevada General Fund Revised Economic Forum Revenues*: 1995–97 Biennium

State Gaming Taxes	37.9%
Casino Entertainment Tax	2.9%
Subtotal Gaming Taxes	**40.8%**
Sales and Use Taxes	35.4%
Business License Tax	4.9%
Insurance Premium Tax	7.2%
Cigarette Tax	2.7%
Mining Tax	1.7%
Other Taxes:	
Liquor Tax	1.1%
Annual Slot Tax Transfer	0.4%
Tobacco & Other Taxes	0.2%
Subtotal Other Taxes	1.7%
Subtotal All Taxes	**94.4%**
Nontax Revenues:	
Licenses	2.6%
Fees and Fines	0.8%
Charges for Services	0.2%
Use of Money and Property	1.2%
Miscellaneous Revenues	0.8%
Subtotal Nontax Revenues	**5.6%**

Source: Legislative Counsel Bureau, *Nevada Legislative Appropriations Report, 1995–1997*. Reprinted with permission.
*By legislative action only.

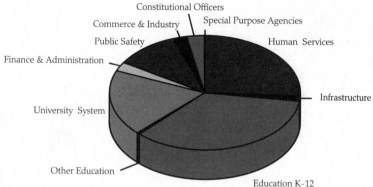

Table 10.4

Nevada General Fund Legislature-Approved Appropriations: 1995–97 Biennium

Constitutional Officers		3.0%
Finance & Administration		2.6%*
Education:		53.9%
K-12	34.8%	
University System	18.6%	
Other	0.5%	
Human Services		25.8%
Commerce & Industry		2.3%
Public Safety		10.9%
Infrastructure		1.4%
Special Purpose Agencies		0.1%

Source: Legislative Counsel Bureau, *Nevada Legislative Appropriations Report, 1995–1997*. Reprinted with permission.

*Includes appropriations for state classified and unclassified employee salary increases.

1995 legislature approved spending $3.2 million on the National Automobile Museum in Reno, $2.5 million for a railway between Boulder City and the Clark County Heritage Museum in Henderson, $5 million to rebuild the V & T Railroad between Carson City and Virginia City, and $250,000 for an animal pavilion at the Clark County Fairgrounds.

Chapter Eleven

Nevada

Past, Present, and Future

Chapters 1 and 2 examined the history of Nevada through 1864. The subsequent eight chapters outlined, within the context of individual topics, the state's historical and political path since it achieved statehood. It seems appropriate, therefore, in this final chapter to discuss and summarize in chronological sequence Nevada's leading historical and political epochs since 1864 and look forward to the state's entry into the twenty-first century.

Nevada Since 1864

In a thoughtful work published in 1986, Nevada historian James Hulse suggested that the state's history tended to fall into three forty-year periods: 1859 to 1899, 1900 to 1939, and 1940 to 1980.[1] Hulse's time lines are certainly not the only ones extant; however, they offer the virtues of simplicity and brevity and constitute an excellent framework for an examination of Nevada history, with the addition of a period beginning in 1980.

The First Period: 1859–1899

The opening of a new frontier brings out the most adventurous and rapacious among a nation's population. That was certainly true in Nevada, where the first forty-year period was characterized by greed, avarice, and unbridled entrepreneurism. In the late 1850s, a California visitor to Nevada wrote in a letter home that

> I have seen more rascality, small and great, in my fairly brief forty days' sojourn to this wilderness of sagebrush, sharpers, and prostitutes, than in a thirteen years' experience in our not squeamishly moral State of California. . . . If I resided here six months I should turn out a consummate rascal.[2]

Organization of the territorial and state governments has been covered in some detail in chapter 2; it is unnecessary to discuss them further here. However, much of what occurred between 1859 and 1864 had a great influence on the first years of Nevada's statehood.

Issues related to mining economics dominated the period from statehood until the end of the nineteenth century, as had been the case prior to statehood. The major difference between the pre-statehood and post-statehood periods, however, was one of mine ownership. Prior to statehood, thousands of miners staked claims to the Comstock Lode. After statehood, ownership of the mines was concentrated in the hands of a wealthy few, the so-called Bank Crowd.

By 1864, it began to appear that the major mining lodes were depleted. In a move that well defines the era, the Bank of California, founded by William C. Ralston in that year, began lending money at discount rates to the state's ore mills. The idea to do so came from Ralston's Virginia City branch manager, William Sharon, about whom it "is probably impossible to find a really kind word that was ever said . . . and preserved in print."[3] Sharon's gamble paid off when the depression continued and the mill owners could not repay the loans: the bank simply took over their mills. Eventually, the bank and its subsidiaries took control of mills and mines, the worth of which was far in excess of the value of the loans they had made. Their hold on the state's mining industry was made complete when in addition to monopolizing water and timber supplies the banks seized control of transportation by incorporating the Virginia and Truckee Railroad Company to build a railway between the ore deposits and Carson City–Reno. Until 1875, the Bank Crowd dominated every aspect of Nevada's mining industry, and thus dominated the state's politics.

In 1875 a run on the Bank of California led to its failure when the bank, weighed down by unsafe investments, was unable to pay its depositors; Ralston responded by committing suicide. After 1875, the Bank of California and its subsidiaries were replaced in prominence by the Bonanza Firm of John W. Mackay, James G. Fair, James C. Flood, and William S. O'Brien. The Bonanza Kings, as these four were known, were responsible for discovering and exploiting the "Big Bonanza" gold and silver ore lode. Like the Bank Crowd before them, they solidified their economic power by coupling their mineral wealth with ownership in milling companies, water companies, and lumber resources.

Because of their economic power within the state, the Bank Crowd and the Bonanza Kings were also able to generally have their way in the political arena. At the federal level, Senator William Stewart did their bidding, and his lasting contribution was the National Mining Act of 1866, which allowed the mining companies to take public lands and water merely by using them. The mining law, still in effect today, also allows mining companies to "patent" (i.e., purchase) public land for five dollars or less an acre; in addition, the mines pay no royalties for the privilege of digging up and carting off the nation's mineral resources.

At the state level, the mining and banking interests were no less successful. In

1865 the first state legislature enacted legislation that would allow a property tax levy of $2.75 per $100 of assessed valuation. However, in its infamous Section 99 the law also provided that the levy on the proceeds of the mines would be limited to $1.00 per $100 of valuation. In addition, a $20 per ton deduction was allowed for working the ore and only three-fourths of the remaining amount could be taxed. As historian Russell Elliott has noted, "The mine owners got a three-way benefit in taxation, first in the state constitution, which specified that mines and mining claims were to be assessed on net proceeds only, and then in the revenue act of 1865, which allowed the deduction for working the ore and then taxed only a portion of the remainder."[4]

The revenue act was declared unconstitutional in 1867,[5] but the Bank Crowd had already convinced the legislature in 1867 and 1871 to pass substitute legislation that would continue preferential tax treatment for the mines. Legislation in 1875 ended that preference, and a series of setbacks in the courts and through gubernatorial vetoes established a more equitable taxation structure in the state.

As discussed in chapter 10, the mines were not the only industry seeking to control the state's politics and economy. Indeed, the railroads were generally more successful than the Bank Crowd and the Bonanza Kings had been in having their way in the state and federal governments. Congress gave the railroads 5 million acres of land in Nevada. And it is beyond dispute that the Central Pacific and Virginia and Truckee railroads overcharged Nevada customers and avoided paying their just due in taxes. Nevada congressman Rollin Daggett, for example, noted in an 1881 speech that the cost of shipping a carload of coal oil from New York to San Francisco was $300; that same carload shipped from New York to Reno would cost $536 and $716 from New York to Winnemucca.[6] In comments reminiscent of those about the wealthy California mining companies that were made at the 1864 state constitutional convention, Daggett observed that "Nevada is an orange which for ten years these railroad vampires have been sucking in silence. We have been, and are still, bleeding at every pore."[7]

That the railroads were so successful in having their way can be attributed to their selection of astute political agents and a win-at-all-costs attitude. The "Big Four" of the Central Pacific Railroad (Leland Stanford, Charles Crocker, Mark Hopkins, and Collis P. Huntington) hired the services of Charles "Black" Wallace, and the V & T Railroad utilized the skills of its agent, H. M. Yerington, to control the state's government. They "literally bought legislators who promised to work for the railroad interest," they controlled delegations to the party conventions "obtaining favorable platforms," and they gave out free railroad passes and other favors to their allies.[8] Yerington gloated in an 1879 letter that

during every Nevada legislature since 1869 bills have been introduced to regulate freight and fares, and many other matters connected with the working of railroads in this state, most of them have been of a blackmailing character requiring *Coin* to prevent them from being introduced or to get them out of the road after introduction. This Co. has put up the Coin in large sums every session and the result has been not one bill inimical to railroads has been passed during all these years.[9]

At the national level, they were able to influence Nevada's U.S. senators, especially William M. Stewart and John P. Jones, through various gifts and favors, including two hundred shares of Central Pacific Railroad stock given to Stewart in 1866.[10] They even managed to get one of their own elected to the Senate in 1875 when William Sharon of the V & T Railroad was chosen by the state legislature, a state legislature filled with men who were, in most respects, in office because of vote buying and the railroads' largess to their campaigns.

The purpose of all this activity on the part of the railroads was, of course, to defeat legislation at both the state and national levels calling for regulation of railroad freight rates. In that, they were generally successful until 1887, when national railroad regulation was passed by Congress in the form of the Interstate Commerce Act.

From the mid-1860s until the end of the first forty-year period in 1899, known ore deposits began to be mined out and the state suffered the blows of a serious mining depression exacerbated by federal monetary policies. In 1873 Congress passed the Mint Act, known in the western United States as the Crime of '73. The Mint Act put the United States on the gold standard and eliminated the minting of silver coins. With government demand for silver down and demand for gold rising, the price paid and the demand for Nevada's chief industrial product decreased dramatically. Attempts by the western states to convince Congress to return to bimetallism were defeated with the exception of a few minor, short-lived victories such as the Sherman Silver Purchase Act in 1890, which required the federal government to purchase 4 1/2 million ounces of silver per month. It was repealed in 1893.

The Crime of '73 led to splits in both the Democratic and Republican parties and the eventual dominance in the state of the newly minted Silver Party. Democrats and Republicans alike fled their parties to join the Silver Party; and in the election of 1892, the Silver Party in Nevada won all three presidential electors, the race for the state's only congressional seat, and numerous seats in the legislature. That trend continued in state elections through 1906, when the Silver or Silver-Democrat Parties won virtually all major state and national elections in Nevada.

By 1900, however, the Silver Party was already in decline with the discovery of other silver and gold ore lodes in the state, the discovery and increased national and international importance of copper, and the decreasing significance of the silver issue at the national level. Before moving on to Nevada's second forty-year period, however, it is also worth noting that during this first period various movements for political and economic reform began to take hold in the state. Although their goals would not be achieved until the early twentieth century, supporters of women's suffrage, direct election of senators, western water projects, and railroad regulation began to see their issues seriously debated in the state during the silver period.

The Second Period: 1900–1939

The end of Nevada's mining depression came in 1900 when silver and gold were found near Tonopah and Goldfield in the southern part of the state. As had been the case in northern Nevada, mining towns in southern Nevada boomed and, eventually, busted. During that period of roughly a quarter century, however, various individuals in the state grew rich and powerful. Among the most influential were Key Pittman and Tasker Oddie, who started their political careers, and George Wingfield, who made his fortune during the Tonopah-Goldfield boom.

By 1912, silver and gold were being replaced by copper, needed to supply the electrical industry of the early twentieth century's industrial revolution, as the state's chief mining export. In 1900 a large vein of copper was discovered in White Pine County near Ely, which accelerated the construction of company towns in the region to house the men who would mine it. These company towns often included stores, schools, and hospitals; they were planned communities, quite unlike the muddy, disorganized, and often dangerous tent cities that had sprung up during the earlier mining period. What is also notable about the mines of the copper era is that unlike the gold and silver mines in the north, they were not dominated by California companies. Those who made their fortunes from the copper mines tended to stay in Nevada and contribute to the state's development. Demand for copper would continue to fuel the state's mining industry through the two world wars and the Korean War, until copper prices dropped in the 1970s.

By far the most important political and historical aspect of the first two decades of the twentieth century in Nevada was the state's support for Progressive Era reforms that gave the voters more control over their own government and reduced the power of the wealthy elite who often dominated the legislature and government officials. As noted in chapter 4, the state adopted the three direct-democracy election methods of initiative, referendum, and recall between 1904 and 1912. In 1909 the legislature established the office of mine inspector to ensure mine safety for Nevada's working miners, and in 1911 a workman's compensation bill was passed to aid those injured on the job. In 1914, the efforts of Dr. Anne Martin, Dr. Jeanne Weir, and Ms. O. H. Mack paid off when women were given the right to vote. The Direct Primary Law was passed in 1909, establishing democratic primaries rather than backroom caucuses as the means for party selection of candidates and requiring that the state legislature abide by a popular vote in its appointment of U.S. senators. The ratification of the Seventeenth Amendment in 1913, providing for direct election of U.S. senators, put an end to vote buying in the state legislature by senate hopefuls.

The domination of the banks and railroads also began to falter during the Progressive Era. The legislature established the Railroad Commission in 1907 to regulate rates and, in that same year, created the Board of Bank Commissioners to oversee the state's banks. In 1913 the Nevada Tax Commission was formed to ensure equity in the assessment of all property, especially railroad property, in the state. More than anything else, these boards and commissions brought an end to the freewheeling, unlimited laissez-faire attitude that had dominated the state's first half-century. Reflecting the moralistic components of the progressive tradition, the legislature also outlawed gambling in 1910. In 1918, the state's voters approved an initiative prohibiting the manufacture and sale of alcohol.

The state's economy staged a comeback during World War I, when demand for silver, gold, and copper increased dramatically. Demand and, consequently, prices for Nevada's agricultural and livestock products also rose during the war, making those marginal industries more profitable. At war's end, however, agricultural prices declined and the industry returned to its pre-war subsistence levels.

In the 1920s the bipartisan political machine of George Wingfield dominated the state's politics. Wingfield, never a candidate for major office himself, pulled the strings and supported Democrats, such as Key Pittman, and Republicans, such as Tasker Oddie. Wingfield's power, however, came crashing down in 1932 with the depression-induced failure of his banking empire.

The 1930s brought about the dominance of the Democratic Party and the federal government in the state. After the depression hit, Nevadans, like others in the nation, supported Democrats rather than Republicans, whom they blamed for bad economic conditions. As a result of the efforts of Nevada's congressional delegation, the state suffered less from the depression than others did. Even before Franklin Roosevelt's New Deal benefited the state through tremendous federal investment, Nevada took advantage of various federal aid programs to the states, programs often initiated by the state's two U.S. senators. The Silver Purchase Act of 1934, introduced into Congress by Senator Key Pittman, aided Nevada's mining economy by providing for the increased purchase of silver by the federal government. In addition to utilizing federal highway assistance programs, Nevada also accepted federal aid that paid the entire cost of roads built through unappropriated federal lands and Indian reservations; with 87 percent of the state's land controlled by the federal government, this was no small matter. The act authorizing this massive road-building project, the Oddie-Colton Act of 1930, was co-authored by Senator Tasker Oddie of Nevada.

The Naval Ammunition Depot opened in Hawthorne in 1929, and in 1931 construction began on Hoover Dam near Las Vegas. The dam project, which employed five thousand workers at its peak in 1934, not only pumped millions of dollars into the local economy but also created what is today Boulder City. Millions more in federal dollars flowed into the state through FDR's various relief projects, including the Civilian Conservation Corps (CCC) and the Works Progress Administration (WPA), which built many of Nevada's streets, sewers, sidewalks, and parks. From 1933 to 1939, Nevada had the distinction among all states of the highest total per capita expenditures by the federal government.[11]

The state's economy was further aided during the depression by two bills signed into law by Governor Fred Balzar on the same day in 1931. With one of those bills, the twenty-one-year-old ban on gambling was ended; the other, a divorce bill, allowed residency to be established in six weeks rather than six months, as had been the case since 1915. Both bills had the effect of bringing newcomers and their money to the state, even if only for a short time. Although the ramifications of the gaming bill would not be seen for a decade, the divorce bill had the immediate effect of creating a booming industry in the Reno area for dude ranches, hotels, boardinghouses, and, of course, lawyers.

As noted earlier, the 1930s were a time of Democratic Party ascendance in the state. After twelve years in the U.S. Senate, Republican Tasker Oddie was defeated in the election of 1932 by Democrat Pat McCarran. In state elections of 1932, 1934, 1936, and 1938, Nevada Democrats won virtually every seat at the state and national level. The death of Nevada's senior senator, Key Pittman, in November 1940, brought McCarran to the forefront of state and national politics where he would stay until his own death in 1954.

The Third Period: 1940–1980

The beginning of World War II in Europe in 1939 increased not only demand for Nevada's copper but also federal investment in the state. Unlike federal funds in the second period, which had been directed almost exclusively to public works projects such as roads, dams, sewers, and sidewalks, these new federal moneys went toward the creation of military bases and industrial plants vital to the war effort.

In 1941, Camp Sibert was established in Boulder City to guard against sabotage at Hoover Dam, and an Army Air Corps gunnery school that would later become Nellis Air Force Base was created in the desert near Las Vegas. Stead Air Force Base near Reno was established in 1942, and a naval air station was situated in Fallon. In 1950, the Atomic Energy Commission began building what would ultimately become known as the Nevada Test Site. The Basic Magnesium plant was opened near Las Vegas in 1942 to manufacture magnesium needed for the war effort. All of these projects brought thousands of civilian and military workers to the state, and with them, their paychecks. In addition, the war created tremendous growth in the number and size of defense plants in southern California and a rising tide of California tourists to the state's gaming tables. Tourism and gaming were further aided by the federal government with passage in 1956 of the Interstate Highway Act, which would ultimately provide two major interstate highways through the state, easy routes by which tourists could travel easily and quickly to Reno and Las Vegas.

Mining continued to be important in the state during the war and post-war periods, but it was during this time that gaming and tourism began to supplant mining as the state's chief industry. It was also during this time that the state began to seriously regulate gaming. As had been the case with mining during the boom of the 1850s and early 1860s, gaming in the state had been the preserve of freewheeling entrepreneurs. Unlike mining, however, many of Nevada's gaming magnates had ties to organized crime. The state's 1931 statute allowing gaming put regulation into the hands of city and county officials who were less concerned with keeping out organized crime than with "fee collection and the control of drunks and cheaters."[12] In 1945 gaming control was transferred to the state Tax Commission, but this move did little to help, since those already holding licenses, many of whom had organized crime connections, were grandfathered in and allowed to keep their licenses with no further background checks.

That the state acted further had much to do with an effort to avoid federal control, or even prohibition, of gambling. Hearings held in 1950 and 1951 by Senator Estes Kefauver (D-Tennessee) confirmed the presence of organized crime in Nevada's casinos, and federal moves were afoot that would damage, if not eliminate, the state's major industry and source of revenue. In 1955, at the urging of Governor Charles Russell, the legislature established a three-member Gaming Control Board within the state Tax Commission to investigate gaming license applicants and recommend approval or disapproval of licenses.

In 1959 Governor Grant Sawyer proposed, and the legislature approved, a bill that removed the Gaming Control Board from the aegis of the state Tax Commission and made it the investigative arm of the newly created five-member Nevada Gaming Commission. The independent commission was given substantial control over licensing and regulation of all gaming in the state. The commission also created the state's official List of Excluded Persons, commonly known as the Black Book, that listed people with unsavory reputations and organized-crime ties who were not to be allowed in Nevada's casinos for fear that their presence would damage the industry's reputation. Allowing a person listed in the Black Book into gaming premises could result in substantial sanctions, including the loss of one's gaming license. This sanction was exercised in 1963 when Frank Sinatra, co-owner of the Cal-Neva Lodge in Lake Tahoe and the Sands Hotel in Las Vegas, had his license stripped from him when he allowed Black Book listee Sam Giancana to stay at the Lodge.

The increased regulation of gaming brought about by the efforts of Russell and Sawyer did not end federal scrutiny of the industry, however. In the 1960s U.S. Attorney General Robert F. Kennedy launched increased surveillance of Nevada gaming when it became clear that Jimmy Hoffa and the Teamsters were expanding their presence in the state through loans to various hotel-casinos from the Teamsters' pension fund. FBI investigations found sufficient evidence of skimming to acquire convictions of four associates of the Flamingo. Governor Sawyer's actions to clean up gaming staved off increased federal control, and in 1969 the state turned a corner when at the urging of Howard Hughes, who had bought the Desert Inn in 1967, the legislature passed the Corporate Gaming Act. That act encouraged normally conservative corporate and banking concerns to invest in gaming and led to an overall increased respectability of the industry throughout the country. Nonetheless, in the late 1970s and early 1980s, the state was rocked with charges of hidden organized crime ownership and skimming at the Tropicana, Aladdin, and Stardust casinos, events portrayed in Martin Scorsese's 1995 film *Casino.*

The Fourth Period: 1980 and the Future

In the 1980s Nevada saw a renaissance in the state's mining industry. As the price of gold in world markets increased and new methods for its recovery were developed, many of the "depleted" mines with small traces of gold returned to profitability. Nevada mines now account for approximately 60 percent of the country's gold and 20 percent of its silver production. In addition, the mining of other minerals, such as mercury and barite, has increased dramatically.

Since 1980, Nevada has been shaped by two primary forces: two-party competition and rapid population growth. For reasons explained in chapter 4, the once-dominant Democrats have found themselves in a competitive situation, similar to that existing prior to the New Deal, in which either party may win or lose any election in the state, depending upon the issues and candidates. Since 1980, the Republicans have won the state's presidential electors three out of four times; the lieutenant governor, secretary of state, and attorney general races on two of four occasions; state treasurer and state controller in all four elections; two of six U.S. Senate races; and the U.S. House eight out of fifteen times. At the state legislature, Democrats have been the majority party in the senate in four of the past eight sessions and in the assembly six times, with the Republicans the majority in 1985 and an even split between the two parties in 1995. Even Democrats once thought invincible have fallen to the Republicans' new-found fourth-period vitality; in 1982, four-term incumbent senator Howard Cannon was defeated by the relatively unknown Chic Hecht, and in 1994, the year the Republicans recaptured both houses of the U.S. Congress, four-term congressman James Bilbray was ousted by John Ensign.

The state's tremendous growth in population began, not in the 1980s, but as far back as the 1940s, when federal investment in the state began to take off. Between the 1940 and 1950 censuses, Nevada's population increased more than 45 percent; by the time of the 1960 census, it had charged forward by another 78

Table 11.1

Population of Nevada, 1860–1995

Census Date	Population	Percentage Increase Over Preceding Census
1860	6,857	NA
1870	42,491	519.7
1880	62,266	46.5
1890	47,355	-23.9
1900	42,335	-10.6
1910	81,875	93.4
1920	77,407	-5.5
1930	91,058	17.6
1940	110,247	21.1
1950	160,083	45.2
1960	285,278	78.2
1970	488,738	71.3
1980	800,508	63.8
1990	1,201,833	50.1
1995 (est.)	1,582,280	31.7

Source: Department of Commerce, Bureau of the Census, for data through 1990. 1995 estimate from the Nevada Department of Taxation.

percent; by the 1970 census, population had grown to almost half a million, an increase of more than 70 percent since 1960; and by 1980, the state was home to more than 800,000 people, an increase of more than 60 percent since 1970. At the time of the 1990 census, Nevada had more than 1 million residents, an increase of almost 50 percent since 1980.[13] By 1995 it was estimated that the state's population was in excess of 1.5 million, more than ten times the number of residents in 1940. Nevada has had the distinction of being the fastest growing state in the nation in recent years (see Table 11.1).

The effects of this phenomenal growth rate have been dramatic for the state. As noted in chapter 10, new residents require immediate services, and the state has been hard-pressed to keep pace with the need for new schools, roads, and other infrastructure required for a burgeoning population. Not surprisingly, the construction industry and its suppliers have experienced a boom in the past few decades, building these public projects and providing the newcomers with houses, apartments, grocery stores, movie theaters, and other structural needs.

The state's gaming industry has seen some of its best times ever during this fourth period, although its good fortune is not necessarily tied directly to population growth. Gaming has taken off in hitherto unrecognized areas such as Laughlin and Mesquite as well as in the traditional centers of Reno and Las Vegas. In the first half of the decade of the 1990s, megaresorts such as the MGM Grand, the Mirage, the Excalibur, the Luxor, and Treasure Island have been built and existing casinos such as Circus Circus, the Sahara, the Golden Nugget, Binion's Horseshoe, and others have completed enormous expansion plans. Even more large Las Vegas resorts are on the way. In Reno, the Silver Legacy, tallest hotel-casino in the state, opened in 1995.

Gaming and tourism have also led to major expansions at the state's airports. McCarran International Airport in Las Vegas now serves as a hub for major airlines, including America West and Southwest, and is the eighth busiest air terminal in the nation. That the Las Vegas airport is named after Senator McCarran and the Reno airport was formerly named after Senator Cannon should come as no surprise; both men were at the forefront of aviation legislation that made airports and air travel more convenient and less expensive to the average American. Just as the Interstate Highway Act made travel to the gaming meccas of Las Vegas and Reno easier in its day, the actions of McCarran and Cannon have brought more tourists to the state's gaming tables by reducing travel time and making a weekend or weeklong trip from anywhere in the country as convenient as a short plane trip.

Las Vegas, once a small railroad stop between Los Angeles and Salt Lake City, is now the state's commercial and population center. Approximately two-thirds of Nevada's population resides in Clark County. The transition of the state from one dominated politically and economically by Washoe and the rural counties to one living in the shadow of Las Vegas has not been without its difficulties. In the mid-1980s, Clark County residents and their elected officials took on the issue of "fair share." As noted in chapter 10, the 1981 legislature approved a shift in the state's tax structure from a reliance on property taxes to sales taxes. Part of that sales tax came from a city-county relief tax that was returned to local governments in the state. Under the formula for distribution approved by the legislature, Washoe County, because it had lost more funds in the shift, received more of the city-county relief tax funds than it paid, whereas Clark County received less than it paid. After a great deal of turmoil, bickering, and name-calling, the 1991 legislature approved a new formula that in 1996 returned to both Washoe and Clark Counties approximately 97 percent of the amount each paid into the fund. The rural counties receive slightly more than their contribution.[14]

The "fair share" issue, however, did not end in 1991. During the 1995 legislature, the City of Las Vegas and Clark County went to war over distribution of sales tax revenues between them. In a successful eleventh-hour move, the county was able to convince the legislature to include the unincorporated town of Spring

Valley and an area that has now become the unincorporated town of Summerlin South in the tax distribution formula. The move will mean that by the turn of the century, Clark County will gain and Las Vegas will lose approximately $1.2 million annually.

Many of Nevada's new residents are retirees, many of whom derive their support from government pensions, Social Security, and Medicare and require above-average medical care and social services. In other states where they have moved in large numbers, such as Florida and Arizona, they have been notorious for their refusal to support increased funding for government services they do not perceive as directly benefiting them. Whether this will also occur in Nevada remains to be seen. However, in recent years, voters in the southern portion of the state, where the vast majority of retirees live, have turned down one bond issue after another that would have gone to support more police, schools, parks, and libraries.

To the extent that retirees living on government assistance exhibit hypocrisy in their failure to support these increased government services, they are merely reflecting an attitude long prevalent in the state. It is doubtful that any other state in the Union has been so dependent for its existence and survival on the federal government; yet Nevadans are among the most vociferous critics of the federal government and the first to tout themselves as "rugged individualists" who pulled themselves up by their own bootstraps. As we have noted in this chapter and others, Nevada came into existence as a result of the federal government's nurturing; it has grown and prospered as a result of vast federal investment in dams, roads, military bases, and industrial complexes. But for the federal government's largess, it is doubtful that Nevada would have achieved all that it has. Federal decisions *not* to regulate gaming have contributed to the state's prosperity and economic strength, too.

Yet, Nevada was in the forefront of the failed Sagebrush Rebellion in the 1970s, fomenters of which hoped to turn federal lands over to the states. It has also provided tremendous support in the mid-1990s for Sagebrush II and a county supremacy movement that claims control over all federal lands within county borders. Mining companies and livestock owners, with their representatives in Congress, have successfully fought off one attempt after another to raise the rents on grazing lands and the royalties on mining claims to something akin to their fair market value. Officers with the Bureau of Land Management and the Forest Service have been threatened, and they sometimes even drive their own automobiles while working so as not to be targeted. This sentiment is not isolated: in 1995 the legislature passed a bill that would have required federal officers to seek the approval of state and local officials before they could enforce state laws on public lands. The bill died when Governor Miller vetoed it and the assembly, which had previously passed it unanimously, came up a mere five votes short of an override.

Nevada residents' demand for low taxes and the state's increased urban population, however, may ultimately determine the political success of ranchers and mining companies in the state. In fiscal year 1995, the Bureau of Land Management pumped more than $73 million into the state in support of the 67 percent of Nevada's land under its stewardship. Turning this land over to the state would require Nevadans to pick up that tab with their own tax dollars or sell off the land to private interests. The vast majority of Nevada's new residents are moving into urban areas such as Las Vegas and Reno, and their concern for keeping these wilderness areas from being locked up by mining and grazing interests or sold off to private owners may ultimately prevail.

These urban residents also need water, which has already created conflict between Las Vegas and the surrounding rural areas. In addition to seeking additional water from the Colorado River, the Las Vegas Valley Water District has proposed buying up water rights from ranchers and farmers and tapping into other water sources in the state. As a result of an extended drought, northern Nevada is also feeling the strain of increasing population and decreasing water supplies; residents there, too, must seek additional sources of the vital liquid, and the rural areas seem the most likely target of opportunity.

Conclusion

Nevadans have a great deal of which they may be justly proud. In slightly more than 130 years the state has gone from a Wild West, lawless region to a modern, urban one that offers opportunity to those willing to work for it. Nevada was among the first states in the nation to grant suffrage to women; to ratify the Thirteenth, Fourteenth, and Fifteenth Amendments to the U.S. Constitution; to provide for workman's compensation; to initiate a direct primary; and to put government in the hands of the people through initiative, referendum, and recall. It is a state that has dealt with astonishing growth over a short period of time, one that has passed statutes protecting its minorities from discrimination, and one that has established a community college and university system that is growing not only in numbers but in the quality of its students, faculty, and national reputation.

As Nevada enters the final half of the twentieth century and prepares for the twenty-first, many challenges lie on the horizon. Clearly the state must seek to diversify its economy to an even greater extent than it already has. Development of manufacturing and banking centers has already occurred to some degree; more must be done. If the state's history tells us nothing else, it surely informs us that reliance upon a single industry, whether mining or gaming, is a dangerous path. Today, gaming is at an all-time high in Nevada. Yet, it is not recession-proof, as the downturns in the early 1980s and 1990s taught us, and the state's gamers face increased competition in other states and nations.

Even if we could guarantee the perpetual solvency of gaming in the state, we must ask ourselves if a gaming-based economy is what we truly want. Do we truly want a tax base founded primarily on unstable and volatile gaming and sales tax revenues, or are we willing to raise property taxes in order to stabilize that base? Do we truly want a single industry that arguably has the power to dictate to state government in the way that mining, the Bank Crowd, and the railroads once did? Do we truly want a state government so dependent upon the tax revenues of a single industry that it dare not tax or regulate it too much for fear that the state's budget may come crashing down? Are policies that are in the best interests of gaming corporations also in the best interests of the state? These are issues that will not go away; they will have to be addressed in the coming years.

Nevada must also come to terms once more with attempts at colonization and exploitation by outsiders. Just as California mining companies, railroads, and banks once sought to take what they could out of Nevada with little regard for the state's needs, new colonizers have arisen in the latter twentieth century to take their place. Tons of precious gold, silver, and other metals are taken from the state every year by companies that pay the state no more than 5 percent on these millions of dollars in net proceeds. That these companies are primarily owned by corporations outside the United States makes their colonialism and exploitation even more apparent. In 1994, for example, a Canadian-owned mining company, American Barrick Resources, Inc., paid only $10,000 to buy a mine with $10 million in gold deposits.[15] Within the United States, eastern politicians and nuclear power plant owners are single-minded in their goal to place a high-level nuclear waste repository at Yucca Mountain, just outside of Las Vegas; that Nevadans are almost unanimously opposed means little. To these corporations and politicians, Nevada seems a place good only for pillaging precious minerals and dumping unwanted and dangerous waste.

Nevada's prison system too is in a state of impending crisis. The state has one of the highest incarceration rates in the country, and its prisons are frequently overcrowded. In the past that overcrowding could be relieved by releasing nonviolent offenders on parole and probation. The days of such simple solutions may be over, however. The 1995 legislature passed legislation that increases the penalties for serious criminal offenses and allows many nonviolent offenders to repay their debt to society without doing prison time. Although in the short run this may reduce the prison population somewhat, it may create long-term problems. With only major, violent offenders serving prison time, it will be more difficult in the future to remediate inevitable overcrowding by releasing them on probation and parole. It is estimated by the state that Nevada must achieve a parole rate of 35 percent in order to avoid prison overcrowding and cost overruns. In 1994, prior to the passage of these stricter crime laws, the rate was only 32 percent;[16]

the new crime laws are likely to make that rate drop even lower over the next several years, thus resulting in a deeper crisis.

Nevada must also come to terms in the next few years with its provision of social services. A 1988 fiscal study showed that the state spent $550 per primary and secondary student and $198 per university and community college student, compared to a national average of $600 and $235, respectively. In the area of public welfare, Nevada's expenditures were only $155 per capita, while the national average was $318.[17] A 1988 study by the National Alliance for the Mentally Ill and the Public Citizens' Research Group ranked the state forty-fourth of the fifty states in its provision of services to the mentally ill.[18] Although Nevada is among the lowest ranked states in terms of education, welfare, and mental health spending, the state is among those with the highest rates of poverty, infant mortality, high school dropouts, unwed mothers (and fathers), suicide, alcoholism, and gambling addiction in the nation. How and whether those figures will change are dependent upon Nevada's decisions over the next few years.

In short, Nevada is a state that will enter the twenty-first century as it chooses to; its ability to prosper and continue as a land of dreams and opportunity rests in its own hands. Hard decisions—uncomfortable decisions—will have to be made on taxation, spending, government services, land and water use, and openness in politics. It is to be hoped that we will have the foresight, the skills, and the willingness to do what we must to ensure that all Nevadans enjoy the fruits of their labors and that all share equally the liberties and opportunities available in the Sagebrush State.

Appendix

The Constitution of the State of Nevada

The Nevada constitution was framed by a convention of delegates chosen by the people. The convention met at Carson City on July 4, 1864, and adjourned on July 28 of the same year. On the 1st Wednesday of September 1864, the constitution was approved by the vote of the people of the Territory of Nevada, and on October 31, 1864, President Lincoln proclaimed that the State of Nevada was admitted into the Union on an equal footing with the original states.

The literal text of the original, signed copy of the constitution filed in the office of the secretary of state has been retained, unless it has been repealed or superseded by amendment. Where the original text has been amended or where a new provision has been added to the original constitution, the source of the amendment or addition is indicated in the source note immediately following the text of the amended or new section. Lead lines for sections have been supplied by the Legislative Counsel of the State of Nevada.[1]

[1] The Nevada Constitution is reprinted with permission from the Legislative Counsel Bureau of the State of Nevada.

Preliminary Action

Whereas, The Act of Congress Approved March Twenty First A.D. Eighteen Hundred and Sixty Four "To enable the People of the Territory of Nevada to form a Constitution and State Government and for the admission of such State into the Union on an equal footing with the Original States," requires that the Members of the Convention for framing said Constitution shall, after Organization, on behalf of the people of said Territory, adopt the Constitution of the United States.—Therefore, Be it Resolved, That the Members of this Convention, elected by the Authority of the aforesaid enabling Act of Congress, Assembled in Carson City the Capital of said Territory of Nevada, and immediately subsequent to its Organization, do adopt, on behalf of the people of said Territory the Constitution of the United States[.]

Ordinance

Slavery prohibited; freedom of religious worship; disclaimer of public lands. [Effective until the date Congress consents to amendment or a legal determination is made that such consent is not necessary, and after that date if the proposed amendment is not approved by the people at the 1996 general election.] In obedience to the requirements of an act of the Congress of the United States, approved March twenty-first, A.D. eighteen hundred and sixty-four, to enable the people of Nevada to form a constitution and state government, this convention, elected and convened in obedience to said enabling act, do ordain as follows, and this ordinance shall be irrevocable, without the consent of the United States and the people of the State of Nevada:

First. That there shall be in this state neither slavery nor involuntary servitude, otherwise than in the punishment for crimes, whereof the party shall have been duly convicted.

Second. That perfect toleration of religious sentiment shall be secured, and no inhabitant of said state shall ever be molested, in person or property, on account of his or her mode of religious worship.

Third. That the people inhabiting said territory do agree and declare, that they forever disclaim all right and title to the unappropriated public lands lying within said territory, and that the same shall be and remain at the sole and entire disposition of the United States; and that lands belonging to citizens of the United States, residing without the said state, shall never be taxed higher than the land belonging to the residents thereof; and that no taxes shall be imposed by said state on lands or property therein belonging to, or which may hereafter be purchased by, the United States, unless otherwise provided by the congress of the United States.

[Amended in 1956. Proposed and passed by the 1953 legislature; agreed to and passed by the 1955 legislature; approved and ratified by the people at the 1956 general election. See: Statutes of Nevada 1953, p. 718; Statutes of Nevada 1955, p. 926.]

Preamble

We the people of the State of Nevada Grateful to Almighty God for our freedom in order to secure its blessings, insure domestic tranquility, and form a more perfect Government, do establish this Constitution.

Article 1
Declaration of Rights

Sec. 1. Inalienable rights.
2. Purpose of government; paramount allegiance to United States.
3. Trial by jury; waiver in civil cases.
4. Liberty of conscience.
5. Suspension of habeas corpus.
6. Excessive bail and fines; cruel or unusual punishments; detention of witnesses.
7. Bail; exception for capital offenses and certain murders.
8. Rights of accused in criminal prosecutions; jeopardy; due process of law; eminent domain. [Effective until November 27, 1996, and after that date if the proposed amendment is not approved by the people at the 1996 general election.]
8. Rights of accused in criminal prosecutions; jeopardy; rights of victims of crime; due process of law; eminent domain. [Effective November 27, 1996, if the proposed amendment is approved by the people at the 1996 general election.]
9. Liberty of speech and the press.
10. Right to assemble and to petition.
11. Right to keep and bear arms; civil power supreme.
12. Quartering soldier in private house.
13. Representation apportioned according to population.
14. Exemption of property from execution; imprisonment for debt.

15. Bill of attainder; ex post facto law; obligation of contract.
16. Rights of foreigners. [Repealed in 1924.]
17. Slavery and involuntary servitude prohibited.
18. Unreasonable seizure and search; issuance of warrants.
19. Treason.
20. Rights retained by people.

Sec. 1 Inalienable rights. All men are by Nature free and equal and have certain inalienable rights among which are those of enjoying and defending life and liberty; Acquiring Possessing and Protecting property and pursuing and obtaining safety and happiness[.]

Sec. 2. Purpose of government; paramount allegiance to United States. All political power is inherent in the people[.] Government is instituted for the protection, security and benefit of the people; and they have the right to alter or reform the same whenever the public good may require it. But the Paramount Allegiance of every citizen is due to the Federal Government in the exercise of all its Constitutional powers as the same have been or may be defined by the Supreme Court of the United States; and no power exists in the people of this or any other State of the Federal Union to dissolve their connection therewith or perform any act tending to impair[,] subvert, or resist the Supreme Authority of the government of the United States. The Constitution of the United States confers full power on the Federal Government to maintain and Perpetuate its existance [existence], and whensoever any portion of the States, or people thereof attempt to secede from the Federal Union, or forcibly resist the Execution of its laws, the Federal Government may, by warrant of the Constitution, employ armed force in compelling obedience to its Authority.

Sec. 3. Trial by jury; waiver in civil cases. The right of trial by Jury shall be secured to all and remain inviolate forever; but a Jury trial may be waived by the parties in all civil cases in the manner to be prescribed by law; and in civil cases, if three fourths of the Jurors agree upon a verdict it shall stand and have the same force and effect as a verdict by the whole Jury, Provided, the Legislature by a law passed by a two thirds vote of all the members elected to each branch thereof may require a unanimous verdict notwithstanding this Provision.

Sec. 4. Liberty of conscience. The free exercise and enjoyment of religious profession and worship without discrimination or preference shall forever be allowed in this State, and no person shall be rendered incompetent to be a witness on account of his opinions on matters of his religious belief, but the liberty of consciene [conscience] hereby secured, shall not be so construed, as to excuse acts of licentiousness or justify practices inconsistent with the peace, or safety of this State.

Sec. 5. Suspension of habeas corpus. The privilege of the writ of Habeas Corpus, shall not be suspended unless when in cases of rebellion or invasion the public safety may require its suspension.

Sec. 6. Excessive bail and fines; cruel or unusual punishments; detention of witnesses. Excessive bail shall not be required, nor excessive fines imposed, nor shall cruel or unusual punishments be inflicted, nor shall witnesses be unreasonably detained.

Sec. 7. Bail; exception for capital offenses and certain murders. All persons shall be bailable by sufficient sureties; unless for Capital Offenses or murders punishable by life imprisonment without possibility of parole when the proof is evident or the presumption great.

[Amended in 1980. Proposed and passed by the 1977 legislature; agreed to and passed by the 1979 legislature; and approved and ratified by the people at the 1980 general election. See: Statutes of Nevada 1977, p. 1697; Statutes of Nevada 1979, p. 1941.]

Sec. 8. Rights of accused in criminal prosecutions; jeopardy; due process of law; eminent domain. [Effective until November 27, 1996, and after that date if the proposed amendment is not approved by the people at the 1996 general election.] No person shall be tried for a capital or other infamous crime (except in cases of impeachment, and in cases of the militia when in actual service and the land and naval forces in time of war, or which this state may keep, with the consent of congress, in time of peace, and in cases of petit larceny, under the regulation of the legislature) except on presentment or indictment of the grand jury, or upon information duly filed by a district attorney, or attorney-general of the state, and in any trial, in any court whatever, the party accused shall be allowed to appear and defend in person, and with counsel, as in civil actions. No person shall be subject to be twice put in jeopardy for the same offense; nor shall he be compelled, in any criminal case, to be a witness against himself, nor be deprived of life, liberty, or property, without due process of law; nor shall private property be taken for public use without just compensation having been first made, or secured, except in cases of war, riot, fire, or great public peril, in which case compensation shall be afterward made.

[Amended in 1912. Proposed and passed by the 1909 legislature; agreed to and passed by the 1911 legislature; and approved and ratified by the people at the 1912 general election. See: Statutes of Nevada 1909, p. 346; Statutes of Nevada 1911, p. 454.]

Sec. 8. Rights of accused in criminal prosecutions; jeopardy; rights of victims of crime; due process of law; eminent domain. [Effective November 27, 1996, if the proposed amendment is approved by the people at the 1996 general election.]

1. No person shall be tried for a capital or other infamous crime (except in cases of impeachment, and in cases of the militia when in actual service and the

land and naval forces in time of war, or which this state may keep, with the consent of congress, in time of peace, and in cases of petit larceny, under the regulation of the legislature) except on presentment or indictment of the grand jury, or upon information duly filed by a district attorney, or attorney-general of the state, and in any trial, in any court whatever, the party accused shall be allowed to appear and defend in person, and with counsel, as in civil actions. No person shall be subject to be twice put in jeopardy for the same offense; nor shall he be compelled, in any criminal case, to be a witness against himself.

2. The legislature shall provide by law for the rights of victims of crime, personally or through a representative, to be:

    (a) Informed, upon written request, of the status or disposition of a criminal proceeding at any stage of the proceeding;

    (b) Present at all public hearings involving the critical stages of a criminal proceeding; and

    (c) Heard at all proceedings for the sentencing or release of a convicted person after trial.

3. Except as otherwise provided in subsection 4, no person may maintain an action against the state or any public officer or employee for damages or injunctive, declaratory or other legal or equitable relief on behalf of a victim of a crime as a result of a violation of any statute enacted by the legislature pursuant to subsection 2. No such violation authorizes setting aside a conviction or sentence or continuing or postponing a criminal proceeding.

4. A person may maintain an action to compel a public officer or employee to carry out any duty required by the legislature pursuant to subsection 2.

5. No person shall be deprived of life, liberty, or property, without due process of law.

6. Private property shall not be taken for public use without just compensation having been first made, or secured, except in cases of war, riot, fire, or great public peril, in which case compensation shall be afterward made.

[Amended in 1912. Proposed and passed by the 1909 legislature; agreed to and passed by the 1911 legislature; and approved and ratified by the people at the 1912 general election. See: Statutes of Nevada 1909, p. 346; Statutes of Nevada 1911, p. 454.]—(Amendment proposed and passed by the 1993 legislature and agreed to and passed by the 1995 legislature; effective November 27, 1996, if the proposed amendment is approved by the people at the 1996 general election.)

Sec. 9. Liberty of speech and the press. Every citizen may freely speak, write and publish his sentiments on all subjects being responsible for the abuse of that right; and no law shall be passed to restrain or abridge the liberty of speech or of the press. In all criminal prosecutions and civil actions for libels, the truth may be given in evidence to the Jury; and if it shall appear to the Jury that the matter charged as libelous is true and was published with good motives and for justifiable ends, the party shall be acquitted or exonerated.

Sec. 10. Right to assemble and to petition. The people shall have the right freely to assemble together to consult for the common good, to instruct their representatives and to petition the Legislature for redress of Grievances.

Sec. 11. Right to keep and bear arms; civil power supreme.

1. Every citizen has the right to keep and bear arms for security and defense, for lawful hunting and recreational use and for other lawful purposes.

2. The military shall be subordinate to the civil power; No standing army shall be maintained by this State in time of peace, and in time of War, no appropriation for a standing army shall be for a longer time than two years.

[Amended in 1982. Proposed and passed by the 1979 legislature; agreed to and passed by the 1981 legislature; and approved and ratified by the people at the 1982 general election. See: Statutes of Nevada 1979, p. 1986; Statutes of Nevada 1981, p. 2083.]

Sec. 12. Quartering soldier in private house. No soldier shall, in time of Peace be quartered in any house without the consent of the owner, nor in time of War, except in the manner to be prescribed by law.

Sec. 13. Representation apportioned according to population. Representation shall be apportioned according to population.

Sec. 14. Exemption of property from execution; imprisonment for debt. The privilege of the debtor to enjoy the necessary comforts of life shall be recognized by wholesome laws, exempting a reasonable amount of property from seizure or sale for payment of any debts or liabilities hereafter contracted; And there shall be no imprisonment for debt, except in cases of fraud, libel, or slander, and no person shall be imprisioned [imprisoned] for a Militia fine in time of Peace.

Sec. 15. Bill of attainder; ex post facto law; obligation of contract. No bill of attainder, ex-post-facto law, or law impairing the obligation of contracts shall ever be passed.

Sec. 16. Rights of foreigners. [Repealed in 1924.]

[Sec. 16 of the original constitution was repealed by vote of the people at the 1924 general election. See: Statutes of Nevada 1921, p. 416; Statutes of Nevada 1923, p.

407. The original section read: "Foreigners who are, or who may hereafter become Bona-fide residents of this State, shall enjoy the same rights, in respect to the possession, enjoyment and inheritance of property, as native born citizens."]

Sec. 17. Slavery and involuntary servitude prohibited. Neither Slavery nor involuntary servitude unless for the punishment of crimes shall ever be tolerated in this State.

Sec. 18. Unreasonable seizure and search; issuance of warrants. The right of the people to be secure in their persons, houses, papers and effects against unreasonable seizures and searches shall not be violated; and no warrant shall issue but on probable cause, supported by Oath or Affirmation, particularly describing the place or places to be searched, and the person or persons, and thing or things to be seized.

Sec. 19. Treason. Treason against the State shall consist only in levying war against it, adhering to its enemies or giving them Aid and Comfort. And no person shall be convicted of treason unless on the testimony of two witnesses to the same overt act, or on confession in open court.

Sec. 20. Rights retained by people. This enumeration of rights shall not be construed to impair or deny others retained by the people.

Article 2
Right of Suffrage

Sec. 1. Right to vote; qualifications of elector; qualifications of nonelector to vote for President and Vice President of United States.
 2. When residence not gained or lost.
 3. Armed Forces personnel. [Repealed in 1972.]
 4. Privilege of qualified electors on general election day.
 5. Voting by ballot; voting in elections by legislature.
 6. Registration of electors; test of electoral qualifications.
 7. Poll tax: Levy and purpose. [Repealed in 1966.]
 8. Qualifications of voters on adoption or rejection of constitution.
 9. Recall of public officers: Procedure and limitations. [Effective until November 27, 1996, and after that date if the proposed amendment is not approved by the people at the 1996 general election.]
 9. Recall of public officers: Procedure and limitations. [Effective November 27, 1996, if the proposed amendment is approved by the people at the 1996 general election.]
 10. Candidates for Representative in Congress or United States Senator: Placement of name on ballot; appointment as Senator. [Effective upon determination that at least 24 other states have limited the duration of service of their respective Representatives in Congress and United States Senators, if

approved by the people at the 1996 general election.]

[10.]11. Limitation on contributions to campaign. [Effective November 27, 1996, if approved by the people at the 1996 general election.]

Sec. 1. Right to vote; qualifications of elector; qualifications of nonelector to vote for President and Vice President of United States. All citizens of the United States (not laboring under the disabilities named in this constitution) of the age of eighteen years and upwards, who shall have actually, and not constructively, resided in the state six months, and in the district or county thirty days next preceding any election, shall be entitled to vote for all officers that now or hereafter may be elected by the people, and upon all questions submitted to the electors at such election; provided, that no person who has been or may be convicted of treason or felony in any state or territory of the United States, unless restored to civil rights, and no idiot or insane person shall be entitled to the privilege of an elector. There shall be no denial of the elective franchise at any election on account of sex. The legislature may provide by law the conditions under which a citizen of the United States who does not have the status of an elector in another state and who does not meet the residence requirements of this section may vote in this state for President and Vice President of the United States.

[Amended in 1880, 1886, 1914, 1970 and 1971. The first amendment was proposed and passed by the 1877 legislature; agreed to and passed by the 1879 legislature; and approved and ratified by the people at the 1880 general election. See: Statutes of Nevada 1877, p. 213; Statutes of Nevada 1879, p. 149. The second amendment was approved and ratified by the people at the 1886 general election, but no entry of the proposed amendment had been made upon the journal of either house of the legislature, and such omission was fatal to the adoption of the amendment. See: State ex rel. Stevenson v. Tufly, 19 Nev. 391 (1887). The third amendment was proposed and passed by the 1911 legislature; agreed to and passed by the 1913 legislature; and approved and ratified by the people at the 1914 general election. See: Statutes of Nevada 1911, p. 457; Statutes of Nevada 1913, p. 581. The fourth amendment was proposed and passed by the 1967 legislature; agreed to and passed by the 1969 legislature; and approved and ratified by the people at the 1970 general election. See: Statutes of Nevada 1967, p. 1827; Statutes of Nevada 1969, p. 1657. The fifth amendment was proposed and passed by the 1969 legislature; agreed to and passed by the 1971 legislature; and approved and ratified by the people at a special election held on June 8, 1971. See: Statutes of Nevada 1969, p. 1685; Statutes of Nevada 1971, p. 2263.]

Sec. 2. When residence not gained or lost. For the purpose of voting, no person shall be deemed to have gained or lost a residence solely by reason of his presence or absence while employed in the service of the United States, nor while engaged in the navigation of the waters of the United States or of the high seas; nor while a student of any institution of learning; nor while kept at any charitable institution or medical facility at public expense; nor while confined in any public prison.

[Amended in 1972. Proposed and passed by the 1969 legislature; agreed to and passed by the 1971 legislature; approved and ratified by the people at the 1972 general election. See: Statutes of Nevada 1969, p. 1695; Statutes of Nevada 1971, p. 2240.]

Sec. 3. Armed Forces personnel. [Repealed in 1972.]

[Amended in 1956. Proposed and passed by the 1953 legislature; agreed to and passed by the 1955 legislature; approved and ratified by the people at the 1956 general election. See: Statutes of Nevada 1953, p. 732; Statutes of Nevada 1955, p. 952. Repealed in 1972. Repealer proposed and passed by the 1969 legislature; agreed to and passed by the 1971 legislature; approved and ratified by the people at the 1972 general election. See: Statutes of Nevada 1969, p. 1695; Statutes of Nevada 1971, p. 2240. The section as amended in 1956 and repealed in 1972 read: "The right of suffrage shall be enjoyed by all persons, otherwise entitled to the same, who may be in the military or naval service of the United States; provided, the votes so cast shall be made to apply to the county and township of which said voters were bona fide residents at the time of their entry into such service; and provided further, that the payment of a poll tax shall not be required as a condition to the right of voting. Provision shall be made by law, regulating the manner of voting, holding elections, and making returns of such elections, wherein other provisions are not contained in this constitution."]

Sec. 4. Privilege of qualified electors on general election day. During the day on which any General Election shall be held in this State no qualified elector shall be arrested by virtue of any civil process.

Sec. 5. Voting by ballot; voting in elections by legislature. All elections by the people shall be by ballot, and all elections by the Legislature, or by either branch thereof shall be "Viva-Voce."

Sec. 6. Registration of electors; test of electoral qualifications. Provision shall be made by law for the registration of the names of the Electors within the counties of which they may be residents and for the ascertainment by proper proofs of the persons who shall be entitled to the right of suffrage, as hereby established, to preserve the purity of elections, and to regulate the manner of holding and making returns of the same; and the Legislature shall have power to prescribe by law any other or further rules or oaths, as may be deemed necessary, as a test of electoral qualification.

Sec. 7. Poll tax: Levy and purpose. [Repealed in 1966.]

[Amended in 1910. Proposed and passed by the 1907 legislature; agreed to and passed by the 1909 legislature; approved and ratified by the people at the 1910 general election. See: Statutes of Nevada 1907, p. 450; Statutes of Nevada 1909, p. 344.

Repealed in 1966. Repealer proposed and passed by the 1963 legislature; agreed to and passed by the 1965 legislature; approved and ratified by the people at the 1966 general election. See: Statutes of Nevada 1963, p. 1421; Statutes of Nevada 1965, p. 1495. The section as amended in 1910 and repealed in 1966 read: "The Legislature shall provide by law for the payment of an annual poll tax of not less than two, nor exceeding four, dollars from each male resident in the State between the ages of twenty-one and sixty years (uncivilized American Indians excepted) to be expended for the maintenance and betterment of the public roads."]

Sec. 8. Qualifications of voters on adoption or rejection of constitution. All persons qualified by law to vote for representatives to the General Assembly of the Territory of Nevada, on the twenty first day of March A.D. Eighteen hundred and sixty four and all other persons who may be lawful voters in said Territory on the first Wednesday of September next following, shall be entitled to vote directly upon the question of adopting or rejecting this Constitution.

Sec. 9. Recall of public officers: Procedure and limitations. [Effective until November 27, 1996, and after that date if the proposed amendment is not approved by the people at the 1996 general election.] Every public officer in the State of Nevada is subject, as herein provided, to recall from office by the registered voters of the state, or of the county, district, or municipality, from which he was elected. For this purpose a number of registered voters not less than twenty-five per cent (25%) of the number who actually voted in the state or in the county, district, or municipality electing said officer, at the preceding general election, shall file their petition, in the manner herein provided, demanding his recall by the people; they shall set forth in said petition, in not exceeding two hundred (200) words, the reasons why said recall is demanded. If he shall offer his resignation, it shall be accepted and take effect on the day it is offered, and the vacancy thereby caused shall be filled in the manner provided by law. If he shall not resign within five (5) days after the petition is filed, a special election shall be ordered to be held within twenty days (20) after the issuance of the call therefor, in the state, or county, district, or municipality electing said officer, to determine whether the people will recall said officer. On the ballot at said election shall be printed verbatim as set forth in the recall petition, the reasons for demanding the recall of said officer, and in not more than two hundred (200) words, the officer's justification of his course in office. He shall continue to perform the duties of his office until the result of said election shall be finally declared. Other candidates for the office may be nominated to be voted for at said special election. The candidate who shall receive highest number of votes at said special election shall be deemed elected for the remainder of the term, whether it be the person against whom the recall petition was filed, or another. The recall petition shall be filed with the officer with whom the petition for nomination to such office shall be filed, and the same officer shall order the special election when it is required. No such petition shall be circulated or filed against any officer until he has actually held his office six (6) months, save and except that it may be filed against a senator or assemblyman in the legislature at any time after ten (10) days from the beginning of the first session after his election. After one such petition and special election, no further recall petition shall be filed against the same officer during the term for which he was elected, unless such further petitioners shall pay into the public treasury from which the expenses of said special election have been paid, the whole amount paid out of said public treasury as expenses for the preceding special election. Such additional legislation as may aid the operation of this section shall be provided by law.

[Added in 1912 and amended in 1970. The addition was proposed and passed by the 1909 legislature; agreed to and passed by the 1911 legislature; and approved and ratified by the people at the 1912 general election. See: Statutes of Nevada 1909, p. 345; Statutes of Nevada 1911, p. 448. The amendment was proposed and passed by the 1967 legislature; agreed to and passed by the 1969 legislature; and approved and ratified by the people at the 1970 general election. See: Statutes of Nevada 1967, p. 1782; Statutes of Nevada 1969, p. 1663.]

Sec. 9. Recall of public officers: Procedure and limitations. [Effective November 27, 1996, if the proposed amendment is approved by the people at the 1996 general election.] Every public officer in the State of Nevada is subject, as herein provided, to recall from office by the registered voters of the state, or of the county, district, or municipality which he represents. For this purpose, not less than twenty-five per cent (25%) of the number who actually voted in the state or in the county, district, or municipality which he represents, at the election in which he was elected, shall file their petition, in the manner herein provided, demanding his recall by the people. They shall set forth in said petition, in not exceeding two hundred (200) words, the reasons why said recall is demanded. If he shall offer his resignation, it shall be accepted and take effect on the day it is offered, and the vacancy thereby caused shall be filled in the manner provided by law. If he shall not resign within five (5) days after the petition is filed, a special election shall be ordered to be held within thirty (30) days after the issuance of the call therefor, in the state, or county, district, or municipality electing said officer, to determine whether the people will recall said officer. On the ballot at said election shall be printed verbatim as set forth in the recall petition, the reasons for demanding the recall of said officer, and in not more than two hundred (200) words, the officer's justification of his course in office. He shall continue to perform the duties of his office until the result of said election shall be finally declared. Other candidates for the office may be nominated to be voted for at said special election. The candidate who shall receive highest number of votes at said special election shall be deemed elected for the remainder of the term, whether it be the person against whom the recall petition was filed, or another. The recall petition shall be filed with the officer with whom the petition for nomination to such office shall be filed, and the same officer shall order the special election when it is required.

No such petition shall be circulated or filed against any officer until he has actually held his office six (6) months, save and except that it may be filed against a senator or assemblyman in the legislature at any time after ten (10) days from the beginning of the first session after his election. After one such petition and special election, no further recall petition shall be filed against the same officer during the term for which he was elected, unless such further petitioners shall pay into the public treasury from which the expenses of said special election have been paid, the whole amount paid out of said public treasury as expenses for the preceding special election. Such additional legislation as may aid the operation of this section shall be provided by law.

[Added in 1912 and amended in 1970. The addition was proposed and passed by the 1909 legislature; agreed to and passed by the 1911 legislature; and approved and ratified by the people at the 1912 general election. See: Statutes of Nevada 1909, p. 345; Statutes of Nevada 1911, p. 448. The amendment was proposed and passed by the 1967 legislature; agreed to and passed by the 1969 legislature; and approved and ratified by the people at the 1970 general election. See: Statutes of Nevada 1967, p. 1782; Statutes of Nevada 1969, p. 1663.]—(Amendment proposed and passed by the 1993 legislature and agreed to and passed by the 1995 legislature; effective November 27, 1996, if the proposed amendment is approved by the people at the 1996 general election.)

Sec. 10. Candidates for Representative in Congress or United States Senator: Placement of name on ballot; appointment as Senator. [Effective upon determination that at least 24 other states have limited the duration of service of their respective Representatives in Congress and United States Senators, if approved by the people at the 1996 general election.]

1. No person is eligible to have his name placed on a ballot for election as a Representative in Congress if at the end of the current term of that office he will have served, or would have served but for his resignation from that office, as a Representative in Congress from any district of this state, after December 31, 1996, for three full terms or a total of 6 years, whichever is completed first.

2. No person is eligible to have his name placed on a ballot for election as a United States Senator if at the end of the current term of that office he will have served, or would have served but for his resignation from that office, as a United States Senator from this state, after December 31, 1996, for two full terms or a total of 12 years, whichever is completed first. The governor shall not appoint as United States Senator any person ineligible to have his name placed on the ballot under this subsection.

3. The legislature shall provide by law that the name of any person whom this section makes ineligible to have his name placed upon the ballot may be writ-

ten in by a registered voter, and for the counting of the votes so written in.

4. This section does not become effective until it is proclaimed by the secretary of state, or determined by a district court of this state upon the petition of any registered voter, that at least 24 other states have limited the duration of service of their respective Representatives in Congress and United States Senators.

(Proposed by initiative petition and approved by the people at the 1994 general election; effective upon determination that at least 24 other states have limited the duration of service of their respective Representatives in Congress and United States Senators, if approved by the people at the 1996 general election.)

Sec. [10.] 11. Limitation on contributions to campaign. [Effective November 27, 1996, if approved by the people at the 1996 general election.]

1. As used in this section, "contribution" includes the value of services provided in kind for which money would otherwise be paid, such as paid polling and resulting data, paid direct mail, paid solicitation by telephone, any paid campaign paraphernalia printed or otherwise produced, and the use of paid personnel to assist in a campaign.

2. The legislature shall provide by law for the limitation of the total contribution by any natural or artificial person to the campaign of any person for election to any office, except a federal office, to $5,000 for the primary and $5,000 for the general election, and to the approval or rejection of any question by the registered voters to $5,000, whether the office sought or the question submitted is local or for the state as a whole. The legislature shall further provide for the punishment of the contributor, the candidate, and any other knowing party to a violation of the limit, as a felony.

(Proposed by initiative petition and approved by the people at the 1994 general election; effective November 27, 1996, if approved by the people at the 1996 general election.)

Article 3
Distribution of Powers

Sec. 1. Three separate departments; separation of powers. [Effective until November 27, 1996, and after that date if the proposed amendment is not approved by the people at the 1996 general election.]

1. Three separate departments; separation of powers; legislative review of administrative regulations. [Effective November 27, 1996, if the proposed amendment is approved by the people at the 1996 general election.]

Sec. 1. Three separate departments; separation of powers. [Effective until November 27, 1996, and after that date if the proposed amendment is not approved by the people at the 1996 general election.] The powers of the Government of the State of Nevada shall be divided into three separate departments,—the Legislative,—the Executive and the Judicial; and no persons charged with the exercise of powers properly belonging to one of these departments shall exercise any functions, appertaining to either of the others, except in the cases herein expressly directed or permitted.

Sec. 1. Three separate departments; separation of powers; legislative review of administrative regulations. [Effective November 27, 1996, if the proposed amendment is approved by the people at the 1996 general election.]

1. The powers of the Government of the State of Nevada shall be divided into three separate departments,—the Legislative,—the Executive and the Judicial; and no persons charged with the exercise of powers properly belonging to one of these departments shall exercise any functions, appertaining to either of the others, except in the cases expressly directed or permitted in this constitution.

2. If the legislature authorizes the adoption of regulations by an executive agency which bind persons outside the agency, the legislature may provide by law for:

    (a) The review of these regulations by a legislative agency before their effective date to determine initially whether each is within the statutory authority for its adoption;

    (b) The suspension by a legislative agency of any such regulation which appears to exceed that authority, until it is reviewed by a legislative body composed of members of the Senate and Assembly which is authorized to act on behalf of both houses of the legislature; and

    (c) The nullification of any such regulation by a majority vote of that legislative body, whether or not the regulation was suspended.

(Amendment proposed and passed by the 1993 legislature and agreed to and passed by the 1995 legislature; effective November 27, 1996, if the proposed amendment is approved by the people at the 1996 general election.)

Article 4
Legislative Department

Sec. 1. Legislative power vested in senate and assembly.

2. Biennial sessions of legislature; commencement.

3. Members of assembly: Election and term of office. [Effective until November 27, 1996, and after that date if the proposed amendment is not ap-

proved by the people at the 1996 general election.]

3. Members of assembly: Election and term of office; eligibility for office. [Effective November 27, 1996, if the proposed amendment is approved by the people at the 1996 general election.]

4. Senators: Election and term of office. [Effective until November 27, 1996, and after that date if the proposed amendment is not approved by the people at the 1996 general election.]

4. Senators: Election and term of office; eligibility for office. [Effective November 27, 1996, if the proposed amendment is approved by the people at the 1996 general election.]

5. Number of senators and assemblymen; apportionment.

6. Power of each house to judge qualifications of members, choose officers, set rules of proceedings and expel members.

7. Punishment of nonmember.

8. Senators and assemblymen ineligible for certain offices.

9. Federal officers ineligible for state office; exceptions.

10. Embezzler of public money ineligible for office; disqualification for bribery.

11. Privilege of members: Freedom from arrest on civil process.

12. Vacancy.

13. Quorum; compelling attendance.

14. Journal.

15. Open sessions and meetings; adjournment for more than 3 days or to another place.

16. Bills may originate in either house; amendment.

17. Act to embrace one subject only; title; amendment.

18. Reading of bill; vote on final passage; majority necessary to pass bill or joint resolution; signatures; consent calendar. [Effective until November 27, 1996, and after that date if the proposed amendment is not approved by the people at the 1996 general election.]

18. Reading of bill; voting on final passage; number of members necessary to pass bill or joint resolution; signatures; referral of certain measures to voters; consent calendar. [Effective November 27, 1996, if the proposed amendment is approved by the people at the 1996 general election.]

19. Manner of drawing money from treasury.

20. Certain local and special laws prohibited.

21. General laws to have uniform application.

22. Suit against state.

23. Enacting clause; law to be enacted by bill.

24. Lotteries.

25. Uniform county and township government.

26. Boards of county commissioners: Election and duties.
27. Disqualification of jurors; elections.
28. Compensation of legislative officers and employees; increase or decrease of compensation.
29. Duration of regular and special sessions. [Repealed in 1958.]
30. Homesteads: Exemption from forced sale; joint consent required for alienation; recording of declaration.
31. Property of married persons.
32. County officers: Power of legislature; election, duties and compensation; duties of county clerks.
33. Compensation of members of legislature; payment for postage, stationery and other expenses; additional allowances for officers.
34. Election of United States Senators.
35. Bills to be presented to governor; approval; disapproval and reconsideration by legislature; failure of governor to return bill.
[36.] Abolishment of county; approval of voters in county.
37. Continuity of government in case of enemy attack; succession to public offices; legislative quorum requirements; relocation of seat of government.
37[A]. Consolidation of city and county containing seat of government into one municipal government; separate taxing districts.

Sec. 1. Legislative power vested in senate and assembly. The Legislative authority of this State shall be vested in a Senate and Assembly which shall be designated "The Legislature of the State of Nevada" and the sessions of such Legislature shall be held at the seat of government of the State.

Sec. 2. Biennial sessions of legislature; commencement. The sessions of the Legislature shall be biennial, and shall commence on the 3rd Monday of January next ensuing the election of members of the Assembly, unless the Governor of the State shall, in the interim, convene the Legislature by proclamation.

[Amended in 1889, 1958 and 1960. The first amendment was proposed and passed by the 1885 legislature; agreed to and passed by the 1887 legislature; and approved and ratified by the people at a special election held February 11, 1889. See: Statutes of Nevada 1885, p. 151; Statutes of Nevada 1887, p. 165. The second amendment was proposed and passed by the 1955 legislature; agreed to and passed by the 1957 legislature; and approved and ratified by the people at the 1958 general election. See: Statutes of Nevada 1955, p. 946; Statutes of Nevada 1957, p. 793. The third amendment was proposed by initiative petition and approved and ratified by the people at the general election of 1960.]

Sec. 3. Members of assembly: Election and term of office. [Effective until November 27, 1996, and after that date if the proposed amendment is not approved by the people at the 1996 general election.] The members of the Assembly shall be chosen biennialy [biennially] by the qualified electors of their respective districts, on the Tuesday next after the first Monday in November and their term of office shall be two years from the day next after their election.

Sec. 3. Members of assembly: Election and term of office; eligibility for office. [Effective November 27, 1996, if the proposed amendment is approved by the people at the 1996 general election.]

1. The members of the Assembly shall be chosen biennially by the qualified electors of their respective districts, on the Tuesday next after the first Monday in November and their term of office shall be two years from the day next after their election.

2. No person may be elected or appointed as a member of the Assembly who has served in that office, or at the expiration of his current term if he is so serving will have served, 12 years or more, from any district of this state.

(Amendment proposed by initiative petition and approved by the people at the 1994 general election; effective November 27, 1996, if the proposed amendment is approved by the people at the 1996 general election.)

Sec. 4. Senators: Election and term of office. [Effective until November 27, 1996, and after that date if the proposed amendment is not approved by the people at the 1996 general election.] Senators shall be chosen at the same time and places as members of the Assembly by the qualified electors of their respective districts, and their term of Office shall be four Years from the day next after their election.

Sec. 4. Senators: Election and term of office; eligibility for office. [Effective November 27, 1996, if the proposed amendment is approved by the people at the 1996 general election.]

1. Senators shall be chosen at the same time and places as members of the Assembly by the qualified electors of their respective districts, and their term of Office shall be four Years from the day next after their election.

(Amendment proposed by initiative petition and approved by the people at the 1994 general election; effective November 27, 1996, if the proposed amendment is approved by the people at the 1996 general election.)

Sec. 5. Number of senators and assemblymen; apportionment. Senators and members of the assembly shall be duly qualified electors in the respective counties and districts which they represent, and the number of senators shall not be less than one-third nor more than one-half of that of the members of the assembly.

It shall be the mandatory duty of the legislature at its first session after the taking of the decennial census of the United States in the year 1950, and after each subsequent decennial census, to fix by law the number of senators and assemblymen, and apportion them among the several counties of the state, or among legislative districts which may be established by law, according to the number of inhabitants in them, respectively.

[Amended in 1950 and 1970. The first amendment was proposed and passed by the 1947 legislature; agreed to and passed by the 1949 legislature; and approved and ratified by the people at the 1950 general election. See: Statutes of Nevada 1947, p. 881; Statutes of Nevada 1949, p. 685. The second amendment was proposed and passed by the 1967 legislature; agreed to and passed by the 1969 legislature; and approved and ratified by the people at the 1970 general election. See: Statutes of Nevada 1967, p. 1797; Statutes of Nevada 1969, p. 1723.]

Sec. 6. Power of each house to judge qualifications of members, choose officers, set rules of proceedings and expel members. Each House shall judge of the qualifications, elections and returns of its own members, choose its own officers (except the President of the Senate), determine the rules of its proceedings and may punish its members for disorderly conduct, and with the concurrence of two thirds of all the members elected, expel a member.

Sec. 7. Punishment of nonmember. Either House, during the session, may punish, by imprisonment, any person not a member, who shall have been guilty of disrespect to the House by disorderly or contemptuous behavior in its presence; but such imprisonment shall not extend beyond the final adjournment of the session.

Sec. 8. Senators and assemblymen ineligible for certain offices. No Senator or member of Assembly shall, during the term for which he shall have been elected, nor for one year thereafter be appointed to any civil office of profit under this State which shall have been created, or the emoluments of which shall have been increased during such term, except such office as may be filled by elections by the people.

Sec. 9. Federal officers ineligible for state office; exceptions. No person holding any lucrative office under the Government of the United States or any other power, shall be eligible to any civil office of Profit under this State; Provided, that Post-Masters whose compensation does not exceed Five Hundred dollars per annum, or commissioners of deeds, shall not be deemed as holding a lucrative office.

Sec. 10. Embezzler of public money ineligible for office; disqualification for bribery. Any person who shall be convicted of the embezzlement, or defalcation of the public funds of this State or who may be convicted of having given or offered a bribe to procure his election or appointment to office, or received a bribe to aid in the procurement of office for any other person, shall be disqualified from holding any office of profit or trust in this State; and the Legislature shall, as soon as practicable, provide by law for the punishment of such defalcation, bribery, or embezzlement as a felony.

Sec. 11. Privilege of members: Freedom from arrest on civil process. Members of the Legislature shall be privileged from arrest on civil process during the session of the Legislature, and for fifteen days next before the commencement of each session.

Sec. 12. Vacancy. In case of the death or resignation of any member of the legislature, either senator or assemblyman, the county commissioners of the county from which such member was elected shall appoint a person of the same political party as the party which elected such senator or assemblyman to fill such vacancy; provided, that this section shall apply only in cases where no biennial election or any regular election at which county officers are to [be] elected takes place between the time of such death or resignation and the next succeeding session of the legislature.

[Amended in 1922 and 1944. The first amendment was proposed and passed by the 1919 legislature; agreed to and passed by the 1921 legislature; and approved and ratified by the people at the 1922 general election. See: Statutes of Nevada 1919, p. 478; Statutes of Nevada 1921, p. 412. The second amendment was proposed and passed by the 1941 legislature; agreed to and passed by the 1943 legislature; and approved and ratified by the people at the 1944 general election. See: Statutes of Nevada 1941, p. 563; Statutes of Nevada 1943, p. 311.]

Sec. 13. Quorum; compelling attendance. A majority of all the members elected to each House shall constitute a quorum to transact business, but a smaller number may adjourn, from day to day and may compel the attendance of absent members, in such manner, and under such penalties as each house may prescribe[.]

Sec. 14. Journal. Each House shall keep a journal of its own proceedings which shall be published and the yeas and nays of the members of either house on any question shall at the desire of any three members present, be entered on the journal.

Sec. 15. Open sessions and meetings; adjournment for more than 3 days or to another place. The doors of each House shall be kept open during its session, and neither shall, without the consent of the other, adjourn for more than three days nor to any other place than that in which they may be holding their sessions. The meetings of all legislative committees must be open to the public, except meetings held to consider the character, alleged misconduct, professional competence, or physical or mental health of a person.

[Amended in 1994. Proposed and passed by the 1991 legislature; agreed to and passed by the 1993 legislature; and approved and ratified by the people at the 1994 general election. See: Statutes of Nevada 1991, p. 2573; Statutes of Nevada 1993, p. 2974.]

Sec. 16. Bills may originate in either house; amendment. Any bill may originate in either House of the Legislature, and all bills passed by one may be amended in the other.

Sec. 17. Act to embrace one subject only; title; amendment. Each law enacted by the Legislature shall embrace but one subject, and matter, properly connected therewith, which subject shall be briefly expressed in the title; and no law shall be revised or amended by reference to its title only; but, in such case, the act as revised or section as amended, shall be re-enacted and published at length.

Sec. 18. Reading of bill; vote on final passage; majority necessary to pass bill or joint resolution; signatures; consent calendar. [Effective until November 27, 1996, and after that date if the proposed amendment is not approved by the people at the 1996 general election.] Every bill, except a bill placed on a consent calendar adopted as provided in this section, shall be read by sections on three several days, in each House, unless in case of emergency, two thirds of the House where such bill may be pending shall deem it expedient to dispense with this rule; but the reading of a bill by sections, on its final passage, shall in no case be dispensed with, and the vote on the final passage of every bill or joint resolution shall be taken by yeas and nays to be entered on the journals of each House; and a majority of all the members elected to each house, shall be necessary to pass every bill or joint resolution, and all bills or joint resolutions so passed, shall be signed by the presiding officers of the respective Houses and by the Secretary of the Senate and Clerk of the Assembly. Each House may provide by rule for the creation of a consent calendar and establish the procedure for the passage of uncontested bills.

[Amended in 1976. Proposed and passed by the 1973 legislature; agreed to and passed by the 1975 legislature; and approved and ratified by the people at the 1976 general election. See: Statutes of Nevada 1973, p. 1946; Statutes of Nevada 1975, p. 1900.]

Sec. 18. Reading of bill; voting on final passage; number of members necessary to pass bill or joint resolution; signatures; referral of certain measures to voters; consent calendar. [Effective November 27, 1996, if the proposed amendment is approved by the people at the 1996 general election.]

1. Every bill, except a bill placed on a consent calendar adopted as provided in subsection 4, must be read by sections on three several days, in each House, unless in case of emergency, two thirds of the House where such bill is pending shall deem it expedient to dispense with this rule. The reading of a bill by sections, on its final passage, shall in no case be dispensed with, and the vote on the final passage of every bill or joint resolution shall be taken by yeas and nays to be entered on the journals of each House. Except as otherwise provided in subsection 2, a majority of all the members elected to each house is necessary to pass every bill or joint resolution, and all bills or joint resolutions so passed, shall be signed by the presiding officers of the respective Houses and by the Secretary of the Senate and Clerk of the Assembly.

2. Except as otherwise provided in subsection 3, an affirmative vote of not fewer than two-thirds of the members elected to each house is necessary to pass a bill or joint resolution which creates, generates, or increases any public revenue in any form, including but not limited to taxes, fees, assessments and rates, or changes in the computation bases for taxes, fees, assessments and rates.

3. A majority of all of the members elected to each house may refer any measure which creates, generates, or increases any revenue in any form to the people of the State at the next general election, and shall become effective and enforced only if it has been approved by a majority of the votes cast on the measure at such election.

4. Each House may provide by rule for the creation of a consent calendar and establish the procedure for the passage of uncontested bills.

[Amended in 1976. Proposed and passed by the 1973 legislature; agreed to and passed by the 1975 legislature; and approved and ratified by the people at the 1976 general election. See: Statutes of Nevada 1973, p. 1946; Statutes of Nevada 1975, p. 1900.]—(Amendment proposed by initiative petition and approved by the people at the 1994 general election; effective November 27, 1996, if the proposed amendment is approved by the people at the 1996 general election.)

Sec. 19. Manner of drawing money from treasury. No money shall be drawn from the treasury but in consequence of appropriations made by law.

[Amended in 1954. Proposed and passed by the 1951 legislature; agreed to and passed by the 1953 legislature; and approved and ratified by the people at the 1954 general election. See: Statutes of Nevada 1951, p. 584; Statutes of Nevada 1953, p. 717.]

Sec. 20. Certain local and special laws prohibited. The legislature shall not pass local or special laws in any of the following enumerated cases—that is to say:

Regulating the jurisdiction and duties of justices of the peace and of constables, and fixing their compensation;
For the punishment of crimes and misdemeanors;
Regulating the practice of courts of justice;
Providing for changing the venue in civil and criminal cases;
Granting divorces;
Changing the names of persons;
Vacating roads, town plots, streets, alleys, and public squares;
Summoning and impaneling grand and petit juries, and providing for their compensation;

Regulating county and township business;

Regulating the election of county and township officers;

For the assessment and collection of taxes for state, county, and township purposes;

Providing for opening and conducting elections of state, county, or township officers, and designating the places of voting;

Providing for the sale of real estate belonging to minors or other persons laboring under legal disabilities;

Giving effect to invalid deeds, wills, or other instruments;

Refunding money paid into the state treasury, or into the treasury of any county;

Releasing the indebtedness, liability, or obligation of any corporation, association, or person to the state, or to any county, town, or city of this state; but nothing in this section shall be construed to deny or restrict the power of the legislature to establish and regulate the compensation and fees of county officers, to authorize and empower the boards of county commissioners of the various counties of the state to establish and regulate the compensation and fees of township officers in their respective counties, to establish and regulate the rates of freight, passage, toll, and charges of railroads, tollroads, ditch, flume, and tunnel companies incorporated under the laws of this state or doing business therein.

[Amended in 1889 and 1926. The first amendment was proposed and passed by the 1885 legislature; agreed to and passed by the 1887 legislature; and approved and ratified by the people at a special election held February 11, 1889. See: Statutes of Nevada 1885, p. 152; Statutes of Nevada 1887, p. 166. The second amendment was proposed and passed by the 1923 legislature; agreed to and passed by the 1925 legislature; and approved and ratified by the people at the 1926 general election. See: Statutes of Nevada 1923, p. 411; Statutes of Nevada 1925, p. 357.]

Sec. 21. General laws to have uniform application. In all cases enumerated in the preceding section, and in all other cases where a general law can be made applicable, all laws shall be general and of uniform operation throughout the State.

Sec. 22. Suit against state. Provision may be made by general law for bringing suit against the State as to all liabilities originating after the adoption of this Constitution[.]

Sec. 23. Enacting clause; law to be enacted by bill. The enacting clause of every law shall be as follows: "The people of the State of Nevada represented in Senate and Assembly, do enact as follows," and no law shall be enacted except by bill.

Sec. 24. Lotteries.

1. Except as otherwise provided in subsection 2, no lottery may be authorized by

this State, nor may lottery tickets be sold.

2. The State and the political subdivisions thereof shall not operate a lottery. The legislature may authorize persons engaged in charitable activities or activities not for profit to operate a lottery in the form of a raffle or drawing on their own behalf. All proceeds of the lottery, less expenses directly related to the operation of the lottery, must be used only to benefit charitable or nonprofit activities in this state. A charitable or nonprofit organization shall not employ or otherwise engage any person to organize or operate its lottery for compensation. The legislature may provide by law for the regulation of such lotteries.

[Amended in 1990. Proposed and passed by the 1987 legislature; agreed to and passed by the 1989 legislature; and approved and ratified by the people at the 1990 general election. See: Statutes of Nevada 1987, p. 2468; Statutes of Nevada 1989, p. 2249.]

Sec. 25. Uniform county and township government. The Legislature shall establish a system of County and Township Government which shall be uniform throughout the State.

Sec. 26. Boards of county commissioners: Election and duties. The Legislature shall provide by law, for the election of a Board of County Commissioners in each County, and such County Commissioners shall jointly and individually perform such duties as may be prescribed by law.

Sec. 27. Disqualification of jurors; elections. Laws shall be made to exclude from serving on juries, all persons not qualified electors of this State, and all persons who shall have been convicted of bribery, perjury, foregery [forgery,] larceny or other high crimes, unless restored to civil rights; and laws shall be passed regulating elections, and prohibiting under adequate penalties, all undue influence thereon from power, bribery, tumult, or other improper practice.

Sec. 28. Compensation of legislative officers and employees; increase or decrease of compensation. No money shall be drawn from the State Treasury as salary or compensation to any officer or employee of the Legislature, or either branch thereof, except in cases where such salary or compensation has been fixed by a law in force prior to the election or appointment of such officer or employee; and the salary or compensation so fixed, shall neither be increased nor diminished so as to apply to any officer or employee of the Legislature, or either branch thereof at such Session; Provided, that this restriction shall not apply to the first session of the Legislature.

Sec. 29. Duration of regular and special sessions. [Repealed in 1958.]

[Sec. 29 of Art. 4 of the original constitution was repealed by vote of the people at the 1958 general election. See: Statutes of Nevada 1955, p. 945; Statutes of Nevada

1957, p. 793. The original section read: "The first regular session of the Legislature under this Constitution may extend to Ninety days, but no subsequent regular session shall exceed sixty days, nor any special session convened by the Governor exceed twenty days."]

Sec. 30. Homesteads: Exemption from forced sale; joint consent required for alienation; recording of declaration. A homestead as provided by law, shall be exempt from forced sale under any process of law, and shall not be alienated without the joint consent of husband and wife when that relation exists; but no property shall be exempt from sale for taxes or for the payment of obligations contracted for the purchase of said premises, or for the erection of improvements thereon; Provided, the provisions of this Section shall not apply to any process of law obtained by virtue of a lien given by the consent of both husband and wife, and laws shall be enacted providing for the recording of such homestead within the County in which the same shall be situated[.]

Sec. 31. Property of married persons. All property, both real and personal, of a married person owned or claimed by such person before marriage, and that acquired afterward by gift, devise or descent, shall be the separate property of such person. The legislature shall more clearly define the rights of married persons in relation to their separate property and other property.

[Amended in 1978. Proposed and passed by the 1975 legislature; agreed to and passed by the 1977 legislature; and approved and ratified by the people at the 1978 general election. See: Statutes of Nevada 1975, p. 1917; Statutes of Nevada 1977, p. 1703.]

Sec. 32. County officers: Power of legislature; election, duties and compensation; duties of county clerks. The Legislature shall have power to increase, diminish, consolidate or abolish the following county officers: County Clerks, County Recorders, Auditors, Sheriffs, District Attorneys and Public Administrators. The Legislature shall provide for their election by the people, and fix by law their duties and compensation. County Clerks shall be ex-officio Clerks of the Courts of Record and of the Boards of County Commissioners in and for their respective counties.

[Amended in 1889 and 1972. The first amendment was proposed and passed by the 1887 legislature; agreed to and passed by the 1889 legislature; and approved and ratified by the people at a special election held February 11, 1889. See: Statutes of Nevada 1887, p. 161; Statutes of Nevada 1889, p. 151. The second amendment was proposed and passed by the 1969 legislature; agreed to and passed by the 1971 legislature; and approved and ratified by the people at the 1972 general election. See: Statutes of Nevada 1969, p. 1723; Statutes of Nevada 1971, p. 2232.]

Sec. 33. Compensation of members of legislature; payment for postage, stationery and other expenses; additional allowances for officers. The members of the Legislature shall receive for their services, a compensation to be fixed by law and paid out of the public treasury, for not to exceed 60 days during any regular session of the legislature and not to exceed 20 days during any special session convened by the governor; but no increase of such compensation shall take effect during the term for which the members of either house shall have been elected Provided, that an appropriation may be made for the payment of such actual expenses as members of the Legislature may incur for postage, express charges, newspapers and stationery not exceeding the sum of Sixty dollars for any general or special session to each member; and Furthermore Provided, that the Speaker of the Assembly, and Lieutenant Governor, as President of the Senate, shall each, during the time of their actual attendance as such presiding officers receive an additional allowance of two dollars per diem.

[Amended in 1958. Proposed and passed by the 1955 legislature; agreed to and passed by the 1957 legislature; approved and ratified by the people at the 1958 general election. See: Statutes of Nevada 1955, p. 946; Statutes of Nevada 1957, p. 794.]

Sec. 34. Election of United States Senators. In all elections for United States Senators, such elections shall be held in joint convention of both Houses of the Legislature. It shall be the duty of the Legislature which convenes next preceding the expiration of the term of such Senator, to elect his successor. If a vacancy in such Senatorial representation from any cause occur, it shall be the duty of the Legislature then in Session or at the succeeding Session thereof, to supply such vacancy[.] If the Legislature shall at any time as herein provided, fail to unite in a joint convention within twenty days after the commencement of the Session of the Legislature for the election [of] such Senator it shall be the duty of the Governor, by proclamation to convene the two Houses of the Legislature in joint convention, within not less than five days nor exceeding ten days from the publication of his proclamation, and the joint convention when so assembled shall proceed to elect the Senator as herein provided.

[This section became obsolete in 1913 with the adoption of Amendment XVII to the Constitution of the United States of America.]

Sec. 35. Bills to be presented to governor; approval; disapproval and reconsideration by legislature; failure of governor to return bill. Every bill which may have passed the Legislature, shall, before it becomes a law be presented to the Governor. If he approve it, he shall sign it, but if not he shall return it with his objections, to the House in which it originated, which House shall cause such objections to be entered upon its journal, and proceed to reconsider it; If after such reconsideration it again pass both Houses by yeas and nays, by a vote of two thirds of the members elected to each House it shall become a law notwithstanding the Governors objections. If any bill shall not be returned within five days after it shall have been presented to him (Sunday excepted) exclusive of the day on which he received it, the same shall be a law, in like manner as if he had signed it, unless the Legislature by its final adjournment, prevent such return, in which case it shall be a law, unless the Governor within ten days next after the adjournment (Sundays excepted) shall file such bill with his objections thereto, in the office of the Secretary of State, who shall lay the same before the Legislature at its next Session, in like manner as if it had been returned by the Governor, and if the same shall receive the vote of two-thirds of the members elected to each branch of the Legislature, upon a vote taken by yeas and nays to be entered upon the journals of each house, it shall become a law.

[Sec. 36.] Abolishment of county; approval of voters in county. The legislature shall not abolish any county unless the qualified voters of the county affected shall at a general or special election first approve such proposed abolishment by a majority of all the voters voting at such election. The legislature shall provide by law the method of initiating and conducting such election.

[Added in 1940. Proposed and passed by the 1937 legislature; agreed to and passed by the 1939 legislature; and approved and ratified by the people at the 1940 general election. See: Statutes of Nevada 1937, p. 564; Statutes of Nevada 1939, p. 360.]

Sec. 37. Continuity of government in case of enemy attack; succession to public offices; legislative quorum requirements; relocation of seat of government. The legislature, in order to insure continuity of state and local governmental operations in periods of emergency resulting from disasters caused by enemy attack, shall have the power and the immediate duty to provide for immediate and temporary succession to the powers and duties of public offices, of whatever nature and whether filled by election or appointment, the incumbents of which may become unavailable for carrying on the powers and duties of such offices, and to adopt such other measures as may be necessary and proper for insuring the continuity of governmental operations, including changes in quorum requirements in the legislature and the relocation of the seat of government. In the exercise of the powers hereby conferred, the legislature shall conform to the requirements of this constitution except to the extent that in the judgment of the legislature so to do would be impracticable or would admit of undue delay.

[Added in 1964. Proposed and passed by the 1961 legislature; agreed to and passed by the 1963 legislature; and approved and ratified by the people at the 1964 general election. See Statutes of Nevada 1961, p. 831; Statutes of Nevada 1963, p. 1416.]

Sec. 37[A]. Consolidation of city and county containing seat of government into one municipal government; separate taxing districts. Notwithstanding the general provisions of sections 20, 25, 26, and 36 of this article, the legislature may by law consolidate into one municipal government, with one set of officers, the city designated as the seat of government of this state and the county in which such city is situated. Such consolidated municipality shall be considered as a county for the purpose of representation in the legislature, shall have all the powers conferred upon counties by this constitution or by general law, and shall have such other powers as may be conferred by its charter. Notwithstanding the general provisions of section 1 of article 10, the legislature may create two or more separate taxing districts within such consolidated municipality.

[Added in 1968. Proposed and passed by the 1965 legislature; agreed to and passed by the 1967 legislature; and approved and ratified by the people at the 1968 general election. See: Statutes of Nevada 1965, p. 1515; Statutes of Nevada 1967, p. 1797.]

Article 5
Executive Department

Sec. 1. Supreme executive power vested in governor.
2. Election and term of governor.
3. Eligibility; qualifications; number of terms.
4. Returns of general election transmitted to secretary of state; canvass by supreme court; declaration of election.
5. Governor is commander in chief of state military forces.
6. Transaction of executive business; reports of executive officers.
7. Responsibility for execution of laws.
8. Vacancies filled by governor.
9. Special sessions of legislature; business at special session.
10. Governor's message.
11. Adjournment of legislature by governor.
12. Person holding federal office ineligible for office of governor.
13. Pardons, reprieves and commutations of sentence; remission of fines and forfeitures.
14. Remission of fines and forfeitures; commutations and pardons; suspension of sentence; probation.
15. The Great Seal.
16. Grants and commissions: Signatures and seal.
17. Lieutenant governor: Election, term, qualifications and duties; vacancy or disability during vacancy in office of governor.
18. Vacancy in office of governor; duties to devolve upon lieutenant governor.
19. Other state officers: Election, term and qualifications. [Effective until November 27, 1996, and after that date if the proposed amendment is not approved by the people at the 1996 general election.]
19. Other state officers: Election and term of office; eligibility for office. [Effective November 27, 1996, if the proposed amendment is approved by the people at the 1996 general election.]

Sec. 1. Supreme executive power vested in governor. The supreme executive power of this State, shall be vested in a Chief Magistrate who shall be Governor of the State of Nevada.

Sec. 2. Election and term of governor. The Governor shall be elected by the qualified electors at the time and places of voting for members of the Legislature, and shall hold his office for Four Years from the time of his installation, and until his successor shall be qualified.

Sec. 3. Eligibility; qualifications; number of terms. No person shall be eligible to the office of Governor, who is not a qualified elector, and who, at the time of such election, has not attained the age of twenty five years; and who shall not have been a citizen resident of this State for two years next preceding the election; nor shall any person be elected to the office of Governor more than twice; and no person who has held the office of Governor, or acted as Governor for more than two years of a term to which some other person was elected Governor shall be elected to the office of Governor more than once.

[Amended in 1970. Proposed and passed by the 1967 legislature; agreed to and passed by the 1969 legislature; and approved and ratified by the people at the 1970 general election. See: Statutes of Nevada 1967, p. 1794; Statutes of Nevada 1969, p. 1668.]

Sec. 4. Returns of general election transmitted to secretary of state; canvass by supreme court; declaration of election. The returns of every election for United States senator and member of Congress, district and state officers, and for and against any questions submitted to the electors of the State of Nevada, voted for at the general election, shall be sealed up and transmitted to the seat of government, directed to the secretary of state, and the chief justice of the supreme court, and the associate justices, or a majority thereof, shall meet at the office of the secretary of state, on a day to be fixed by law, and open and canvass the election returns for United States senator and member of Congress, district and state officers, and for and against any questions submitted to the electors of the State of Nevada, and forthwith declare the result and publish the names of the persons elected and the results of the vote cast upon any question submitted to the electors of the State of Nevada. The persons having the highest number of votes for the respective offices shall be declared elected, but in case any two or more have an equal and the highest number of votes for the same office, the legislature shall, by joint vote of both houses, elect one of said persons to fill said office.

[Amended in 1940. Proposed and passed by the 1937 legislature; agreed to and passed by the 1939 legislature; and approved and ratified by the people at the 1940 general election. See: Statutes of Nevada 1937, p. 553; Statutes of Nevada 1939, p. 361.]

Sec. 5. Governor is commander in chief of state military forces. The Governor shall be Commander in Chief of the Military forces of this State except when they shall be called into the service of the United States.

Sec. 6. Transaction of executive business; reports of executive officers. He shall transact all executive business with the Officers of the Government Civil and Military; and may require information in writing, from the Officers of the Executive Department, upon any subject relating to the duties of their respective Offices.

Sec. 7. Responsibility for execution of laws. He shall see that the laws are faithfully executed.

Sec. 8. Vacancies filled by governor. When any Office shall, from any cause become vacant and no mode is provided by the Constitution and laws for filling such vacancy, the Governor shall have the power to fill such vacancy by granting a commission which shall expire at the next election and qualification of the person elected to such Office.

Sec. 9. Special sessions of legislature; business at special session. The Governor may on extraordinary occasions, convene the Legislature by Proclamation and shall state to both houses when organized, the purpose for which they have been convened, and the Legislature shall transact no legislative business, except that for which they were specially convened, or such other legislative business as the Governor may call to the attention of the Legislature while in Session.

Sec. 10. Governor's message. He shall communicate by Message to the Legislature at every regular Session the condition of the State and recommend such measures as he may deem expedient[.]

Sec. 11. Adjournment of legislature by governor. In case of a disagreement between the two Houses with respect to the time of adjournment, the Governor shall have power to adjourn the Legislature to such time as he may think proper; Provided, it be not beyond the time fixed for the meeting of the next Legislature.

Sec. 12. Person holding federal office ineligible for office of governor. No person shall, while holding any office under the United States Government hold the office of Governor, except as herein expressly provided.

Sec. 13. Pardons, reprieves and commutations of sentence; remission of fines and forfeitures. The Governor shall have the power to suspend the collection of fines and forfeitures and grant reprieves for a period not exceeding sixty days dating from the time of conviction, for all offenses, except in cases of impeachment. Upon conviction for treason he shall have power to suspend the execution of the sentence until the case shall be reported to the Legislature at its next meeting, when the Legislature shall either pardon, direct the execution of the sentence, or grant a further reprieve. And if the Legislature should fail or refuse to make final disposition of such case, the sentence shall be enforced at such time and place as the Governor by his order may direct. The Governor shall communicate to the Legislature, at the beginning of every session, every case of fine or forfeiture remitted, or reprieve, pardon, or commutation granted, stating the name of the convict, the crime of which he was convicted, the Sentence, its date, and the date of the remission, commutation, pardon or reprieve.

Sec. 14. Remission of fines and forfeitures; commutations and pardons; suspension of sentence; probation.

1. The governor, justices of the supreme court, and attorney general, or a major part of them, of whom the governor shall be one, may, upon such conditions and with such limitations and restrictions as they may think proper, remit fines and forfeitures, commute punishments, except as provided in subsection 2, and grant pardons, after convictions, in all cases, except treason and impeachments, subject to such regulations as may be provided by law relative to the manner of applying for pardons.

2. Except as may be provided by law, a sentence of death or a sentence of life imprisonment without possibility of parole may not be commuted to a sentence which would allow parole.

3. The legislature is authorized to pass laws conferring upon the district courts authority to suspend the execution of sentences, fix the conditions for, and to grant probation, and within the minimum and maximum periods authorized by law, fix the sentence to be served by the person convicted of crime in said courts.

[Amended in 1950 and 1982. The first amendment was proposed and passed by the 1947 legislature; agreed to and passed by the 1949 legislature; and approved and ratified by the people at the 1950 general election. See: Statutes of Nevada 1947, p. 875; Statutes of Nevada 1949, p. 684. The second amendment was proposed and passed by the 1979 legislature; agreed to and passed by the 1981 legislature; and approved and ratified by the people at the 1982 general election. See: Statutes of Nevada 1979, p. 2005; Statutes of Nevada 1981, p. 2097.]

Sec. 15. The Great Seal. There shall be a Seal of this State, which shall be kept by the Governor and used by him Officially, and shall be called "The Great Seal of the State of Nevada."

Sec. 16. Grants and commissions: Signatures and seal. All grants and commissions shall be in the name and by the authority of the State of Nevada, sealed with the Great Seal of the State, signed by the Governor and counter-signed by the Secretary of State.

Sec. 17. Lieutenant governor: Election, term, qualifications and duties; vacancy or disability during vacancy in office of governor. A Lieutenant Governor shall be elected at the same time and places and in the same manner as the Governor and his term of Office, and his eligibility, shall also be the same. He shall be President of the Senate, but shall only have a casting vote therein. If during a Vacancy of the office of Governor, the Lieutenant Governor shall be impeached, displaced, resign, die, or become incapable of performing the duties of the office, or be absent from the State, the President pro-tempore of the Senate shall act as Governor until the vacancy be filled or the disability cease.

Sec. 18. Vacancy in office of governor; duties to devolve upon lieutenant governor. In case of the impeachment of the Governor, or his removal from Office, death, inability to discharge the duties of the said Office, resignation or absence from the State, the powers and duties of the Office shall devolve upon the Lieutenant Governor for the residue of the term, or until the disability shall cease. But when the Governor shall with the consent of the Legislature be out of the State, in time of War, and at the head of any military force thereof, he shall continue Commander in Chief of the military forces of the State.

Sec. 19. Other state officers: Election, term and qualifications. [Effective until November 27, 1996, and after that date if the proposed amendment is not approved by the people at the 1996 general election.] A secretary of state, a treasurer, a controller, and an attorney general, shall be elected at the same time and places, and in the same manner as the governor. The term of office of each shall be the same as is prescribed for the governor. Any elector shall be eligible to either of said offices.

[Amended in 1954. Proposed and passed by the 1951 legislature; agreed to and passed by the 1953 legislature; and approved and ratified by the people at the 1954 general election. See: Statutes of Nevada 1951, p. 581; Statutes of Nevada 1953, p. 715.]

Sec. 19. Other state officers: Election and term of office; eligibility for office. [Effective November 27, 1996, if the proposed amendment is approved by the people at the 1996 general election.]

1. A secretary of state, a treasurer, a controller, and an attorney general, shall be elected at the same time and places, and in the same manner as the governor. The term of office of each shall be the same as is prescribed for the governor.

2. Any elector shall be eligible to any of these offices, but no person may be elected to any of them more than twice, or more than once if he has previously

held the office by election or appointment.

[Amended in 1954. Proposed and passed by the 1951 legislature; agreed to and passed by the 1953 legislature; and approved and ratified by the people at the 1954 general election. See: Statutes of Nevada 1951, p. 581; Statutes of Nevada 1953, p. 715.]—(Amendment proposed by initiative petition and approved by the people at the 1994 general election; effective November 27, 1996, if the proposed amendment is approved by the people at the 1996 general election.)

Sec. 20. Secretary of state: Duties. The Secretary of State shall keep a true record of the Official Acts of the Legislative and Executive Departments of the Government, and shall when required, lay the same and all matters relative thereto, before either branch of the Legislature.

Sec. 21. Board of state prison commissioners; board of examiners; examination of claims. The Governor, Secretary of State and Attorney General shall constitute a Board of State Prison Commissioners, which Board shall have such supervision of all matters connected with the State Prison as may be provided by law. They shall also constitute a Board of Examiners, with power to examine all claims against the State (except salaries or compensation of Officers fixed by law) and perform such other duties as may be prescribed by law, and no claim against the State (except salaries or compensation of Officers fixed by law) shall be passed upon by the Legislature without having been considered and acted upon by said "Board of Examiners."

Sec. 22. Duties of certain state officers. The secretary of state, state treasurer, state controller, attorney general, and superintendent of public instruction shall perform such other duties as may be prescribed by law.

[Amended in 1954. Proposed and passed by the 1951 legislature; agreed to and passed by the 1953 legislature; and approved and ratified by the people at the 1954 general election. See: Statutes of Nevada 1951, p. 581; Statutes of Nevada 1953, p. 716.]

Article 6
Judicial Department

Sec. 1. Judicial power vested in court system.
2. Supreme court: Composition; staggered terms of justices; holding of court by panels of justices and full court.
3. Justices of supreme court: Election; terms; chief justice.
4. Jurisdiction of supreme court; appointment of district judge to sit for disabled or disqualified justice.
5. Judicial districts; election and terms of district judges.
6. District Courts: Jurisdiction; referees; family court.

7. Terms of court.

8. Number, qualifications, terms of office and jurisdiction of justices of the peace; appeals; courts of record.

9. Municipal courts.

10. Fees or perquisites of judicial officers.

11. Justices and judges ineligible for other offices. [Effective until November 27, 1996, and after that date if the proposed amendment is not approved by the people at the 1996 general election.]

11. Justices and judges ineligible for other offices; limitation on terms of office. [Effective November 27, 1996, if the proposed amendment is approved by the people at the 1996 general election.]

12. Judge not to charge jury respecting matters of fact; statement of testimony and declaration of law.

13. Style of process.

14. One form of civil action.

15. Compensation of judges.

16. Special fee in civil action for compensation of judges.

17. Absence of judicial officer from state; vacation of office.

18. Territorial judicial officers not superseded until election and qualification of successors.

19. Administration of court system by chief justice.

20. Commission on judicial selection.

21. Commission on judicial discipline.

Sec. 1. Judicial power vested in court system. The Judicial power of this State shall be vested in a court system, comprising a Supreme Court, District Courts, and Justices of the Peace. The Legislature may also establish, as part of the system, Courts for municipal purposes only in incorporated cities and towns.

[Amended in 1976. Proposed and passed by the 1973 legislature; agreed to and passed by the 1975 legislature; and approved and ratified by the people at the 1976 general election. See: Statutes of Nevada 1973, p. 1960; Statutes of Nevada 1975, p. 1934.]

Sec. 2. Supreme court: Composition; staggered terms of justices; holding of court by panels of justices and full court.

1. The supreme court consists of the chief justice and two or more associate justices, as may be provided by law. In increasing or diminishing the number of associate justices, the legislature shall provide for the arrangement of their terms so that an equal number of terms, as nearly as may be, expire every 2 years.

2. The legislature may provide by law:

   (a) If the court consists of more than five justices, for the hearing and decision of cases by panels of no fewer than three justices, the resolution by the full court of any conflicts between decisions so rendered, and the kinds of cases which must be heard by the full court.
   (b) For the places of holding court by panels of justices if established, and by the full court.

[Amended in 1976. Proposed and passed by the 1973 legislature; agreed to and passed by the 1975 legislature; and approved and ratified by the people at the 1976 general election. See: Statutes of Nevada 1973, p. 1952; Statutes of Nevada 1975, p. 1980.]

Sec. 3. Justices of supreme court: Election; terms; chief justice. The Justices of the Supreme Court, shall be elected by the qualified electors of the State at the general election, and shall hold office for the term of Six Years from and including the first Monday of January next succeeding their election; Provided, that there shall be elected, at the first election under this Constitution, Three Justices of the Supreme Court who shall hold Office from and including the first Monday of December A.D. Eighteen hundred and Sixty four, and continue in Office thereafter, Two, Four and Six Years respectively, from and including the first Monday of January next suceeding [succeeding] their election. They shall meet as soon as practicable after their election and qualification, and at their first meeting shall determine by lot, the term of Office each shall fill, and the Justice drawing the shortest term shall be Chief Justice, and after the expiration of his term, the one having the next shortest term shall be Chief Justice, after which the Senior Justice in Commission shall be Chief Justice; and in case the commission of any two or more of said Justices shall bear the same date, they shall determine by lot, who shall be Chief Justice.

Sec. 4. Jurisdiction of supreme court; appointment of district judge to sit for disabled or disqualified justice. The supreme court shall have appellate jurisdiction in all civil cases arising in district courts, and also on questions of law alone in all criminal cases in which the offense charged is within the original jurisdiction of the district courts. The court shall also have power to issue writs of mandamus, certiorari, prohibition, quo warranto, and habeas corpus and also all writs necessary or proper to the complete exercise of its appellate jurisdiction. Each of the justices shall have power to issue writs of habeas corpus to any part of the state, upon petition by, or on behalf of, any person held in actual custody, and may make such writs returnable, before himself or the supreme court, or before any district court in the state or before any judge of said courts.

In case of the disability or disqualification, for any cause, of the chief justice or one of the associate justices of the supreme court, or any two of them, the governor is authorized and empowered to designate any district judge or judges to sit in the place or places of such disqualified or disabled justice or justices, and said judge or judges so designated shall receive their actual expense of travel and otherwise while sitting in the supreme court.

[Amended in 1920, 1976 and 1978. The first amendment was proposed and passed by the 1917 legislature; agreed to and passed by the 1919 legislature; and approved and ratified by the people at the 1920 general election. See: Statutes of Nevada 1917, p. 491; Statutes of Nevada 1919, p. 485. The second amendment was proposed and passed by the 1973 legislature; agreed to and passed by the 1975 legislature; and approved and ratified by the people at the 1976 general election. See: Statutes of Nevada 1973, p. 1953; Statutes of Nevada 1975, p. 1981. The third amendment was proposed and passed by the 1975 legislature; agreed to and passed by the 1977 legislature; and approved and ratified by the people at the 1978 general election. See: Statutes of Nevada 1975, p. 1951; Statutes of Nevada 1977, p. 1690.]

Sec. 5. Judicial districts; election and terms of district judges. The state is hereby divided into Nine Judicial Districts of which the county of Storey shall constitute the First; The county of Ormsby the Second; the county of Lyon the Third; The county of Washoe the Fourth; The counties of Nye and Churchill the Fifth; The county of Humboldt the Sixth; The county of Lander the Seventh; The county of Douglas the Eighth; and the county of Esmeralda the Ninth. The county of Roop shall be attached to the county of Washoe for judicial purposes until otherwise provided by law. The Legislature may, however, provide by law for an alteration in the boundaries or divisions of the Districts herein prescribed, and also for increasing or diminishing the number of the Judicial Districts and Judges therein. But no such change shall take effect, except in case of a vacancy, or the expiration of the term of an incumbent of the Office. At the first general election under this Constitution there shall be elected in each of the respective Districts (except as in this Section hereafter otherwise provided) One District Judge, who shall hold Office from and including the first Monday of December A.D. Eighteen hundred and Sixty four and until the first Monday of January in the year Eighteen hundred and Sixty seven. After the said first election, there shall be elected at the General election which immediately precedes the expiration of the term of his predecessor, One District Judge in each of the respective Judicial Districts (except in the First District as in this Section hereinafter provided.) The District Judges shall be elected by the qualified electors of their respective districts, and shall hold office for the term of 6 years (excepting those elected at said first election) from and including the first Monday of January, next succeeding their election and qualification; Provided, that the First Judicial District shall be entitled to, and shall have Three District Judges, who shall possess co-extensive and concurrent jurisdiction, and who shall be elected at the same times, in the same manner, and shall hold office for the like terms as herein prescribed, in relation to the Judges in other Judicial Districts, any one of said Judges may preside on the empanneling [empaneling] of Grand Juries and the presentment and trial on indictments, under such rules and regulations as may be prescribed by law.

[Amended in 1976. Proposed and passed by the 1973 legislature; agreed to and passed by the 1975 legislature; and approved and ratified by the people at the 1976 general election. See: Statutes of Nevada 1973, p. 1955; Statutes of Nevada 1975, p. 1932.]

Sec. 6. District Courts: Jurisdiction; referees; family court.

1. The District Courts in the several Judicial Districts of this State have original jurisdiction in all cases excluded by law from the original jurisdiction of justices' courts. They also have final appellate jurisdiction in cases arising in Justices Courts and such other inferior tribunals as may be established by law. The District Courts and the Judges thereof have power to issue writs of Mandamus, Prohibition, Injunction, Quo-Warranto, Certiorari, and all other writs proper and necessary to the complete exercise of their jurisdiction. The District Courts and the Judges thereof shall also have power to issue writs of Habeas Corpus on petition by, or on behalf of any person who is held in actual custody in their respective districts, or who has suffered a criminal conviction in their respective districts and has not completed the sentence imposed pursuant to the judgment of conviction.

2. The legislature may provide by law for:

    (a) Referees in district courts.
    (b) The establishment of a family court as a division of any district court and may prescribe its jurisdiction.

[Amended in 1978, 1986 and 1990. The first amendment was proposed and passed by the 1975 legislature; agreed to and passed by the 1977 legislature; and approved and ratified by the people at the 1978 general election. See: Statutes of Nevada 1975, p. 1951; Statutes of Nevada 1977, p. 1690. The second amendment was proposed and passed by the 1983 legislature; agreed to and passed by the 1985 legislature; and approved and ratified by the people at the 1986 general election. See: Statutes of Nevada 1983, p. 2188; Statutes of Nevada 1985, p. 2332. The third amendment was proposed and passed by the 1987 legislature; agreed to and passed by the 1989 legislature; and approved and ratified by the people at the 1990 general election. See: Statutes of Nevada 1987, p. 2444; Statutes of Nevada 1989, p. 2222. The fourth amendment was proposed and passed by the 1989 legislature; agreed to and passed by the 1991 legislature; and approved and ratified by the people at the 1992 general election. See Statutes of Nevada 1989, p. 2269; Statutes of Nevada 1991, p. 2494.]

Sec. 7. Terms of court. The times of holding the Supreme Court and District Courts shall be as fixed by law. The terms of the Supreme Court shall be held at the seat of Government unless the Legislature otherwise provides by law, except that the Supreme Court may hear oral argument at other places in the state. The terms of the District Courts shall be held at the County seats of their respective counties; Provided, that in case any county shall be hereafter divided into two or more districts, the Legislature may by law, designate the places of holding Courts in such Districts.

[Amended in 1976. Two amendments were proposed and passed by the 1973 legislature; agreed to and passed by the 1975 legislature; and approved and ratified by the people at the 1976 general election. See: Statutes of Nevada 1973, pp. 1940 and 1953; Statutes of Nevada 1975, pp. 1870 and 1981. The amendments were combined pursuant to Nev. Art. 16, ° 1.]

Sec. 8. Number, qualifications, terms of office and jurisdiction of justices of the peace; appeals; courts of record. The Legislature shall determine the number of Justices of the Peace to be elected in each city and township of the State, and shall fix by law their qualifications, their terms of office and the limits of their civil and criminal jurisdiction, according to the amount in controversy, the nature of the case, the penalty provided, or any combination of these.

The provisions of this section affecting the number, qualifications, terms of office and jurisdiction of Justices of the Peace become effective on the first Monday of January, 1979.

The Legislature shall also prescribe by law the manner, and determine the cases in which appeals may be taken from Justices and other courts. The Supreme Court, the District Courts, and such other Courts, as the Legislature shall designate, shall be Courts of Record.

[Amended in 1978. Proposed and passed by the 1975 legislature; agreed to and passed by the 1977 legislature; and approved and ratified by the people at the 1978 general election. See: Statutes of Nevada 1975, p. 1952; Statutes of Nevada 1977, p. 1691.]

Sec. 9. Municipal courts. Provision shall be made by law prescribing the powers[,] duties and responsibilities of any Municipal Court that may be established in pursuance of Section One, of this Article; and also fixing by law the jurisdiction of said Court so as not to conflict with that of the several courts of Record.

Sec. 10. Fees or perquisites of judicial officers. No Judicial Officer, except Justices of the Peace and City Recorders shall receive to his own use any fees or perquisites of Office[.]

Sec. 11. Justices and judges ineligible for other offices. [Effective until November

27, 1996, and after that date if the proposed amendment is not approved by the people at the 1996 general election.] The justices of the supreme court and the district judges shall be ineligible to any office, other than a judicial office, during the term for which they shall have been elected or appointed; and all elections or appointments of any such judges by the people, legislature, or otherwise, during said period, to any office other than judicial, shall be void.

[Amended in 1950. Proposed and passed by the 1947 legislature; agreed to and passed by the 1949 legislature; and approved and ratified by the people at the 1950 general election. See: Statutes of Nevada 1947, p. 878; Statutes of Nevada 1949, p. 684.]

Sec. 11. Justices and judges ineligible for other offices; limitation on terms of office. [Effective November 27, 1996, if the proposed amendment is approved by the people at the 1996 general election.]

1. The justices of the supreme court and the district judges shall be ineligible to any office, other than a judicial office, during the term for which they shall have been elected or appointed; and all elections or appointments of any such judges by the people, legislature, or otherwise, during said period, to any office other than judicial, shall be void.

2. No person may be elected a justice of the supreme court, judge of any other court, or justice of the peace more than twice for the same court, or more than once if he has previously served upon that court by election or appointment.

[Amended in 1950. Proposed and passed by the 1947 legislature; agreed to and passed by the 1949 legislature; and approved and ratified by the people at the 1950 general election. See: Statutes of Nevada 1947, p. 878; Statutes of Nevada 1949, p. 684.]—(Amendment proposed by initiative petition and approved by the people at the 1994 general election; effective November 27, 1996, if the proposed amendment is approved by the people at the 1996 general election.)

Sec. 12. Judge not to charge jury respecting matters of fact; statement of testimony and declaration of law. Judges shall not charge juries in respect to matters of fact, but may state the testimony and declare the law.

Sec. 13. Style of process. The style of all process shall be "The State of Nevada" and all prosecutions shall be conducted in the name and by the authority of the same.

Sec. 14. One form of civil action. There shall be but one form of civil action, and law and equity may be administered in the same action.

Sec. 15. Compensation of judges. The Justices of the Supreme Court and District Judges shall each receive for their services a compensation to be fixed by law and paid in the manner provided by law, which shall not be increased or diminished during the term for which they shall have been elected, unless a Vacancy occurs, in which case the successor of the former incumbent shall receive only such salary as may be provided by law at the time of his election or appointment; and provision shall be made by law for setting apart from each year's revenue a sufficient amount of Money, to pay such compensation.

[Amended in 1968. Proposed and passed by the 1965 legislature; agreed to and passed by the 1967 legislature; and approved and ratified by the people at the 1968 general election. See: Statutes of Nevada 1965, p. 1487; Statutes of Nevada 1967, p. 1787.]

Sec. 16. Special fee in civil action for compensation of judges. The Legislature at its first Session, and from time to time thereafter shall provide by law, that upon the institution of each civil action, and other proceedings, and also upon the perfecting of an appeal in any civil action or proceeding, in the several Courts of Record in this State, a special Court fee, or tax shall be advanced to the Clerks of said Courts, respectively by the party or parties bringing such action or proceeding, or taking such appeal and the money so paid in shall be accounted for by such Clerks, and applied towards the payment of the compensation of the Judges of said Courts, as shall be directed by law.

Sec. 17. Absence of judicial officer from state; vacation of office. The Legislature shall have no power to grant leave of absence to a Judicial Officer, and any such Officer who shall absent himself from the State for more than Ninety consecutive days, shall be deemed to have vacated his Office[.]

Sec. 18. Territorial judicial officers not superseded until election and qualification of successors. No Judicial Officer shall be superceeded [superseded] nor shall the Organization of the several Courts of the Territory of Nevada be changed until the election and qualification of the several Officers provided for in this article[.]

Sec. 19. Administration of court system by chief justice.

1. The chief justice is the administrative head of the court system. Subject to such rules as the supreme court may adopt, the chief justice may:

    (a) Apportion the work of the supreme court among justices.
    (b) Assign district judges to assist in other judicial districts or to specialized functions which may be established by law.
    (c) Recall to active service any retired justice or judge of the court system who consents to such recall and who has not been removed or retired for cause or defeated for retention in office, and may assign him to appropriate temporary duty within the court system.

2. In the absence or temporary disability of the chief justice, the associate justice senior in commission shall act as chief justice.

3. This section becomes effective July 1, 1977.

[Added in 1976. Proposed and passed by the 1973 legislature; agreed to and passed by the 1975 legislature; and approved and ratified by the people at the 1976 general election. See: Statutes of Nevada 1973, p. 1960; Statutes of Nevada 1975, p. 1934.]

Sec. 20. Commission on judicial selection.

1. When a vacancy occurs before the expiration of any term of office in the supreme court or among the district judges, the governor shall appoint a justice or judge from among three nominees selected for such individual vacancy by the commission on judicial selection.

2. The term of office of any justice or judge so appointed expires on the first Monday of January following the next general election.

3. Each nomination for the supreme court shall be made by the permanent commission, composed of:

    (a) The chief justice or an associate justice designated by him;
    (b) Three members of the State Bar of Nevada, a public corporation created by statute, appointed by its board of governors; and
    (c) Three persons, not members of the legal profession, appointed by the governor.

4. Each nomination for the district court shall be made by a temporary commission composed of:

    (a) The permanent commission;
    (b) A member of the State Bar of Nevada resident in the judicial district in which the vacancy occurs, appointed by the board of governors of the State Bar of Nevada; and
    (c) A resident of such judicial district, not a member of the legal profession, appointed by the governor.

5. If at any time the State Bar of Nevada ceases to exist as a public corporation or ceases to include all attorneys admitted to practice before the courts of this state, the legislature shall provide by law, or if it fails to do so the court shall provide by rule, for the appointment of attorneys at law to the positions designated in this section to be occupied by members of the State Bar of Nevada.

6. The term of office of each appointive member of the permanent commission, except the first members, is 4 years. Each appointing authority shall appoint

one of the members first appointed for a term of 2 years. If a vacancy occurs, the appointing authority shall fill the vacancy for the unexpired term. The additional members of a temporary commission shall be appointed when a vacancy occurs, and their terms shall expire when the nominations for such vacancy have been transmitted to the governor.

7. An appointing authority shall not appoint to the permanent commission more than:

   (a) One resident of any county.
   (b) Two members of the same political party.

No member of the permanent commission may be a member of a commission on judicial discipline.

8. After the expiration of 30 days from the date on which the commission on judicial selection has delivered to him its list of nominees for any vacancy, if the governor has not made the appointment required by this section, he shall make no other appointment to any public office until he has appointed a justice or judge from the list submitted.

If a commission on judicial selection is established by another section of this constitution to nominate persons to fill vacancies on the supreme court, such commission shall serve as the permanent commission established by subsection 3 of this section.

[Added in 1976. Proposed and passed by the 1973 legislature; agreed to and passed by the 1975 legislature; and approved and ratified by the people at the 1976 general election. See: Statutes of Nevada 1973, p. 1954; Statutes of Nevada 1975, p. 1872.]

Sec. 21. Commission on judicial discipline.

1. A justice of the supreme court, a district judge, a justice of the peace or a municipal judge may, in addition to the provision of article 7 for impeachment, be censured, retired, removed or otherwise disciplined by the commission on judicial discipline. A justice or judge may appeal from the action of the commission to the supreme court, which may reverse such action or take any alternative action provided in this subsection.

2. The commission is composed of:

   (a) Two justices or judges appointed by the supreme court;
   (b) Two members of the State Bar of Nevada, a public corporation created by statute, appointed by its board of governors; and
   (c) Three persons, not members of the legal profession, appointed by the governor.

The commission shall elect a chairman from among its three lay members.

3. If at any time the State Bar of Nevada ceases to exist as a public corporation or ceases to include all attorneys admitted to practice before the courts of this state, the legislature shall provide by law, or if it fails to do so the court shall provide by rule, for the appointment of attorneys at law to the positions designated in this section to be occupied by members of the State Bar of Nevada.

4. The term of office of each appointive member of the commission, except the first members, is 4 years. Each appointing authority shall appoint one of the members first appointed for a term of 2 years. If a vacancy occurs, the appointing authority shall fill the vacancy for the unexpired term. An appointing authority shall not appoint more than one resident of any county. The governor shall not appoint more than two members of the same political party. No member may be a member of a commission on judicial selection.

5. The supreme court shall make appropriate rules for:

   (a) The confidentiality of all proceedings before the commission, except a decision to censure, retire or remove a justice or judge.
   (b) The grounds of censure and other forms of discipline which may be imposed by the commission.
   (c) The conduct of investigations and hearings.

6. No justice or judge may by virtue of this section be:

   (a) Removed except for willful misconduct, willful or persistent failure to perform the duties of his office or habitual intemperance; or
   (b) Retired except for advanced age which interferes with the proper performance of his judicial duties, or for mental or physical disability which prevents the proper performance of his judicial duties and which is likely to be permanent in nature.

7. Any person may bring to the attention of the commission any matter relating to the fitness of a justice or judge. The commission shall, after preliminary investigation, dismiss the matter or order a hearing to be held before it. If a hearing is ordered, a statement of the matter shall be served upon the justice or judge against whom the proceeding is brought. The commission in its discretion may suspend a justice or judge from the exercise of his office pending the determination of the proceedings before the commission. Any justice or judge whose removal is sought is liable to indictment and punishment according to law. A justice or judge retired for disability in accordance with this section is entitled thereafter to receive such compensation as the legislature may provide.

8. If a proceeding is brought against a justice of the supreme court, no justice of the supreme court may sit on the commission for that proceeding. If a proceeding is brought against a district judge, no district judge from the same judicial district may sit on the commission for that proceeding. If a proceeding is brought against a justice of the peace, no justice of the peace from the same township may sit on the commission for that proceeding. If a proceeding is brought against a municipal judge, no municipal judge from the same city may sit on the commission for that proceeding. If an appeal is taken from an action of the commission to the supreme court, any justice who sat on the commission for that proceeding is disqualified from participating in the consideration or decision of the appeal. When any member of the commission is disqualified by this subsection, the supreme court shall appoint a substitute from among the eligible judges.

9. The commission may:

    (a) Designate for each hearing an attorney or attorneys at law to act as counsel to conduct the proceeding;

    (b) Summon witnesses to appear and testify under oath and compel the production of books, papers, documents and records;

    (c) Grant immunity from prosecution or punishment when the commission deems it necessary and proper in order to compel the giving of testimony under oath and the production of books, papers, documents and records; and

    (d) Exercise such further powers as the legislature may from time to time confer upon it.

[Added in 1976 and amended in 1994. The addition was proposed and passed by the 1973 legislature; agreed to and passed by the 1975 legislature; and approved and ratified by the people at the 1976 general election. See: Statutes of Nevada 1973, p. 1956; Statutes of Nevada 1975, p. 1932. The amendment was proposed and passed by the 1991 legislature; agreed to and passed by the 1993 legislature; and approved and ratified by the people at the 1994 general election. See: Statutes of Nevada 1991, p. 2590; Statutes of Nevada 1993, p. 2969.]

Article 7
Impeachment and Removal from Office

Sec. 1. Impeachment: Trial; conviction.
     2. Officers subject to impeachment.
     3. Removal of supreme court justice or district judge.
     4. Removal of other civil officers.

Sec. 1. Impeachment: Trial; conviction. The Assembly shall have the sole power of impeaching. The concurrence of a majority of all the members elected, shall be necessary to an impeachment. All impeachments shall be tried by the Senate, and when sitting for that purpose, the Senators shall be upon Oath or Affirmation, to do justice according to Law and Evidence. The Chief Justice of the Supreme court, shall preside over the Senate while sitting to try the Governor or Lieutenant Governor upon impeachment. No person shall be convicted without the concurrence of two thirds of the Senators elected.

Sec. 2. Officers subject to impeachment. The Governor and other State and Judicial Officers, except Justices of the Peace shall be liable to impeachment for Misdemeanor or Malfeasance in Office; but judgment in such case shall not extend further than removal from Office and disqualification to hold any Office of honor, profit, or trust under this State. The party whether convicted or acquitted, shall, nevertheless, be liable to indictment, trial, judgment and punishment according to law.

Sec. 3. Removal of supreme court justice or district judge. For any reasonable cause to be entered on the journals of each House, which may, or may not be sufficient grounds for impeachment, the Chief Justice and Associate Justices of the Supreme Court and Judges of the District Courts shall be removed from Office on the vote of two thirds of the Members elected to each branch of the Legislature, and the Justice or Judge complained of, shall be served with a copy of the complaint against him, and shall have an opportunity of being heard in person or by counsel in his defense, Provided, that no member of either branch of the Legislature shall be eligible to fill the vacancy occasioned by such removal.

Sec. 4. Removal of other civil officers. Provision shall be made by law for the removal from Office of any Civil Officer other than those in this Article previously specified, for Malfeasance, or Nonfeasance in the Performance of his duties.

Article 8
Municipal and Other Corporations

Sec. 1. Corporations formed under general laws; municipal corporations formed under special acts.

2. Corporate property subject to taxation; exemptions.

3. Individual liability of corporators.

4. Regulation of corporations incorporated under territorial law.

5. Corporations may sue and be sued.

6. Circulation of certain bank notes or paper as money prohibited.

7. Eminent domain by corporations.

8. Municipal corporations formed under general laws.
9. Gifts or loans of public money to certain corporations prohibited. [Effective until November 27, 1996, and after that date if the proposed amendment is not approved by the people at the 1996 general election.]
9. Use of public money for certain corporations restricted. [Effective November 27, 1996, if the proposed amendment is approved by the people at the 1996 general election.]
10. Loans of public money to or ownership of stock in certain corporations by county or municipal corporation prohibited.

Sec. 1. Corporations formed under general laws; municipal corporations formed under special acts. The Legislature shall pass no Special Act in any manner relating to corporate powers except for Municipal purposes; but corporations may be formed under general laws; and all such laws may from time to time, be altered or repealed.

Sec. 2. Corporate property subject to taxation; exemptions. All real property, and possessory rights to the same, as well as personal property in this State, belonging to corporations now existing or hereafter created shall be subject to taxation, the same as property of individuals; Provided, that the property of corporations formed for Municipal, Charitable, Religious, or Educational purposes may be exempted by law.

Sec. 3. Individual liability of corporators. Dues from corporations shall be secured by such means as may be prescribed by law; Provided, that corporators in corporations formed under the laws of this State shall not be individually liable for the debts or liabilities of such corporation.

Sec. 4. Regulation of corporations incorporated under territorial law. Corporations created by or under the laws of the Territory of Nevada shall be subject to the provisions of such laws until the Legislature shall pass laws regulating the same, in pursuance of the provisions of this Constitution[.]

Sec. 5. Corporations may sue and be sued. Corporations may sue and be sued in all courts, in like manner as individuals.

Sec. 6. Circulation of certain bank notes or paper as money prohibited. No bank notes or paper of any kind shall ever be permitted to circulate as money in this State, except the Federal currency, and the notes of banks authorized under the laws of Congress.

Sec. 7. Eminent domain by corporations. No right of way shall be appropriated to the use of any corporation until full compensation be first made or secured therefor.

Sec. 8. Municipal corporations formed under general laws. The legislature shall provide for the organization of cities and towns by general laws and shall restrict their power of taxation, assessment, borrowing money, contracting debts and loaning their credit, except for procuring supplies of water; provided, however, that the legislature may, by general laws, in the manner and to the extent therein provided, permit and authorize the electors of any city or town to frame, adopt and amend a charter for its own government, or to amend any existing charter of such city or town.

[Amended in 1924. Proposed and passed by the 1921 legislature; agreed to and passed by the 1923 legislature; and approved and ratified by the people at the 1924 general election. See: Statutes of Nevada 1921, p. 420; Statutes of Nevada 1923, p. 403.]

Sec. 9. Gifts or loans of public money to certain corporations prohibited. [Effective until November 27, 1996, and after that date if the proposed amendment is not approved by the people at the 1996 general election.]

The State shall not donate or loan money, or its credit, subscribe to or be, interested in the Stock of any company, association, or corporation, except corporations formed for educational or charitable purposes.

Sec. 9. Use of public money for certain corporations restricted. [Effective November 27, 1996, if the proposed amendment is approved by the people at the 1996 general election.]

1. Except as otherwise provided in subsections 2 and 3, the State shall not donate or loan money or its credit to, or subscribe to or be interested in the Stock of any company, association, or corporation.

2. The legislature may by law, approved by a vote of two-thirds of the members elected to each house, authorize the investment of state money in a company, association or corporation subject to the following conditions:

   (a) Before any investment is authorized, a determination must be made, by a person or entity designated in the authorizing legislation, that:
      (1) The investment is for the economic development of this state or the creation of new employment opportunities in this state; and
      (2) The state can reasonably expect to achieve a reasonable rate of return on the investment, adjusted for the relative degree of risk; and
   (b) Each investment by the state must be made through a cooperative venture with private investors of reasonable sophistication who participate in the venture on terms that are the same as or less favorable than the terms on which the state is participating. Revenue received from investments pursuant to this subsection may be reinvested subject to the same conditions.

3. The provisions of this section do not apply to corporations formed for educational or charitable purposes.

(Amendment proposed and passed by the 1993 legislature and agreed to and passed by the 1995 legislature; effective November 27, 1996, if the proposed amendment is approved by the people at the 1996 general election.)

Sec. 10. Loans of public money to or ownership of stock in certain corporations by county or municipal corporation prohibited. No county, city, town, or other municipal corporation shall become a stockholder in any joint stock company, corporation or association whatever, or loan its credit in aid of any such company, corporation or association, except, rail-road corporations[,] companies or associations.

Article 9
Finance and State Debt

Sec. 1. Fiscal year.
2. Annual tax for state expenses; trust funds for compensation for industrial accidents, occupational diseases and public employees' retirement system. [Effective until November 27, 1996, and after that date if the proposed amendment is not approved by the people at the 1996 general election.]
2. Annual tax for state expenses; trust funds for industrial accidents, occupational diseases and public employees' retirement system; administration of public employees' retirement system. [Effective November 27, 1996, if the proposed amendment is approved by the people at the 1996 general election.]
3. State indebtedness: Limitations and exceptions. [Effective until November 27, 1996, and after that date if the proposed amendment is not approved by the people at the 1996 general election.]
3. State indebtedness: Limitations and exceptions. [Effective November 27, 1996, if the proposed amendment is approved by the people at the 1996 general election.]
4. Assumption of debts of county, city or corporation by state.
5. Proceeds from fees for licensing and registration of motor vehicles and excise taxes on fuel reserved for construction, maintenance and repair of public highways; exception.

Sec. 1. Fiscal year. The fiscal year shall commence on the first day of July of each year.

[Amended in 1930. Proposed and passed by the 1927 legislature; agreed to and passed by the 1929 legislature; and approved and ratified by the people at the 1930 general election. See: Statutes of Nevada 1927, p. 346; Statutes of Nevada 1929, p. 429.]

Sec. 2. Annual tax for state expenses; trust funds for compensation for industrial accidents, occupational diseases and public employees' retirement system. [Effective until November 27, 1996, and after that date if the proposed amendment is not approved by the people at the 1996 general election.] The legislature shall provide by law for an annual tax sufficient to defray the estimated expenses of the state for each fiscal year; and whenever the expenses of any year shall exceed the income, the legislature shall provide for levying a tax sufficient, with other sources of income, to pay the deficiency, as well as the estimated expenses of such ensuing year or two years. Any moneys paid for the purpose of providing compensation for industrial accidents and occupational diseases, and for administrative expenses incidental thereto, and for the purpose of funding and administering a public employees'retirement system, shall be segregated in proper accounts in the state treasury, and such moneys shall never be used for any other purposes, and they are hereby declared to be trust funds for the uses and purposes herein specified.

[Amended in 1956 and 1974. The first amendment was proposed and passed by the 1953 legislature; agreed to and passed by the 1955 legislature; and approved and ratified by the people at the 1956 general election. See: Statutes of Nevada 1953, p. 729; Statutes of Nevada 1955, p. 927. The second amendment was proposed and passed by the 1971 legislature; agreed to and passed by the 1973 legislature; and approved and ratified by the people at the 1974 general election. See: Statutes of Nevada 1971, p. 2267; Statutes of Nevada 1973, p. 1948.]

Sec. 2. Annual tax for state expenses; trust funds for industrial accidents, occupational diseases and public employees' retirement system; administration of public employees'retirement system. [Effective November 27, 1996, if the proposed amendment is approved by the people at the 1996 general election.]

1. The legislature shall provide by law for an annual tax sufficient to defray the estimated expenses of the state for each fiscal year; and whenever the expenses of any year exceed the income, the legislature shall provide for levying a tax sufficient, with other sources of income, to pay the deficiency, as well as the estimated expenses of such ensuing year or two years.

2. Any money paid for the purpose of providing compensation for industrial accidents and occupational diseases, and for administrative expenses incidental thereto, and for the purpose of funding and administering a public employees' retirement system, must be segregated in proper accounts in the state treasury, and such money must never be used for any other purposes, and they are hereby declared to be trust funds for the uses and purposes herein specified.

3. Any money paid for the purpose of funding and administering a public employees'retirement system must not be loaned to the state or invested to purchase any obligations of the state.

4. The public employees' retirement system must be governed by a public employees' retirement board. The board shall employ an executive officer who

serves at the pleasure of the board. In addition to any other employees authorized by the board, the board shall employ an independent actuary. The board shall adopt actuarial assumptions based upon the recommendations made by the independent actuary it employs.

[Amended in 1956 and 1974. The first amendment was proposed and passed by the 1953 legislature; agreed to and passed by the 1955 legislature; and approved and ratified by the people at the 1956 general election. See: Statutes of Nevada 1953, p. 729; Statutes of Nevada 1955, p. 927. The second amendment was proposed and passed by the 1971 legislature; agreed to and passed by the 1973 legislature; and approved and ratified by the people at the 1974 general election. See: Statutes of Nevada 1971, p. 2267; Statutes of Nevada 1973, p. 1948.]—(Amendment proposed and passed by the 1993 legislature and agreed to and passed by the 1995 legislature; effective November 27, 1996, if the proposed amendment is approved by the people at the 1996 general election.)

Sec. 3. State indebtedness: Limitations and exceptions. [Effective until November 27, 1996, and after that date if the proposed amendment is not approved by the people at the 1996 general election.] The state may contract public debts; but such debts shall never, in the aggregate, exclusive of interest, exceed the sum of two per cent of the assessed valuation of the state, as shown by the reports of the county assessors to the state controller, except for the purpose of defraying extraordinary expenses, as hereinafter mentioned. Every such debt shall be authorized by law for some purpose or purposes, to be distinctly specified therein; and every such law shall provide for levying an annual tax sufficient to pay the interest semiannually, and the principal within twenty years from the passage of such law, and shall specially appropriate the proceeds of said taxes to the payment of said principal and interest; and such appropriation shall not be repealed nor the taxes postponed or diminished until the principal and interest of said debts shall have been wholly paid. Every contract of indebtedness entered into or assumed by or on behalf of the state, when all its debts and liabilities amount to said sum before mentioned, shall be void and of no effect, except in cases of money borrowed to repel invasion, suppress insurrection, defend the state in time of war, or, if hostilities be threatened, provide for the public defense.

The state, notwithstanding the foregoing limitations, may, pursuant to authority of the legislature, make and enter into any and all contracts necessary, expedient or advisable for the protection and preservation of any of its property or natural resources, or for the purposes of obtaining the benefits thereof, however arising and whether arising by or through any undertaking or project of the United States or by or through any treaty or compact between the states, or otherwise. The legislature may from time to time make such appropriations as may be necessary to carry out the obligations of the state under such contracts, and shall levy such tax as may be necessary to pay the same or carry them into effect.

[Amended in 1916, 1934 and 1989. The first amendment was proposed and passed by the 1913 legislature; agreed to and passed by the 1915 legislature; and approved and ratified by the people at the 1916 general election. See: Statutes of Nevada 1913, p. 585; Statutes of Nevada 1915, p. 516. The second amendment was proposed and passed by the 1931 legislature; agreed to and passed by the 1933 legislature; and approved and ratified by the people at the 1934 general election. See: Statutes of Nevada 1933, p. 357. The third amendment was proposed and passed by the 1987 legislature; agreed to and passed by the 1989 legislature; and approved and ratified by the people at a special election held on May 2, 1989. See: Statutes of Nevada 1987, p. 2422; Statutes of Nevada 1989, p. 2230.]

Sec. 3. State indebtedness: Limitations and exceptions. [Effective November 27, 1996, if the proposed amendment is approved by the people at the 1996 general election.] The state may contract public debts; but such debts shall never, in the aggregate, exclusive of interest, exceed the sum of two per cent of the assessed valuation of the state, as shown by the reports of the county assessors to the state controller, except for the purpose of defraying extraordinary expenses, as hereinafter mentioned. Every such debt shall be authorized by law for some purpose or purposes, to be distinctly specified therein; and every such law shall provide for levying an annual tax sufficient to pay the interest semiannually, and the principal within twenty years from the passage of such law, and shall specially appropriate the proceeds of said taxes to the payment of said principal and interest; and such appropriation shall not be repealed nor the taxes postponed or diminished until the principal and interest of said debts shall have been wholly paid. Every contract of indebtedness entered into or assumed by or on behalf of the state, when all its debts and liabilities amount to said sum before mentioned, shall be void and of no effect, except in cases of money borrowed to repel invasion, suppress insurrection, defend the state in time of war, or, if hostilities be threatened, provide for the public defense.

The state, notwithstanding the foregoing limitations, may, pursuant to authority of the legislature, make and enter into any and all contracts necessary, expedient or advisable for the protection and preservation of any of its property or natural resources, or for the purposes of obtaining the benefits thereof, however arising and whether arising by or through any undertaking or project of the United States or by or through any treaty or compact between the states, or otherwise, including contracts for the retrofitting of state buildings to make the use of energy in the buildings more efficient. The legislature may from time to time make such appropriations as may be necessary to carry out the obligations of the state under such contracts, and shall levy such tax as may be necessary to pay the same or carry them into effect.

[Amended in 1916, 1934 and 1989. The first amendment was proposed and passed by the 1913 legislature; agreed to and passed by the 1915 legislature; and approved and ratified by the people at the 1916 general election. See: Statutes of Nevada 1913,

p. 585; Statutes of Nevada 1915, p. 516. The second amendment was proposed and passed by the 1931 legislature; agreed to and passed by the 1933 legislature; and approved and ratified by the people at the 1934 general election. See: Statutes of Nevada 1933, p. 357. The third amendment was proposed and passed by the 1987 legislature; agreed to and passed by the 1989 legislature; and approved and ratified by the people at a special election held on May 2, 1989. See: Statutes of Nevada 1987, p. 2422; Statutes of Nevada 1989, p. 2230.]—(Amendment proposed and passed by the 1993 legislature and agreed to and passed by the 1995 legislature; effective November 27, 1996, if the proposed amendment is approved by the people at the 1996 general election.)

Sec. 4. Assumption of debts of county, city or corporation by state. The State shall never assume the debts of any county, town, city or other corporation whatever, unless such debts have been created to repel invasion[,] suppress insurrection or to provide for the public defense.

Sec. 5. Proceeds from fees for licensing and registration of motor vehicles and excise taxes on fuel reserved for construction, maintenance and repair of public highways; exception. The proceeds from the imposition of any license or registration fee and other charge with respect to the operation of any motor vehicle upon any public highway in this state and the proceeds from the imposition of any excise tax on gasoline or other motor vehicle fuel shall, except costs of administration, be used exclusively for the construction, maintenance, and repair of the public highways of this state. The provisions of this section do not apply to the proceeds of any tax imposed upon motor vehicles by the legislature in lieu of an ad valorem property tax.

[Added in 1940 and amended in 1962. The addition was proposed and passed by the 1937 legislature; agreed to and passed by the 1939 legislature; and approved and ratified by the people at the 1940 general election. See: Statutes of Nevada 1937, p. 567; Statutes of Nevada 1939, p. 359. The amendment was proposed and passed by the 1960 legislature; agreed to and passed by the 1961 legislature; and approved and ratified by the people at the 1962 general election. See: Statutes of Nevada 1960, p. 509; Statutes of Nevada 1961, p. 825.]

Article 10
Taxation

Sec. 1. Uniform and equal rate of assessment and taxation; exceptions and exemptions; inheritance and income taxes prohibited.

2. Total tax levy for public purposes limited.

[3]. Household goods and furniture of single household exempt from taxation.

3[A]. Food exempt from taxes on retail sales; exceptions.

4. Taxation of estates taxed by United States; limitations.

5. Tax on proceeds of minerals; appropriation to counties; apportionment; assessment and taxation of mines.

Sec. 1. Uniform and equal rate of assessment and taxation; exceptions and exemptions; inheritance and income taxes prohibited.

1. The legislature shall provide by law for a uniform and equal rate of assessment and taxation, and shall prescribe such regulations as shall secure a just valuation for taxation of all property, real, personal and possessory, except mines and mining claims, which shall be assessed and taxed only as provided in section 5 of this article.

2. Shares of stock, bonds, mortgages, notes, bank deposits, book accounts and credits, and securities and choses in action of like character are deemed to represent interest in property already assessed and taxed, either in Nevada or elsewhere, and shall be exempt.

3. The legislature may constitute agricultural and open-space real property having a greater value for another use than that for which it is being used, as a separate class for taxation purposes and may provide a separate uniform plan for appraisal and valuation of such property for assessment purposes. If such plan is provided, the legislature shall also provide for retroactive assessment for a period of not less than 7 years when agricultural and open-space real property is converted to a higher use conforming to the use for which other nearby property is used.

4. Personal property which is moving in interstate commerce through or over the territory of the State of Nevada, or which was consigned to a warehouse, public or private, within the State of Nevada from outside the State of Nevada for storage in transit to a final destination outside the State of Nevada, whether specified when transportation begins or afterward, shall be deemed to have acquired no situs in Nevada for purposes of taxation and shall be exempt from taxation. Such property shall not be deprived of such exemption because while in the warehouse the property is assembled, bound, joined, processed, disassembled, divided, cut, broken in bulk, relabeled or repackaged.

5. The legislature may exempt motor vehicles from the provisions of the tax required by this section, and in lieu thereof, if such exemption is granted, shall provide for a uniform and equal rate of assessment and taxation of motor vehicles, which rate shall not exceed five cents on one dollar of assessed valuation.

6. The legislature shall provide by law for a progressive reduction in the tax upon business inventories by 20 percent in each year following the adoption of this provision, and after the expiration of the 4th year such inventories are exempt

from taxation. The legislature may exempt any other personal property, including livestock.

7. No inheritance tax shall ever be levied.

8. The legislature may exempt by law property used for municipal, educational, literary, scientific or other charitable purposes, or to encourage the conservation of energy or the substitution of other sources for fossil sources of energy.

9. No income tax shall be levied upon the wages or personal income of natural persons. Notwithstanding the foregoing provision, and except as otherwise provided in subsection 1 of this section, taxes may be levied upon the income or revenue of any business in whatever form it may be conducted for profit in the state.

[Amended in 1902, 1906, 1942, 1960, 1962, 1974, 1978, 1982, 1986, 1989 and 1990. The first amendment was proposed and passed by the 1899 legislature; agreed to and passed by the 1901 legislature; and approved and ratified by the people at the 1902 general election. See: Statutes of Nevada 1899, p. 139; Statutes of Nevada 1901, p. 136. The second amendment was proposed and passed by the 1903 legislature; agreed to and passed by the 1905 legislature; and approved and ratified by the people at the 1906 general election. See: Statutes of Nevada 1903, p. 240; Statutes of Nevada 1905, p. 277. The third amendment was proposed and passed by the 1939 legislature; agreed to and passed by the 1941 legislature; and approved and ratified by the people at the 1942 general election. See: Statutes of Nevada 1939, p. 360; Statutes of Nevada 1941, p. 559. The fourth amendment was proposed and passed by the 1957 legislature; agreed to and passed by the 1959 legislature; and approved and ratified by the people at the 1960 general election. See: Statutes of Nevada 1957, p. 805; Statutes of Nevada 1959, p. 939. The fifth amendment was proposed and passed by the 1960 legislature; agreed to and passed by the 1961 legislature; and approved and ratified by the people at the 1962 general election. See: Statutes of Nevada 1960, p. 509; Statutes of Nevada 1961, p. 825. The sixth amendment was proposed and passed by the 1971 legislature; agreed to and passed by the 1973 legislature; and approved and ratified by the people at the 1974 general election. See: Statutes of Nevada 1971, p. 2299; Statutes of Nevada 1973, p. 1938. The seventh amendment was proposed and passed by the 1975 legislature; agreed to and passed by the 1977 legislature; and approved and ratified by the people at the 1978 general election. See: Statutes of Nevada 1975, p. 1925; Statutes of Nevada 1977, p. 1727. The eighth amendment was proposed and passed by the 1979 legislature; agreed to and passed by the 1981 legislature; and approved and ratified by the people at the 1982 general election. See: Statutes of Nevada 1979, p. 1983, Statutes of Nevada 1981, p. 2070. The ninth and tenth amendments were proposed and passed by the 1983 legislature; agreed to and passed by the 1985 legislature; and approved and ratified by the people at the 1986 general election. See:

Statutes of Nevada 1983; pp. 2141 and 2225; Statutes of Nevada 1985, pp. 2331 and 2401. The amendments were combined pursuant to Nev. Art. 16, ° 1. The eleventh amendment was proposed and passed by the 1987 legislature; agreed to and passed by the 1989 legislature; and approved and ratified by the people at a special election held on May 2, 1989. See: Statutes of Nevada 1987, p. 2442; Statutes of Nevada 1989, p. 2228. The twelfth amendment was proposed by initiative petition and approved and ratified by the people at the general elections of 1988 and 1990.]

Sec. 2. Total tax levy for public purposes limited. The total tax levy for all public purposes including levies for bonds, within the state, or any subdivision thereof, shall not exceed five cents on one dollar of assessed valuation.

[Added in 1936. Proposed and passed by the 1933 legislature; agreed to and passed by the 1935 legislature; and approved and ratified by the people at the 1936 general election. See: Statutes of Nevada 1933, p. 369; Statutes of Nevada 1935, p. 428.]

Sec. [3]. Household goods and furniture of single household exempt from taxation. All household goods and furniture used by a single household and owned by a member of that household are exempt from taxation.

[Added in 1982. Proposed by initiative petition and approved by the people at the 1980 and 1982 general elections.]

Sec. 3[A]. Food exempt from taxes on retail sales; exceptions. The legislature shall provide by law for:

1. The exemption of food for human consumption from any tax upon the sale, storage, use or consumption of tangible personal property; and

2. These commodities to be excluded from any such exemption:

    (a) Prepared food intended for immediate consumption.
    (b) Alcoholic beverages.

[Added in 1984. Proposed and passed by the 1981 legislature; agreed to and passed by the 1983 legislature; and approved and ratified by the people at the 1984 general election. See: Statutes of Nevada 1981, p. 2093; Statutes of Nevada 1983, p. 2113.]

Sec. 4. Taxation of estates taxed by United States; limitations. The legislature may provide by law for the taxation of estates taxed by the United States, but only to the extent of any credit allowed by federal law for the payment of the state tax and only for the purpose of education, to be divided between the common schools and the state university for their support and maintenance. The combined amount of these federal and state taxes may not exceed the estate tax which would be imposed by federal law alone. If another state of the United States imposes and collects death taxes against an estate which is taxable by the State of Nevada under this section, the amount of estate tax to be collected by the State of Nevada must be reduced by the amount of the death taxes collected by the other state. Any lien for the estate tax attaches no sooner than the time when the tax is due and payable, and no restriction on possession or use of a decedent's property may be imposed by law before the time when the tax is due and payable in full under federal law. The State of Nevada shall:

1. Accept the determination by the United States of the amount of the taxable estate without further audit.

2. Accept payment of the tax in installments proportionate to any which may be permitted under federal law.

3. Impose no penalty for such a deferred payment.

4. Not charge interest on a deferred or belated payment at any rate higher than may be provided in similar circumstances by federal law.

[Added in 1986. Proposed and passed by the 1983 legislature; agreed to and passed by the 1985 legislature; and approved and ratified by the people at the 1986 general election. See: Statutes of Nevada 1983, p. 2224; Statutes of Nevada 1985, p. 2400.]

Sec. 5. Tax on proceeds of minerals; appropriation to counties; apportionment; assessment and taxation of mines.

1. The legislature shall provide by law for a tax upon the net proceeds of all minerals, including oil, gas and other hydrocarbons, extracted in this state, at a rate not to exceed 5 percent of the net proceeds. No other tax may be imposed upon a mineral or its proceeds until the identity of the proceeds as such is lost.

2. The legislature shall appropriate to each county that sum which would be produced by levying a tax upon the entire amount of the net proceeds taxed in each taxing district in the county at the rate levied in that district upon the assessed valuation of real property. The total amount so appropriated to each county must be apportioned among the respective governmental units and districts within it, including the county itself and the school district, in the same proportion as they share in the total taxes collected on property according to value.

3. Each patented mine or mining claim must be assessed and taxed as other real property is assessed and taxed, except that no value may be attributed to any mineral known or believed to underlie it, and no value may be attributed to the surface of a mine or claim if one hundred dollars' worth of labor has been actually performed on the mine or claim during the year preceding the assessment.

[Added in 1989. Proposed and passed by the 1987 legislature; agreed to and passed by the 1989 legislature; and approved and ratified by the people at a special election held on May 2, 1989. See: Statutes of Nevada 1987, p. 2443; Statutes of Nevada 1989, p. 2229.]

Article 11
Education

Sec. 1. Legislature to encourage education; appointment, term and duties of superintendent of public instruction.

2. Uniform system of common schools.
3. Pledge of certain property and money, escheated estates and fines collected under penal laws for educational purposes; apportionment and use of interest.
4. Establishment of state university; control by board of regents.
5. Establishment of normal schools and grades of schools; oath of teachers and professors.
6. Support of university and common schools by direct legislative appropriation.
7. Board of regents: Election and duties.
8. Immediate organization and maintenance of state university.
9. Sectarian instruction prohibited in common schools and university.
10. No public money to be used for sectarian purposes.

Sec. 1. Legislature to encourage education; appointment, term and duties of superintendent of public instruction. The legislature shall encourage by all suitable means the promotion of intellectual, literary, scientific, mining, mechanical, agricultural, and moral improvements, and also provide for a superintendent of public instruction and by law prescribe the manner of appointment, term of office and the duties thereof.

[Amended in 1956. Proposed and passed by the 1953 legislature; agreed to and passed by the 1955 legislature; approved and ratified by the people at the 1956 general election. See: Statutes of Nevada 1953, p. 716; Statutes of Nevada 1955, p. 926.]

Sec. 2. Uniform system of common schools. The legislature shall provide for a uniform system of common schools, by which a school shall be established and maintained in each school district at least six months in every year, and any school district which shall allow instruction of a sectarian character therein may be deprived of its proportion of the interest of the public school fund during such neglect or infraction, and the legislature may pass such laws as will tend to secure a general attendance of the children in each school district upon said public schools.

[Amended in 1938. Proposed and passed by the 1935 legislature; agreed to and passed by the 1937 legislature; and approved and ratified by the people at the 1938 general election. See: Statutes of Nevada 1935, p. 440; Statutes of Nevada 1937, p. 550.]

Sec. 3. Pledge of certain property and money, escheated estates and fines collected under penal laws for educational purposes; apportionment and use of interest. All lands granted by Congress to this state for educational purposes, all estates that escheat to the state, all property given or bequeathed to the state for educational purposes, and the proceeds derived from these sources, together with that percentage of the proceeds from the sale of federal lands which has been granted by Congress to this state without restriction or for educational purposes and all fines collected under the penal laws of the state are hereby pledged for educational purposes and the money therefrom must not be transferred to other funds for other uses. The interest only earned on the money derived from these sources must be apportioned by the legislature among the several counties for educational purposes, and, if necessary, a portion of that interest may be appropriated for the support of the state university, but any of that interest which is unexpended at the end of any year must be added to the principal sum pledged for educational purposes.

[Amended in 1886, 1889, 1912, 1916, 1980, and 1988. The first amendment was approved and ratified by the people at the 1886 general election, but no entry of the proposed amendment had been made upon the journal of either house of the legislature, and such omission was fatal to the adoption of the amendment. See: State ex rel. Stevenson v. Tufly, 19 Nev. 391 (1887). The second amendment was proposed and passed by the 1885 legislature; agreed to and passed by the 1887 legislature; and approved and ratified by the people at a special election held February 11, 1889. See: Statutes of Nevada 1885, p. 160; Statutes of Nevada 1887, p. 168. The third amendment was proposed and passed by the 1909 legislature; agreed to and passed by the 1911 legislature; and approved and ratified by the people at the 1912 general election. See: Statutes of Nevada 1909, p. 340; Statutes of Nevada 1911, p. 453. The fourth amendment was proposed and passed by the 1913 legislature; agreed to and passed by the 1915 legislature; and approved and ratified by the people at the 1916 general election. See: Statutes of Nevada 1913, p. 591; Statutes of Nevada 1915, p. 513. The fifth amendment was proposed and passed by the 1977 legislature; agreed to and passed by the 1979 legislature; and approved and ratified by the people at the 1980 general election. See: Statutes of Nevada 1977, p. 1716; Statutes of Nevada 1979, p. 1953. The sixth amendment was proposed and passed by the 1985 legislature; agreed to and passed by the 1987 legislature; and approved and ratified by the people at the 1988 general election. See: Statutes of Nevada 1985, p. 2361; Statutes of Nevada 1987, p. 2355.]

Sec. 4. Establishment of state university; control by board of regents. The Legislature shall provide for the establishment of a State University which shall embrace departments for Agriculture, Mechanic Arts, and Mining to be controlled by a Board of Regents whose duties shall be prescribed by Law.

Sec. 5. Establishment of normal schools and grades of schools; oath of teachers and professors. The Legislature shall have power to establis [establish] Normal schools, and such different grades of schools, from the primary department to the University, as in their discretion they may deem necessary, and all Professors in said University, or Teachers in said Schools of whatever grade, shall be required to take and subscribe to the oath as prescribed in Article Fifteenth of this Constitution. No Professor or Teacher who fails to comply with the provisions of any law framed in accordance with the provisions of this Section, shall be entitled to receive any portion of the public monies set apart for school purposes.

Sec. 6. Support of university and common schools by direct legislative appropriation. In addition to other means provided for the support and maintenance of said university and common schools, the legislature shall provide for their support and maintenance by direct legislative appropriation from the general fund, upon the presentation of budgets in the manner required by law.

[Amended in 1889, 1938 and 1954. The first amendment was proposed and passed by the 1885 legislature; agreed to and passed by the 1887 legislature; and approved and ratified by the people at a special election held February 11, 1889. See: Statutes of Nevada 1885, p. 161; Statutes of Nevada 1887, p. 169. The second amendment was proposed and passed by the 1935 legislature; agreed to and passed by the 1937 legislature; and approved and ratified by the people at the 1938 general election. See: Statutes of Nevada 1935, p. 440; Statutes of Nevada 1937, p. 550. The third amendment was proposed and passed by the 1951 legislature; agreed to and passed by the 1953 legislature; and approved and ratified by the people at the 1954 general election. See: Statutes of Nevada 1951, p. 591; Statutes of Nevada 1953, p. 716.]

Sec. 7. Board of regents: Election and duties. The Governor, Secretary of State, and Superintendent of Public Instruction, shall for the first Four Years and until their successors are elected and qualified constitute a Board of Regents to control and manage the affairs of the University and the funds of the same under such regulations as may be provided by law. But the Legislature shall at its regular session next preceding the expiration of the term of Office of said Board of Regents provide for the election of a new Board of Regents and define their duties.

Sec. 8. Immediate organization and maintenance of state university. The Board of Regents shall, from the interest accruing from the first funds which come under their control, immediately organize and maintain the said Mining department in such manner as to make it most effective and useful, Provided, that all the proceeds of the public lands donated by Act of Congress approved July second A.D. Eighteen hundred and sixty Two, for a college for the benefit of Agriculture[,] the Mechanics Arts, and including Military tactics shall be invested by the said Board of Regents in a separate fund to be appropriated exclusively for the benefit of the first named departments to the University as set forth in Section Four above; And the Legislature shall provide that if through neglect or any other contingency, any portion of the fund so set apart, shall be lost or misappropriated, the State of Nevada shall replace said amount so lost or misappropriated in said fund so that the principal of said fund shall remain forever undiminished[.]

Sec. 9. Sectarian instruction prohibited in common schools and university. No sectarian instruction shall be imparted or tolerated in any school or University that may be established under this Constitution.

Sec. 10. No public money to be used for sectarian purposes. No public funds of any kind or character whatever, State, County or Municipal, shall be used for sectarian purpose.

[Added in 1880. Proposed and passed by the 1877 legislature; agreed to and passed by the 1879 legislature; and approved and ratified by the people at the 1880 general election. See: Statutes of Nevada 1877, p. 221; Statutes of Nevada 1879, p. 149.]

Article 12
Militia

Sec. 1. Legislature to provide for militia.

    2. Power of governor to call out militia.

Sec. 1. Legislature to provide for militia. The Legislature shall provide by law for organizing and disciplining the Militia of this State, for the effectual encouragement of Volunteer Corps and the safe keeping of the public Arms.

Sec. 2. Power of governor to call out militia. The Governor shall have power to call out the Militia to execute the laws of the State or to suppress insurrection or repel invasion.

Article 13
Public Institutions

Sec. 1. Institutions for insane, blind, deaf and dumb to be fostered and supported by state.

    2. State prison: Establishment and maintenance; juvenile offenders.

    3. County public welfare. [Repealed in 1937.]

Sec. 1. Institutions for insane, blind, deaf and dumb to be fostered and supported by state. Institutions for the benefit of the Insane, Blind and Deaf and Dumb, and such other benevolent institutions as the public good may require, shall be fostered and supported by the State, subject to such regulations as may be prescribed by law.

Sec. 2. State prison: Establishment and maintenance; juvenile offenders. A State Prison shall be established and maintained in such manner as may be prescribed by law, and provision may be made by law for the establishment and maintainance [maintenance] of a House of Refuge for Juvenile Offenders.

Sec. 3. County public welfare. [Repealed in 1937.]

[Sec. 3 of the original constitution was repealed by vote of the people at a special election held March 17, 1937. See: Statutes of Nevada 1937, pp. 19, 50. The original section read: "The respective counties of the State shall provide as may be prescribed by law, for those inhabitants who, by reason of age and infirmity or misfortunes, may have claim upon the sympathy and aid of Society."]

Article 14
Boundary

Sec. 1. Boundary of the State of Nevada. The boundary of the State of Nevada is as follows:

Commencing at a point formed by the intersection of the forty-third degree of longitude West from Washington with the forty-second degree of North latitude; thence due East along the forty-second degree of North latitude to its intersection with the thirty-seventh degree of longitude West from Washington; thence South on the thirty-seventh degree of longitude West from Washington to its intersection with the middle line of the Colorado River of the West; thence down the middle line of the Colorado River of the West to its intersection with the Eastern boundary of the State of California; thence in a North Westerly direction along the Eastern boundary line of the State of California to the forty-third degree of Longitude West from Washington; Thence North along the forty-third degree of West Longitude, and the Eastern boundary line of the State of California to the place of beginning. All territory lying West of and adjoining the boundary line herein prescribed, which the State of California may relinquish to the Territory or State of Nevada, shall thereupon be embraced within and constitute a part of this State.

[Amended in 1982. Proposed and passed by the 1979 legislature; agreed to and passed by the 1981 legislature; and approved and ratified by the people at the 1982 general election. See: Statutes of Nevada 1979, p. 1978; Statutes of Nevada 1981, p. 2140.]

Article 15
Miscellaneous Provisions

Sec. 1. Carson City seat of government. The seat of Government shall be at Carson City, but no appropriation for the erection or purchase of Capitol buildings shall be made during the next three Years[.]

Sec. 2. Oath of office. Members of the legislature, and all officers, executive, judicial and ministerial, shall, before they enter upon the duties of their respective offices, take and subscribe to the following oath:

I, ..., do solemnly [solemnly] swear (or affirm) that I will support, protect and defend the constitution and government of the United States, and the constitution and government of the State of Nevada, against all enemies, whether domestic or foreign, and that I will bear true faith, allegiance and loyalty to the same, any ordinance, resolution or law of any state notwithstanding, and that I will well and faithfully perform all the duties of the office of ...., on which I am about to enter; (if an oath) so help me God; (if an affirmation) under the pains and penalties of perjury.

[Amended in 1914. Proposed and passed by the 1911 legislature; agreed to and passed by the 1913 legislature; and approved and ratified by the people at the 1914 general election. See: Statutes of Nevada 1911, p. 458; Journal of the Assembly, 26th Session, p. 20 and Journal of the Senate, 26th Session, p. 37.]

Sec. 3. Eligibility for public office. [Effective until November 27, 1996, and after that date if the proposed amendment is not approved by the people at the 1996 general election.] No person shall be eligible to any office who is not a qualified elector under this constitution.

[Amended in 1889, 1912 and 1978. The first amendment was proposed and passed by the 1887 legislature; agreed to and passed by the 1889 legislature; and approved and ratified by the people at a special election held February 11, 1889. See: Statutes of Nevada 1887, p. 162; Statutes of Nevada 1889, p. 151. The second amendment was proposed and passed by the 1909 legislature; agreed to and passed by the 1911 legislature; and approved and ratified by the people at the 1912 general election. See: Statutes of Nevada 1909, p. 349; Statutes of Nevada 1911, p. 454. The third amendment was proposed and passed by the 1975 legislature; agreed to and passed by the 1977 legislature; and approved and ratified by the people at the 1978 general election. See: Statutes of Nevada 1975, p. 1902; Statutes of Nevada 1977, p. 1687.]

Sec. 3. Eligibility for public office. [Effective November 27, 1996, if the proposed amendment is approved by the people at the 1996 general election.]

1. No person shall be eligible to any office who is not a qualified elector under this constitution.

2. No person may be elected to any state office or local governing body who has served in that office, or at the expiration of his current term if he is so serving will have served, 12 years or more, unless the permissible number of terms or duration of service is otherwise specified in this constitution.

[Amended in 1889, 1912 and 1978. The first amendment was proposed and passed by the 1887 legislature; agreed to and passed by the 1889 legislature; and approved and ratified by the people at a special election held February 11, 1889. See: Statutes of Nevada 1887, p. 162; Statutes of Nevada 1889, p. 151. The second amendment was proposed and passed by the 1909 legislature; agreed to and passed by the 1911 legislature; and approved and ratified by the people at the 1912 general election. See: Statutes of Nevada 1909, p. 349; Statutes of Nevada 1911, p. 454. The third amendment was proposed and passed by the 1975 legislature; agreed to and passed by the 1977 legislature; and approved and ratified by the people at the 1978 general election. See: Statutes of Nevada 1975, p. 1902; Statutes of Nevada 1977, p. 1687.]— (Amendment proposed by initiative petition and approved by the people at the 1994 general election; effective November 27, 1996, if the proposed amendment is approved by the people at the 1996 general election.)

Sec. 4. Perpetuities; eleemosynary purposes. No perpetuities shall be allowed except for eleemosynary purposes.

Sec. 5. Time of general election. The general election shall be held on the Tuesday next after the first Monday of November.

Sec. 6. Number of members of legislature limited. The aggregate number of members of both branches of the Legislature shall never exceed Seventy five.

Sec. 7. County offices at county seats. All county Officers shall hold their Offices at the County seat of their respective Counties.

Sec. 8. Publication of general statutes and opinions of supreme court; effective date of opinions of supreme court. The Legislature shall provide for the speedy publication of all Statute laws of a general nature, and such decisions of the Supreme Court, as it may deem expedient; and all laws and judicial decisions shall be free for publication by any person; Provided, that no judgment of the Supreme Court shall take effect and be operative until the Opinion of the Court in such case shall be filed with the Clerk of said Court.

Sec. 9. Increase or decrease of compensation of officers whose compensation fixed by constitution. The Legislature may, at any time, provide by law for increasing or diminishing the salaries or compensation of any of the Officers, whose salaries or compensation is fixed in this Constitution; Provided, no such change of Salary or compensation shall apply to any Officer during the term for which he may have been elected.

Sec. 10. Election or appointment of officers. All officers whose election or appointment is not otherwise provided for, shall be chosen or appointed as may be prescribed by law.

Sec. 11. Term of office when not fixed by constitution; limitation; municipal officers and employees. The tenure of any office not herein provided for may be declared by law, or, when not so declared, such office shall be held during the pleasure of the authority making the appointment, but the legislature shall not create any office the tenure of which shall be longer than four (4) years, except as herein otherwise provided in this constitution. In the case of any officer or employee of any municipality governed under a legally adopted charter, the provisions of such charter with reference to the tenure of office or the dismissal from office of any such officer or employee shall control.

[Amended in 1946. Proposed and passed by the 1943 legislature; agreed to and passed by the 1945 legislature; and approved and ratified by the people at the 1946 general election. See: Statutes of Nevada 1943, p. 325; Statutes of Nevada 1945, p. 505.]

Sec. 12. Certain state officers to keep offices at Carson City. The Governor, Secretary of State, State Treasurer, State Controller, and Clerk of the Supreme Court, shall keep their respective offices at the seat of Government.

Sec. 13. Census by legislature and Congress: Basis of representation in houses of legislature. The enumeration of the inhabitants of this State shall be taken under the direction of the Legislature if deemed necessary in A.D. Eighteen hundred and Sixty five, A.D. Eighteen hundred and Sixty seven, A.D. Eighteen hundred and Seventy five, and every ten years thereafter; and these enumerations, together with the census that may be taken under the direction of the Congress of the United States in A.D. Eighteen hundred and Seventy, and every subsequent ten years shall serve as the basis of representation in both houses of the Legislature.

Sec. 14. Election by plurality. A plurality of votes given at an election by the people, shall constitute a choice, where not otherwise provided by this Constitution[.]

Sec. 15. Merit system governing employment in executive branch of state government. The legislature shall provide by law for a state merit system governing the employment of employees in the executive branch of state government.

[Added in 1970. Proposed and passed by the 1967 legislature; agreed to and passed by the 1969 legislature; and approved and ratified by the people at the 1970 general election. See: Statutes of Nevada 1967, p. 1829; Statutes of Nevada 1969, p. 1720.]

Article 16
Amendments

Sec. 1. Constitutional amendments: Procedure; concurrent and consecutive amendments.

   2. Convention for revision of constitution: Procedure.

Sec. 1. Constitutional amendments: Procedure; concurrent and consecutive amendments.

1. Any amendment or amendments to this Constitution may be proposed in the Senate or Assembly; and if the same shall be agreed to by a Majority of all the members elected to each of the two houses, such proposed amendment or amendments shall be entered on their respective journals, with the Yeas and Nays taken thereon, and referred to the Legislature then next to be chosen, and shall be published for three months next preceding the time of making such choice. And if in the Legislature next chosen as aforesaid, such proposed amendment or amendments shall be agreed to by a majority of all the members elected to each house, then it shall be the duty of the Legislature to submit such proposed amendment or amendments to the people, in such man-

ner and at such time as the Legislature shall prescribe; and if the people shall approve and ratify such amendment or amendments by a majority of the electors qualified to vote for members of the Legislature voting thereon, such amendment or amendments shall, unless precluded by subsection 2, become a part of the Constitution.

2. If two or more amendments which affect the same section of the constitution are ratified by the people at the same election:

(a) If all can be given effect without contradiction in substance, each shall become a part of the constitution.

(b) If one or more contradict in substance the other or others, that amendment which received the largest favorable vote, and any other amendment or amendments compatible with it, shall become a part of the constitution.

3. If after the proposal of an amendment, another amendment is ratified which affects the same section of the constitution but is compatible with the proposed amendment, the next legislature if it agrees to the proposed amendment shall submit such proposal to the people as a further amendment to the amended section. If, after the proposal of an amendment, another amendment is ratified which contradicts in substance the proposed amendment, such proposed amendment shall not be submitted to the people.

[Amended in 1972. Proposed and passed by the 1969 legislature; agreed to and passed by the 1971 legislature; and approved and ratified by the people at the 1972 general election. See: Statutes of Nevada 1969, p. 1728; Statutes of Nevada 1971, p. 2265. A previous amendment to this section was approved and ratified by the people at the 1886 general election, but no entry of the proposed amendment had been made upon the journal of either house of the legislature, and such omission was fatal to the adoption of the amendment. See: State ex rel. Stevenson v. Tufly, 19 Nev. 391 (1887).]

Sec. 2. Convention for revision of constitution: Procedure. If at any time the Legislature by a vote of two thirds of the Members elected to each house, shall determine that it is necessary to cause a revision of this entire Constitution they shall recommend to the electors at the next election for Members of the Legislature, to vote for or against a convention, and if it shall appear that a majority of the electors voting at such election, shall have voted in favor of calling a Convention, the Legislature shall, at its next session provide by law for calling a Convention to be holden within six months after the passage of such law, and such Convention shall consist of a number of Members not less than that of both branches of the Legislature. In determining what is a majority of the electors voting at such election, reference shall be had to the highest number of votes cast at such election for the candidates for any office or on any question.

[An amendment to this section was approved and ratified by the people at the 1886 general election, but no entry of the proposed amendment had been made upon the journal of either house of the legislature, and such omission was fatal to the adoption of the amendment. See: State ex rel. Stevenson v. Tufly, 19 Nev. 391 (1887).]

Article 17
Schedule

Sec. 1. Saving existing rights and liabilities.
   2. Territorial laws to remain in force.
   3. Fines, penalties and forfeitures to inure to state.
   4. Existing obligations and pending suits.
   5. Salaries of state officers for first term of office.
   6. Apportionment of senators and assemblymen.
   7. Assumption of territorial debts and liabilities.
   8. Terms of elected state officers.
   9. Terms of senators.
   10. Terms of senators and assemblymen after 1866.
   11. Terms of assemblymen: Elected at first general election and in 1865.
   12. First biennial legislative session to commence in 1867.
   13. Continuation of territorial county and township officers; probate judges.
   14. Duties of certain territorial officers continued.
   15. Terms of supreme court and district courts.
   16. Salaries of district judges.
   17. Alteration of salary of district judge authorized.
   18. Qualification and terms of certain elective state officers.
   19. When justices of supreme court and district judges enter upon duties.
   20. State officers and district judges to be commissioned by territorial governor; state controller and treasurer to furnish bonds.
   21. Support of county and city officers.
   22. Vacancies in certain state offices: How filled.
   23. Civil and criminal cases pending in probate courts transferred to district courts.
   24. Levy of tax limited for 3 years.
   25. Roop County attached to Washoe County.
   26. Constitutional debates and proceedings: Publication; payment of reporter.

Sec. 1. Saving existing rights and liabilities. That no inconvenience may arise by reason of a change from a Territorial to a permanent State Government, it is declared, that all rights, actions, prosecutions, judgements[,] Claims and Contracts, as well of individuals, as of bodies corporate, including counties, towns and cities, shall continue as if no change had taken place; and all process which may issue under the

Authority of the Territory of Nevada, previous to its admission into the Union as one of the United States, shall be as valid as if issued in the name of the State of Nevada.

Sec. 2. Territorial laws to remain in force. All laws of the Territory of Nevada in force at the time of the admission of this State, not repugnant to this Constitution, shall remain in force until they expire by their own limitations or be altered or repealed by the Legislature.

Sec. 3. Fines, penalties and forfeitures to inure to state. All fines, penalties and forfeitures accruing to the Territory of Nevada or to the people of the United States in the Territory of Nevada, shall inure to the State of Nevada.

Sec. 4. Existing obligations and pending suits. All recognizances heretofore taken, or which may be taken before the change from a Territorial, to a State Government, shall remain valid, and shall pass to, and may be prosecuted in the name of the State, and all bonds, executed to the Governor of the Territory or to any other Officer or Court in his or their official capacity, or to the people of the United States in the Territory of Nevada, shall pass to the Governor, or other officer or court, and his or their successors in office for the uses therein respectively expressed, and may be sued on, and recovery had accordingly; And all property real, personal or mixed, and all judgements, bonds, specialties, choses in Action, claims and debts of whatsoever description, and all records, and public Archives of the Territory of Nevada, shall issue to and vest in the State of Nevada, and may be sued for and recovered in the same manner and to the same extent by the State of Nevada, as the same could have been by the Territory of Nevada. All criminal prosecutions and penal Actions, which may have arisen, or which may arise before the change from a Territorial to a State Government, and which shall then be pending, shall be prosecuted to judgement and execution in the name of the State. All offenses committed against the laws of the Territory of Nevada, before the change from a Territorial to a State Government, and which shall not be prosecuted before such change, may be prosecuted in the name and by the Authority of the State of Nevada, with like effect as though such change had not taken place; And all penalties incurred, shall remain the same as if this Constitution had not been adopted; All actions at law, and suits in equity, and other legal proceedings, which may be pending in any of the Courts of the Territory of Nevada at the time of the change from a Territorial to a State Government may be continued and transferred to, and determined by, any court of the State, which shall have jurisdiction of the subject matter thereof. All actions at law and suits in Equity, and all other legal proceedings, which may be pending in any of the Courts of the Territory of Nevada at the time of the change from a Territorial to a State Government, shall be continued and transferred to, and may be prosecuted to judgement and execution in any Court of the State which shall have jurisdiction of the subject matter thereof; And all books, papers and records, relating to the same shall be transferred in like manner to such Court.

Sec. 5. Salaries of state officers for first term of office. For the first term of office succeeding the formation of a State Government, the Salary of the Governor shall be Four Thousand Dollars per annum; The salary of the Secretary of State shall be Three Thousand, Six hundred Dollars per annum; The salary of the State Controller shall be Three Thousand, Six hundred Dollars per annum; The salary of the State Treasurer shall be Three Thousand Six hundred Dollars per Annum; The salary of the Surveyor General shall be One Thousand Dollars per annum; The salary of the Attorney General shall be Two Thousand Five hundred Dollars per annum; The salary of the Superintendent of Public Instruction shall be Two Thousand Dollars per annum; The salary of each judge of the Supreme Court shall be Seven Thousand Dollars per annum; The salaries of the foregoing officers, shall be paid quarterly, out of the State Treasury. The pay of State Senators and Members of Assembly shall be Eight Dollars per day, for each day of actual service, and forty cents per mile for mileage going to, and returning from, the place of meeting. No officer mentioned in this Section, shall receive any fee or perquisites, to his own use for the performance of any duty connected with his office, or for the performance of any additional duty imposed upon him by law.

Sec. 6. Apportionment of senators and assemblymen. Until otherwise provided by Law the apportionment of Senators and Assemblymen in the different counties shall be as follows, to Wit: Storey County four Senators and Twelve Assemblymen, Douglas County One Senator and Two Assemblymen; Esmeralda County, Two Senators and Four Assemblymen; Humboldt County, Two Senators and Three Assemblymen; Lander County Two Senators and Four Assemblymen; Lyon County, One Senator and Three Assemblymen; Lyon and Churchill Counties, One Senator jointly; Churchill County One Assemblyman; Nye County One Senator and one Assemblyman; Ormsby County Two Senators and Three Assemblymen; Washoe and Roop Counties, Two Senators and Three Assemblymen.

Sec. 7. Assumption of territorial debts and liabilities. All debts and liabilities of the Territory of Nevada, lawfully incurred and which remain unpaid, at the time of the admission of this State into the Union shall be assumed by and become the debt of the State of Nevada; Provided that the assumption of such indebtedness shall not prevent the State from contracting the additional indebtedness as provided in Section Three of Article Nine of this Constitution.

Sec. 8. Terms of elected state officers. The term of State Officers, except Judicial, elected at the first election under this Constitution shall continue until the Tuesday after the first Monday of January A.D. Eighteen hundred and sixty seven, and until the election and qualification of their successors.

Sec. 9. Terms of senators. The Senators to be elected at the first election under this Constitution shall draw lots, so that, the term of one half of the number as nearly as may be, shall expire on the day succeeding the general election in A.D. Eighteen Hundred and Sixty Six; and the term of the other half shall expire on the day succeeding the general election in A.D. Eighteen hundred and sixty eight, Provided, that in drawing lots for all Senatorial terms, the Senatorial representation shall be allotted, so that in the Counties having two or more Senators, the terms thereof shall be divided as nearly as may be between the long and short terms.

Sec. 10. Terms of senators and assemblymen after 1866. At the general election in A.D. Eighteen hundred and Sixty Six; and thereafter, the term of Senators shall be for Four Years from the day succeeding such general election, and members of Assembly for Two Years from the day succeeding such general election, and the terms of Senators shall be allotted by the Legislature in long and short terms as hereinbefore provided; so that one half the number as nearly as may be, shall be elected every Two Years.

Sec. 11. Terms of assemblymen: Elected at first general election and in 1865. The term of the members of the Assembly elected at the first general election under this Constitution shall expire on the day succeeding the general election in A.D. Eighteen hundred and Sixty Five; and the terms of those elected at the general election in A.D. Eighteen hundred and Sixty Five, shall expire on the day succeeding the general election in A.D. Eighteen hundred and Sixty six.

Sec. 12. First biennial legislative session to commence in 1867. The first regular session of the Legislature shall commence on the second Monday of December A.D. Eighteen hundred and Sixty Four, and the second regular session of the same shall commence on the first Monday of January A.D. Eighteen hundred and Sixty Six; and the third regular session of the Legislature shall be the first of the biennial sessions, and shall commence on the first Monday of January A.D. Eighteen hundred and Sixty Seven; and the regular sessions of the Legislature shall be held thereafter biennially, commencing on the first Monday of January.

[See Art. 4, Sec. 2, as amended in 1889.]

Sec. 13. Continuation of territorial county and township officers; probate judges. All county officers under the laws of the Territory of Nevada at the time when the Constitution shall take effect, whose offices are not inconsistent with the provisions of this Constitution, shall continue in office until the first Monday of January A.D. Eighteen hundred and Sixty Seven, and until their successors are elected and qualified; and all township officers shall continue in office until the expiration of their terms of office, and until their successors are elected and qualified; Provided, that the Probate Judges of the several counties respectively, shall continue in office until the election and qualification of the District Judges of the several counties or Judicial Districts; And Provided further, that the term of office of the present county officers of Lander County, shall expire on the first Monday of January A.D. Eighteen hundred and Sixty Five, except the Probate Judge of said County whose term of office shall expire upon the first Monday of December A.D. Eighteen hundred and Sixty Four, and there shall be an election for County Officers of Lander County at the general election in November A.D. Eighteen hundred and Sixty Four, and the officers then elected, shall hold office from the first Monday of January A.D. Eighteen hundred and Sixty five until the first Monday of January A.D. Eighteen hundred and sixty seven, and until their successors are elected and qualified.

Sec. 14. Duties of certain territorial officers continued. The Governor, Secretary, Treasurer and Superintendent of Public Instruction of the Territory of Nevada shall each continue to discharge the duties of their respective offices after the admission of this State into the Union, and until the time designated for the qualification of the above named officers to be elected under the State Government, and the Territorial Auditor shall continue to discharge the duties of his said office until the time appointed for the qualification of the State Controller; Provided, that the said officers shall each receive the salaries, and be subject to the restrictions and conditions provided in this Constitution; And Provided further, that none of them shall receive to his own use any fees or perquisites for the performance of any duty connected with his office.

Sec. 15. Terms of supreme court and district courts. The terms of the Supreme Court shall, until provision be made by law, be held at such times as the Judges of the said Court or a majority of them may appoint. The first terms of the several District Courts (except as hereinafter mentioned) shall commence on the first Monday of December A.D. Eighteen Hundred and Sixty Four. The first term of the District Court in the Fifth Judicial District, shall commence on the first Monday of December A.D. Eighteen Hundred and Sixty Four in the County of Nye; and shall commence on the first Monday of January A.D. Eighteen Hundred and Sixty Five in the County of Churchill. The terms of the Fourth Judicial District Court shall until otherwise provided by law be held at the County Seat of Washoe County, and the first term thereof commence on the first Monday of December, A.D. Eighteen Hundred and Sixty Four.

Sec. 16. Salaries of district judges. The Judges of the several District Courts of this State shall be paid as hereinbefore provided Salaries at the following rates per Annum: First Judicial District (Each Judge) Six Thousand Dollars; Second Judicial District Four Thousand Dollars; Third Judicial District, Five Thousand Dollars; Fourth Judicial District Five Thousand Dollars; Fifth Judicial District Thirty Six Hundred Dollars; Sixth Judicial District Four Thousand Dollars; Seventh Judicial District Six Thousand Dollars; Eighth Judicial District Thirty Six Hundred Dollars; Ninth Judicial District Five Thousand Dollars.

Sec. 17. Alteration of salary of district judge authorized. The salary of any Judge in said Judicial Districts may by law be altered or changed, subject to the provisions contained in this Constitution.

Sec. 18. Qualification and terms of certain elective state officers. The Governor, Lieutenant Governor, Secretary of State, State Treasurer, State Controller, Attorney General, Surveyor General, Clerk of the Supreme Court and Superintendent of Public Instruction, to be elected at the first election under this Constitution shall each qualify and enter upon the duties of their respective offices on the first Monday of December succeeding their election and shall continue in office until the first Tuesday after the first Monday of January A.D. Eighteen hundred and Sixty Seven, and until the election and qualification of their successors respectively.

Sec. 19. When justices of supreme court and district judges enter upon duties. The Judges of the Supreme Court and District Judges to be elected at the first election under this Constitution shall qualify and enter upon the duties of their respective offices on the first Monday of December succeeding their election.

Sec. 20. State officers and district judges to be commissioned by territorial governor; state controller and treasurer to furnish bonds. All officers of State, and District Judges first elected under this Constitution shall be commissioned by the Governor of this Territory, which commission shall be countersigned by the Secretary of the same, and shall qualify before entering upon the discharge of their duties, before any officer authorized to administer oaths under the Laws of this Territory; and also the State Controller and State Treasurer shall each respectively, before they qualify, and enter upon the discharge of their duties, execute and deliver to the Secretary of the Territory of Nevada an Official Bond, made payable to the People of the State of Nevada in the sum of Thirty Thousand Dollars, to be approved by the Governor of the Territory of Nevada; and shall also execute and deliver to the Secretary of State such other or further official Bond or Bonds as may be required by law.

Sec. 21. Support of county and city officers. Each County, Town, City, and Incorporated Village shall make provision for the support of its own officers, subject to such regulations as may be prescribed by law.

Sec. 22. Vacancies in certain state offices: How filled. In case the office of any State officer, except a judicial officer, shall become vacant before the expiration of the regular term for which he was elected, the vacancy may be filled by appointment by the Governor until it shall be supplied at the next general election, when it shall be filled by election for the residue of the unexpired term.

[Amended in 1976. Proposed and passed by the 1973 legislature; agreed to and passed by the 1975 legislature; and approved and ratified by the people at the 1976 general election. See: Statutes of Nevada 1973, p. 1955; Statutes of Nevada 1975, p. 1873.]

Sec. 23. Civil and criminal cases pending in probate courts transferred to district courts. All cases both civil and criminal, which may be pending and undetermined in the Probate Courts of the several counties at the time when under the provisions of this Constitution, said Probate Courts are to be abolished, shall be transferred to and determined by the District Courts of such counties respectively.

Sec. 24. Levy of tax limited for 3 years. For the first Three Years after the adoption of this Constitution the Legislature shall not levy a tax for State purposes, exceeding one per cent per annum on the taxable property in the State, Provided, the Legislature may levy a special tax not exceeding one fourth of one per cent per annum, which shall be appropriated to the payment of the indebtedness of the Territory of Nevada, assumed by the State of Nevada, and for that purpose only, until all of said indebtedness is paid.

Sec. 25. Roop County attached to Washoe County. The County of Roop shall be attached to the County of Washoe for Judicial[,] Legislative, Revenue and County purposes, until otherwise provided by law.

Sec. 26. Constitutional debates and proceedings: Publication; payment of reporter. At the first regular session of the Legislature to convene under the requirements of this Constitution, provisions shall be made by law for paying for the publication of Six Hundred copies of the Debates and proceedings of this Convention in Book form, to be disposed of as the Legislature may direct; and the Hon. J Neely Johnson President of this Convention, shall contract for, and A. J Marsh, official reporter of this convention under the direction of the President, shall supervise the publication of such debates and proceedings. Provision shall be made by law, at such first session of the Legislature for the compensation of the official reporter of this convention, and he shall be paid in coin or its equivalent. He shall receive for his services in reporting the debates and proceedings, Fifteen Dollars per day during the session of the Convention, and Seven and one half dollars additional for each evening session, and thirty cents per folio of one hundred words for preparing the same for publication, and for supervising and indexing such publication the sum of Fifteen Dollars per day during the time actually engaged in such service.

Article 18
Right of Suffrage

Rights of suffrage and office-holding. [Repealed in 1992.]

[Added in 1880. Art. XVIII was proposed and passed by the 1877 legislature; agreed to and passed by the 1879 legislature; and approved and ratified by the people at the 1880 general election. See: Statutes of Nevada 1877, p. 213; Statutes of Nevada 1879, p. 149. Article XVIII was repealed by vote of the people at the 1992 general election. See Statutes of Nevada 1989, p. 2295; Statutes of Nevada 1991, p. 2498. The original section read: "The rights of suffrage and office-holding shall not be withheld from any male citizen of the United States by reason of his color or previous condition of servitude."]

Article 19
Initiative and Referendum

Sec. 1. Referendum for approval or disapproval of statute or resolution enacted by legislature.
   2. Initiative petition for enactment or amendment of statute or amendment of constitution.
   3. Referendum and initiative petitions: Contents and form; signatures; enacting clause; manner of verification of signatures.
   4. Powers of initiative and referendum of registered voters of counties and municipalities.
   5. Provisions of article self-executing; legislative procedures.
   6. Limitation on initiative making appropriation or requiring expenditure of money.

Sec. 1. Referendum for approval or disapproval of statute or resolution enacted by legislature.

1. A person who intends to circulate a petition that a statute or resolution or part thereof enacted by the legislature be submitted to a vote of the people, before circulating the petition for signatures, shall file a copy thereof with the secretary of state. He shall file the copy not earlier than August 1 of the year before the year in which the election will be held.

2. Whenever a number of registered voters of this state equal to 10 percent or more of the number of voters who voted at the last preceding general election shall express their wish by filing with the secretary of state, not less than 120 days before the next general election, a petition in the form provided for in section 3 of this article that any statute or resolution or any part thereof enacted by the legislature be submitted to a vote of the people, the officers charged with the duties of announcing and proclaiming elections and of certifying nominations or questions to be voted upon shall submit the question of approval or disapproval of such statute or resolution or any part thereof to a vote of the voters at the next succeeding election at which such question may be voted upon by the registered voters of the entire state. The circulation of the petition shall cease on the day the petition is filed with the secretary of state or such other date as may be prescribed for the verification of the number of signatures affixed to the petition, whichever is earliest.

3. If a majority of the voters voting upon the proposal submitted at such election votes approval of such statute or resolution or any part thereof, such statute or resolution or any part thereof shall stand as the law of the state and shall not be amended, annulled, repealed, set aside, suspended or in any way made inoperative except by the direct vote of the people. If a majority of such voters votes disapproval of such statute or resolution or any part thereof, such statute or resolution or any part thereof shall be void and of no effect.

[Added in 1904, amended in 1962 and 1988. The addition was proposed and passed by the 1901 legislature; agreed to and passed by the 1903 legislature; and approved and ratified by the people at the 1904 general election. See: Statutes of Nevada 1901, p. 139. The first amendment was proposed and passed by the 1960 legislature; agreed to and passed by the 1961 legislature; and approved and ratified by the people at the 1962 general election. See: Statutes of Nevada 1960, p. 512; Statutes of Nevada 1961, p. 813. The second amendment was proposed and passed by the 1985 legislature; agreed to and passed by the 1987 legislature; and approved and ratified by the people at the 1988 general election. See: Statutes of Nevada 1985, p. 2363; Statutes of Nevada 1987, p. 2347.]

Sec. 2. Initiative petition for enactment or amendment of statute or amendment of constitution.

1. Notwithstanding the provisions of section 1 of article 4 of this constitution, but subject to the limitations of section 6 of this article, the people reserve to themselves the power to propose, by initiative petition, statutes and amendments to statutes and amendments to this constitution, and to enact or reject them at the polls.

2. An initiative petition shall be in the form required by section 3 of this article and shall be proposed by a number of registered voters equal to 10 percent or more of the number of voters who voted at the last preceding general election in not less than 75 percent of the counties in the state, but the total number of registered voters signing the initiative petition shall be equal to 10 percent or more of the voters who voted in the entire state at the last preceding general election.

3. If the initiative petition proposes a statute or an amendment to a statute, the person who intends to circulate it shall file a copy with the secretary of state before beginning circulation and not earlier than January 1 of the year preceding the year in which a regular session of the legislature is held. After its circulation, it shall be filed with the secretary of state not less than 30 days prior to any regular session of the legislature. The circulation of the petition shall cease on the day the petition is filed with the secretary of state or such other date as

may be prescribed for the verification of the number of signatures affixed to the petition, whichever is earliest. The secretary of state shall transmit such petition to the legislature as soon as the legislature convenes and organizes. The petition shall take precedence over all other measures except appropriation bills, and the statute or amendment to a statute proposed thereby shall be enacted or rejected by the legislature without change or amendment within 40 days. If the proposed statute or amendment to a statute is enacted by the legislature and approved by the governor in the same manner as other statutes are enacted, such statute or amendment to a statute shall become law, but shall be subject to referendum petition as provided in section 1 of this article. If the statute or amendment to a statute is rejected by the legislature, or if no action is taken thereon within 40 days, the secretary of state shall submit the question of approval or disapproval of such statute or amendment to a statute to a vote of the voters at the next succeeding general election. If a majority of the voters voting on such question at such election votes approval of such statute or amendment to a statute, it shall become law and take effect upon completion of the canvass of votes by the supreme court. An initiative measure so approved by the voters shall not be amended, annulled, repealed, set aside or suspended by the legislature within 3 years from the date it takes effect. If a majority of such voters votes disapproval of such statute or amendment to a statute, no further action shall be taken on such petition. If the legislature rejects such proposed statute or amendment, the governor may recommend to the legislature and the legislature may propose a different measure on the same subject, in which event, after such different measure has been approved by the governor, the question of approval or disapproval of each measure shall be submitted by the secretary of state to a vote of the voters at the next succeeding general election. If the conflicting provisions submitted to the voters are both approved by a majority of the voters voting on such measures, the measure which receives the largest number of affirmative votes shall thereupon become law.

4. If the initiative petition proposes an amendment to the constitution, the person who intends to circulate it shall file a copy with the secretary of state before beginning circulation and not earlier than September 1 of the year before the year in which the election is to be held. After its circulation it shall be filed with the secretary of state not less than 90 days before any regular general election at which the question of approval or disapproval of such amendment may be voted upon by the voters of the entire state. The circulation of the petition shall cease on the day the petition is filed with the secretary of state or such other date as may be prescribed for the verification of the number of signatures affixed to the petition, whichever is earliest. The secretary of

state shall cause to be published in a newspaper of general circulation, on three separate occasions, in each county in the state, together with any explanatory matter which shall be placed upon the ballot, the entire text of the proposed amendment. If a majority of the voters voting on such question at such election votes disapproval of such amendment, no further action shall be taken on the petition. If a majority of such voters votes approval of such amendment, the secretary of state shall publish and resubmit the question of approval or disapproval to a vote of the voters at the next succeeding general election in the same manner as such question was originally submitted. If a majority of such voters votes disapproval of such amendment, no further action shall be taken on such petition. If a majority of such voters votes approval of such amendment, it shall become a part of this constitution upon completion of the canvass of votes by the supreme court.

[Added in 1912, amended in 1958, 1962, twice in 1972 and in 1988. The addition was proposed and passed by the 1909 legislature; agreed to and passed by the 1911 legislature; and approved and ratified by the people at the 1912 general election. See: Statutes of Nevada 1909, p. 347; Statutes of Nevada 1911, p. 446. The first amendment was proposed by initiative petition and approved and ratified by the people at the general election of 1958. The second amendment was proposed and passed by the 1960 legislature; agreed to and passed by the 1961 legislature; and approved and ratified by the people at the 1962 general election. See: Statutes of Nevada 1960, p. 512; Statutes of Nevada 1961, p. 813. The third and fourth amendments were proposed and passed by the 1969 legislature; agreed to and passed by the 1971 legislature; and approved and ratified by the people at the 1972 general election. See: Statutes of Nevada 1969, pp. 1680, 1719; Statutes of Nevada 1971, pp. 2230, 2260. The fifth amendment was proposed and passed by the 1985 legislature; agreed to and passed by the 1987 legislature; and approved and ratified by the people at the 1988 general election. See: Statutes of Nevada 1985, p. 2364; Statutes of Nevada 1987, p. 2348.]

Sec. 3. Referendum and initiative petitions: Contents and form; signatures; enacting clause; manner of verification of signatures.

1. Each referendum petition and initiative petition shall include the full text of the measure proposed. Each signer shall affix thereto his or her signature, residence address and the name of the county in which he or she is a registered voter. The petition may consist of more than one document, but each document shall have affixed thereto an affidavit made by one of the signers of such document to the effect that all of the signatures are genuine and that each individual who signed such document was at the time of signing a registered voter in the county of his or her residence. The affidavit shall be executed before a person authorized by law to administer oaths in the State of Nevada.

The enacting clause of all statutes or amendments proposed by initiative petition shall be: "The People of the State of Nevada do enact as follows:".

2. The legislature may authorize the secretary of state and the other public officers to use generally accepted statistical procedures in conducting a preliminary verification of the number of signatures submitted in connection with a referendum petition or an initiative petition, and for this purpose to require petitions to be filed no more than 65 days earlier than is otherwise required by this article.

[Added in 1912, amended in 1958, 1962, and 1988. The addition was proposed and passed by the 1909 legislature; agreed to and passed by the 1911 legislature; and approved and ratified by the people at the 1912 general election. See: Statutes of Nevada 1909, p. 347; Statutes of Nevada 1911, p. 446. The first amendment was proposed by initiative petition and approved and ratified by the people at the general election of 1958. The second amendment was proposed and passed by the 1960 legislature; agreed to and passed by the 1961 legislature; and approved and ratified by the people at the 1962 general election. See: Statutes of Nevada 1960, p. 512; Statutes of Nevada 1961, p. 813. The third amendment was proposed and passed by the 1985 legislature; agreed to and passed by the 1987 legislature; and approved and ratified by the people at the 1988 general election. See: Statutes of Nevada 1985, p. 2365; Statutes of Nevada 1987, p. 2349.]

Sec. 4. Powers of initiative and referendum of registered voters of counties and municipalities. The initiative and referendum powers provided for in this article are further reserved to the registered voters of each county and each municipality as to all local, special and municipal legislation of every kind in or for such county or municipality. In counties and municipalities initiative petitions may be instituted by a number of registered voters equal to 15 percent or more of the voters who voted at the last preceding general county or municipal election. Referendum petitions may be instituted by 10 percent or more of such voters.

[Added in 1962. Proposed and passed by the 1960 legislature; agreed to and passed by the 1961 legislature; and approved and ratified by the people at the 1962 general election. See: Statutes of Nevada 1960, p. 512; Statutes of Nevada 1961, p. 813.]

Sec. 5. Provisions of article self-executing; legislative procedures. The provisions of this article are self-executing but the legislature may provide by law for procedures to facilitate the operation thereof.

[Added in 1962. Proposed and passed by the 1960 legislature; agreed to and passed by the 1961 legislature; and approved and ratified by the people at the 1962 general election. See: Statutes of Nevada 1960, p. 512; Statutes of Nevada 1961, p. 813.]

Sec. 6. Limitation on initiative making appropriation or requiring expenditure of money. This article does not permit the proposal of any statute or statutory amendment which makes an appropriation or otherwise requires the expenditure of money, unless such statute or amendment also imposes a sufficient tax, not prohibited by the constitution, or otherwise constitutionally provides for raising the necessary revenue.

[Added in 1972. Proposed and passed by the 1969 legislature; agreed to and passed by the 1971 legislature; and approved and ratified by the people at the 1972 general election. See: Statutes of Nevada 1969, p. 1720; Statutes of Nevada 1971, p. 2262.]

Election Ordinance

Whereas, The enabling act passed by Congress and approved March Twenty first A.D. Eighteen Hundred and Sixty four, requires that the convention charged with the duty of framing a Constitution for a State Government "shall provide by ordinance for submitting said Constitution to the People of the Territory of Nevada, for their ratification or rejection" on a certain day prescribed therein; therefore this Convention organized in pursuance of said enabling act, do establish the following:

Ordinance

Sec. 1. Proclamation by territorial governor; general election. The Governor of the Territory of Nevada is hereby authorized to issue his proclamation for the submission of this Constitution to the people of said Territory for their approval or rejection on the day provided for such submission, by Act of Congress; and this Constitution shall be submitted to the qualified electors of said Territory, in the several counties thereof, for their approval or rejection, at the time provided by such Act of Congress; and further, on the first Tuesday after the first Monday of November A.D. Eighteen hundred and Sixty four, there shall be a general election in the several counties of said Territory for the election of State Officers, Supreme and District Judges, members of the Legislature, Representative in Congress and three Presidential Electors.

Sec. 2. Qualified electors may vote for adoption or rejection of constitution. All persons qualified by the laws of said Territory to vote for Representatives to the General Assembly on the said Twenty first day of March, including those in the Army of the United States, both within and beyond the boundaries of said Territory, and also all persons who may by the aforesaid laws, be qualified to vote on the first Wednesday of September A.D. Eighteen hundred and Sixty four, including those in the aforesaid Army of the United States, within and without the boundaries of said Territory may vote for the adoption or rejection of said Constitution, on the day last above named. In voting upon this Constitution, each elector shall deposite [deposit] in the ballot box a ticket whereon shall be clearly written, or printed "Constitution Yes" or "Constitution No," or other such words that shall clearly indicate the intention of the Elector.

Sec. 3. Qualified electors for first general election. All persons qualified by the laws of said Territory to vote on the Tuesday after the first Monday of November A.D. Eighteen hundred and Sixty four, including those in the Army of the United States, within and beyond the boundaries of said Territory, may vote on the day last above named, for State Officers, Supreme and District Judges, Members of the Legislature, Representative in Congress, and three Presidential electors, to the electoral college.

Sec. 4. Elections: Places, judges, inspectors and procedure. The elections provided in this Ordinance shall be holden at such places as shall be designated by the Boards of Commissioners of the several counties in said Territory. The Judges, and inspectors of said elections, shall be appointed by said Commissioners, and the said elections shall be conducted in conformity with the existing laws of said Territory in relation to holding the General election.

Sec. 5. Election returns. The Judges and Inspectors of said elections shall carefully count each ballot immediately after said elections, and forthwith make duplicate returns thereof to the clerks of the said County Commissioners of their respective Counties, and said Clerks, within fifteen days after said elections shall transmit an abstract of the votes including the soldiers vote, as herein provided, given for State Officers, Supreme and District Judges, Representative in Congress and three Presidential Electors, enclosed in an envelope, by the most safe and expeditious conveyance to the Governor of said Territory marked "Election Returns" [.]

Sec. 6. Canvass of votes; proclamation; issuance of certificates of election. Upon the receipt of said returns, including those of the soldiers vote, or within Twenty days after the election, if said returns be not sooner received, it shall be the duty of the Board of Canvassers, to consist of the Governor, United States District Attorney and Chief Justice of said Territory or any two of them to canvass the returns in the presence of all who may wish to be present, and if a majority of all the votes given upon this Constitution, shall be in its favor, the said Governor shall immediately publish an abstract of the same, and make proclamation of the fact in some newspaper in said Territory and certify the same to the President of the United States, together with a copy of the Constitution and Ordinance. The said Board of Canvassers, after canvassing the votes of the said November elections shall issue certificates of election, to such persons as were elected State Officers, Judges of the Supreme and District Courts, Representative in Congress and three Presidential Electors. When the President of the United States shall issue his proclamation, declaring this State admitted into the Union, on an equal footing, with the original states; This Constitution shall thenceforth be ordained and established as the Constitution of the State of Nevada.

Sec. 7. List of electors in Army of the United States. For the purpose of taking the vote of the Electors of said Territory who may be in the Army of the United States: the Adjutant General of said Territory, shall on or before the fifth day of August next following, make out a list in alphabetical order and deliver the same to the Governor, of the names of all the electors, residents of said Territory, who shall be in the Army of the United States, stating the number of the Regiment, Battalion, Squadron, or Battery, to which he belongs, and also the County or Township, of his residence in said Territory.

Sec. 8. Transmission of lists of electors in Army of the United States. The Governor shall classify and arrange the aforesaid returned list, and shall make therefrom separate lists of the electors belonging to each Reigment [Regiment], Battalion, Squadron and Battery from said Territory in the Service of the United States, and shall, on or before the Fifteenth day of August following, transmit by mail or otherwise, to the Commanding Officer of each Regiment, Battalion[,] Squadron and Battery, a list of electors belonging thereto, which said list shall specify the name[,] residence and rank of each elector, and the company to which he belongs, if to any, and also the County and Township to which he belongs, and in which he is entitled to vote.

Sec. 9. Voting by soldiers: Qualifications. Between the hours of Nine O'Clock a.m. and Three O'Clock p.m. on each of the election days hereinbefore named, a ballot box or suitable receptacle for votes shall be opened under the immediate charge and direction of three of the highest Officers in command, for the reception of Votes from the electors whose names are upon said list, at each place where a Regiment, Battalion[,] Squadron or Battery of Soldiers from said Territory in the Army of the United States may be on that day; at which time and place, said Electors shall be entitled to vote for all Officers for which by reason of their residence in the several counties in said Territory they are authorized to vote, as fully as they would be entitled to vote in the several Counties or Townships in which they reside, and the votes so given by such electors at such time and place, shall be considered, taken and held to have been given by them in the respective Counties and Townships in which they are resident.

Sec. 10. Voting by soldiers: Procedure; count of votes. Each ballot deposited for the adoption or rejection of this Constitution, in the Army of the United States shall have, distinctly written or printed thereon "Constitution Yes," or "Constitution No"; or words of a similar import, and further, for the election of State Officers, Supreme and District Judges, Members of the Legislature, Representative in Congress and three Presidential Electors, the name and Office of the person voted for shall be plainly written or printed on one piece of paper. The name of each elector voting as aforesaid shall be checked upon the said list, at the time of voting by one of the said Officers, having charge of the ballot box. The said Officers having charge of the election shall count the votes and compare them with the checked list, immediately after the closing of the ballot box[.]

Sec. 11. Voting by soldiers: Transmission of results. All the ballots cast, together with the said voting list, checked as aforesaid, shall be immediately sealed up, and sent forthwith to the Governor of said Territory at Carson City by mail or otherwise, by the Commanding Officer, who shall make out and certify duplicate returns of Votes given, according to the forms hereinafter prescribed, seal up and immediately transmit the same to the said Governor at Carson City by mail or otherwise, the day following the transmission of the ballots and the voting list herein named, the said Commanding Officer shall also immediately transmit to the several County Clerks in said Territory an abstract of the votes given at the general election in November, for County Officers marked "Election Returns" [.]

Sec. 12. Voting by soldiers: Form of return. The form of returns of votes to be made by the Commanding Officer to the Governor and County Clerks of said Territory shall be in substance as follows, Viz:

"Returns of Soldiers, votes in the (here insert the regiment, detachment, battalion, squadron or battery)"—(For first election on the Constitution.) .... I, ..., hereby certify, that, on the first Wednesday of September A.D. Eighteen hundred and sixty four the Electors belonging to the (here insert the name of the regiment, detachment, battalion[,] squadron or battery.) cast the following number of votes for and against the Constitution for the State of Nevada, Viz: For "Constitution" (number of votes written in full and in figures.) Against "Constitution" (number of votes written in full and in figures) .... (Second election for State and other Officers) .... I .... hereby certify that on the first Tuesday after the first Monday in November A.D. Eighteen hundred and Sixty four, the Electors belonging to the (here insert as above) cast the following number of votes for the several officers and persons hereinafter named Viz: .... For Governor .... names of persons voted for, number of votes for each person voted for written in full and also in figures, against the name of each person. .... For Lieutenant Governor .... name of Candidates, number of votes cast for each, written out and in figures as above. .... Continue as above till the list is completed .... Attest .... I, A.B. .... Commanding Officer of the (here .... Insert regiment[,] detachment, battalion, squadron, or battery as the case may be).

Sec. 13. Voting by soldiers: Territorial governor to furnish form of return. The Governor of this Territory is requested to furnish each Commanding Officer within and beyond the boundaries of said Territory, proper and sufficient blanks for said returns.

Sec. 14. Applicability to future votes of soldiers. The provisions of this Ordinance in regard to the Soldiers vote shall apply to future elections under this Constitution, and be in full force until the Legislature shall provide by law for taking the votes of citizens of said Territory in the Army of the United States[.]

Done in Convention, at Carson City the Twenty Eighth day of July, in the year of our Lord One Thousand Eight Hundred and Sixty Four and of the Independence of the United States the Eighty-ninth, and signed by the Delegates.

J. Neely Johnson, *President of the Convention and Delegate from Ormsby County*
Wm. M. Gillespie, *Secretary*

[Then follow the names of delegates who signed the constitution.]
Henry B. Brady, *Delegate from Washoe County*
E. F. Dunne, *Delegate from Humboldt County*
J. G. McClinton, *Delegate from Esmeralda County*
G. N. Folsom, *Delegate from Washoe County*
F. H. Kennedy, *Delegate from Lyon County*
W. W. Belden, *Delegate from Washoe County*
F. M. Proctor, *Delegate from Nye County*
Albert T. Hawley, *Delegate from Douglas County*
Geo. L. Gibson, *Delegate from Ormsby County*
F. Tagliabue, *Delegate from Nye County*
Wm. Wetherell, *Delegate from Esmeralda County*
John A. Collins, *Delegate from Storey County*
Jas. A. Banks, *Delegate from Humboldt County*
J. S. Crosman, *Delegate from Lyon County*
Saml. A. Chapin, *Delegate from Storey County*
C. M. Brosnan, *Delegate from Storey County*
John H. Kinkead, *Delegate from Ormsby County*
Geo. A. Hudson, *Delegate from Lyon County*
Israel Crawford, *Delegate from Ormsby County*
A. J. Lockwood, *Delegate from Ormsby County*
H. G. Parker, *Delegate from Lyon County*
J. H. Warwick, *Delegate from Lander County*
C. E. DeLong, *Delegate from Storey County*
Lloyd Frizell, *Delegate from Storey County*
Geo. A. Nourse, *Delegate from Washoe County*
B. S. Mason, *Delegate from Esmeralda County*
Almon Hovey, *Delegate from Storey County*
Thomas Fitch, *Delegate from Storey County*
J. W. Haines, *Delegate from Douglas County*

Notes

Chapter One. Nevada: Origins and Early History

1. Russell R. Elliott, with the assistance of William D. Rowley, *History of Nevada*, 2d ed., rev. (Lincoln: University of Nebraska Press, 1987), 33. James Hulse, however, suggests that whether Father Garcés crossed southern Nevada is still an open question (James W. Hulse, *The Silver State: Nevada's Heritage Reinterpreted* [Reno: University of Nevada Press, 1991], 34).

2. Hulse, *The Silver State*, 35.

3. Ibid., 37.

4. The party is one of the better known as a result of Washington Irving's 1837 book, *The Adventures of Captain Bonneville, U.S.A., in the Rocky Mountains and the Far West.*

5. Elliott and Rowley, *History of Nevada*, 38, and Hulse, *The Silver State*, 40.

6. Eleanore Bushnell and Don W. Driggs, *The Nevada Constitution: Origin and Growth*, 6th ed. (Reno: University of Nevada Press, 1984), 4.

7. Frankie Sue Del Papa, *Political History of Nevada, 1990* (Carson City: State Printing Office, 1990), 33.

8. Mack and Bancroft, among others, mistakenly list the year of this first post as 1849. See Effie Mona Mack, *Nevada: A History of the State from the Earliest Times Through the Civil War* (Glendale, Calif.: Arthur H. Clark, 1935), 147, and Hubert Howe Bancroft, *History of Nevada, Colorado, and Wyoming, 1540–1888*, vol. 25 of *The Works of Hubert Howe Bancroft* (San Francisco: History Company, 1890), 65–66. However, the more recent work of Russell R. Elliott provides conclusive evidence that the 1850 date is correct. See Russell R. Elliott, "Nevada's First Trading Post: A Study in Historiography," *Nevada Historical Society Quarterly* 8 (spring 1965): 11.

9. "History of the Las Vegas Mission," in *Nevada State Historical Society Papers, 1925–1926*, comp. Andrew Jenson (Reno: Nevada State Historical Society, 1926), 152.

10. Ibid., 153.

11. *Los*, rather than *Las*, was used to prevent confusion with Las Vegas, New Mexico. These episodes and many more are described in Eugene P. Moehring, *Resort City in the Sunbelt: Las Vegas, 1930–1970* (Reno: University of Nevada Press, 1989), 1–3.

12. Myron Angel, ed., *History of Nevada, 1881, with Illustrations* (New York: Arno Press, 1973), 32. Angel's work was originally published in 1881 by Thompson and West of Oakland, California.

13. Bancroft, *History of Nevada, Colorado, and Wyoming*, 74–75.

14. Elliott and Rowley, *History of Nevada*, 54.

15. *Pamphlets on California* 26, no. 28. Quoted in Mack, *Nevada*, 157.

16. Elliott and Rowley, *History of Nevada*, 56.

17. Angel, *History of Nevada*, 41.

18. See, for example, Hulse, *The Silver State*, 60, and Elliott and Rowley, *History of Nevada*, 56. Angel, for instance, notes that Judge W. W. Drummond, who had replaced federal Judge Styles in Carson County, erroneously reported to his superiors that the Mormons had burned the library and records of the United States District Court (*History of Nevada*, 168).

19. Angel, *History of Nevada*, 42.

20. Quoted in Bancroft, *History of Nevada, Colorado, and Wyoming*, 83–84.

21. See Angel, *History of Nevada*, 49–51.

22. Gordon Morris Bakken, *Rocky Mountain Constitution Making, 1850–1912* (Westport, Conn.: Greenwood Press, 1987), 9.

23. Bancroft, *History of Nevada, Colorado, and Wyoming*, 88.

24. J. H. Purkitt, "Nevada Territory," *San Francisco Evening Bulletin*, February 15, 1860. Quoted in Mack, *Nevada*, 184.

Chapter Two. Nevada: Territory and Statehood

1. Bushnell and Driggs, *The Nevada Constitution*, 13.

2. Address of Governor Nye to the Territorial Legislature, in *Journal of the Council of the First Legislative Assembly of the Territory of Nevada* (San Francisco: Commercial Steam Printing, 1862), 14–27. Quoted in Elliott and Rowley, *History of Nevada*, 72.

3. Richard G. Lillard, *Desert Challenge: An Interpretation of Nevada* (New York: Alfred A. Knopf, 1942), 25.

4. The actual results are in some dispute. Elliott and Rowley (*History of Nevada*, 77), Angel (*History of Nevada*, 81), Mack (*Nevada*, 249), and Hulse (*The Silver State*, 81) adopt these figures. However, Bancroft (*History of Nevada, Colorado, and Wyoming*, 178) concludes that of a total vote of 8,162, only 5,150 voted for the statehood measure. In any case, support for statehood was overwhelming.

5. Del Papa, *Political History*, 83. However, Mack (*Nevada*, 250) and Elliott and Rowley (*History of Nevada*, 78) claim that all but four came directly from California.

6. Bakken, *Rocky Mountain Constitution Making*, 6.

7. William C. Miller and Eleanore Bushnell, eds., *Reports of the 1863 Constitutional Convention of the Territory of Nevada* (Carson City: Legislative Counsel Bureau, 1972), 273.

8. Mack, *Nevada*, 251.

9. Nevada Constitution (1863), art. X, sec. 1, quoted in Miller and Bushnell, *Reports of the 1863 Constitutional Convention*, 429.

10. See David A. Johnson, *Founding the Far West: California, Oregon, and Nevada, 1840–1890* (Berkeley: University of California Press, 1992), 83–89.

11. Del Papa, *Political History*, 84.

12. Angel, *History of Nevada*, 84.

13. David A. Johnson, "A Case of Mistaken Identity: William M. Stewart and the Rejection of Nevada's First Constitution," *Nevada Historical Society Quarterly* 22 (fall 1979): 188.

14. Quoted in Bushnell and Driggs, *The Nevada Constitution*, 18.

15. Andrew J. Marsh, *Official Report of the Debates and Proceedings in the Constitutional Convention of the State of Nevada* (San Francisco: Frank Eastman, 1866), 325.

16. Ibid., 224.

17. Del Papa, *Political History*, 86. These limits can be found in the "Ordinance" of the Constitution of the State of Nevada.

18. Although many portions of the book are now outdated, Bushnell and Driggs's work still provides one of the best discussions available of the many disputes dividing the delegates of the 1864 convention, and that section is well worth a read by those interested (*Nevada Constitution*, 26–41).

19. Ibid., 27.

20. Bakken, *Rocky Mountain Constitution Making*, 20.

21. Marsh, *Debates and Proceedings*, 224.

22. Quoted in Lillard, *Desert Challenge*, 75.

23. Marsh, *Debates and Proceedings*, 356.

24. Ibid., 361.

25. Ibid., 335.

26. Johnson, *Founding the Far West*, 222–28.

27. Nevada Constitution (1864), art. X, sec. 1.

28. Johnson, *Founding the Far West*, 223.

29. Marsh, *Debates and Proceedings*, 820, 827.

30. Ibid., xiv, 827. This figure is the one generally accepted and is noted in Elliott and Rowley (*History of Nevada*, 88), Bushnell and Driggs (*The Nevada Constitution*, 42), and Hulse (*The Silver State*, 84). Inexplicably, however, Angel (*History of Nevada*, 86) puts the vote at 11,393 to 2,262, and Gilman M. Ostrander counts the tally as 6,530 to 2,260 (*Nevada: The Great Rotten Borough, 1859–1964* [New York: Alfred A. Knopf, 1966], 39).

31. Del Papa, *Political History*, 90.

32. Johnson, "A Case of Mistaken Identity," 198.

33. Johnson, *Founding the Far West*, 226.

34. *Virginia City Territorial Enterprise*, August 19, 1864. Quoted in Johnson, *Founding the Far West*, 315. William M. Stewart also argued in favor of the constitution on the basis that statehood would bring the territory out of its mining depression. See David A. Johnson, "Industry and the Individual on the Far Western Frontier: A Case Study of Politics and Social Change in Early Nevada," *Pacific Historical Review* 51 (August 1982), 243–64.

35. Marsh, *Debates and Proceedings*, 173.

36. Bancroft, *History of Nevada, Colorado, and Wyoming*, 172.

37. Ostrander, *Great Rotten Borough*, 28.

38. Johnson, *Founding the Far West*, 316.

39. Quoted ibid.

40. Samuel P. Davis, ed., *The History of Nevada*, 2 vols. (Reno: Elms Publishing Co., 1913), 302.

41. Daniel J. Elazar, "The Principles and Traditions Underlying State Constitutions," *Publius: The Journal of Federalism* 12 (winter 1982): 21–22.

Chapter Three. Civil Rights and Liberties in Nevada

1. Jack C. Plano and Milton Greenberg, *The American Political Dictionary*, 3d ed. (Hinsdale, Ill.: Dryden Press, 1972), 63.

2. Ibid.

3. Marsh, *Debates and Proceedings*, 786.

4. Elmer R. Rusco, "The Status of Indians in Nevada Law," in *Native American Politics: Power Relationships in the Western Great Basin Today*, ed. Ruth M. Houghton (Reno: Bureau of Governmental Research, 1973), 59–87.

5. Ibid.

6. Johnson, *Founding the Far West*, 328.

7. See Sue Fawn Chung, "The Chinese Experience in Nevada: Success Despite Discrimination," *Nevada Public Affairs Review* no. 2 (1987): 43–51.

8. Russell M. Magnaghi, "Virginia City's Chinese Community, 1860–1880,"*Nevada Historical Society Quarterly* 24 (summer 1981): 153.

9. James Edward Wright, *The Politics of Populism: Dissent in Colorado* (New Haven: Yale University Press, 1974), 26.

10. Moehring, *Resort City in the Sunbelt*, 199.

11. M. L. "Tony" Miranda, *Out of the Shadows: A Critical First Look at the Ethnohistory of Hispanics in Nevada* (working title) (Reno: University of Nevada Press, in press), 80–82.

12. Carey McWilliams, *North from Mexico: The Spanish-Speaking of the United States* (New York: J. B. Lippincott Co., 1968), 168. Quoted in Miranda, *Out of the Shadows*, 126.

13. Miranda, *Out of the Shadows*, 167–68.

14. Jim Frey, "Preliminary Report: Assessment of the Accessibility of HEW Assisted Programs to the Hispanic Population of Clark County, Nevada" (University of Nevada, Las Vegas, report, 1978), 27. Quoted in Miranda, *Out of the Shadows*, 190.

15. M. L. "Tony" Miranda, "Some Observations on Hispanics in Nevada in the Eighties," *Nevada Public Affairs Review* 2 (1987): 39.

16. Ibid., 201–2.

17. 32 U.S. (7 Pet.) 243 (1833).

Chapter Four. Political Parties and Elections

1. The first four of these are noted in Bushnell and Driggs, *The Nevada Constitution*, 66–68. The fifth has come about since the publication of their work.

2. Ibid., 66.

3. *Buckley v. Valeo*, 424 U.S. 1 (1976).

4. *Arvey v. Sheriff*, 93 Nev. 469, 567 P.2d 470 (1977).

5. Steve Kanigher, "Wallets Open, Mouths Shut,"*Las Vegas Sun*, December 24, 1995, sec. K, p. 1.

6. 410 U.S. 113 (1973).

Chapter Five. Interest Groups and Lobbying

1. Don W. Driggs, "Nevada: Powerful Lobbyists and Conservative Politics," in *Interest Group Politics in the American West,* ed. Ronald J. Hrebenar and Clive S. Thomas (Salt Lake City: University of Utah Press, 1987), 85–92.

2. *Reno Gazette-Journal,* July 2, 1993, sec. A, p. 6. Quoted in Don W. Driggs and Leonard E. Goodall, *Nevada Politics and Government: Conservatism in an Open Society* (Lincoln: University of Nebraska Press, in press).

3. Faun Mortara, "Lobbying in Nevada," in *Sagebrush and Neon: Studies in Nevada Politics,* rev. ed., ed. Eleanore Bushnell (Reno: Bureau of Governmental Research, 1976), 45.

4. Ibid., 44.

5. Driggs, "Powerful Lobbyists," 86.

6. Jane Ann Morrison, "Casinos Gamble on Politicians," *Las Vegas Review-Journal,* May 22, 1993, sec. B, pp. 1, 3.

7. Driggs and Goodall, *Nevada Politics.*

8. Ed Vogel, "Gaming Wins and Losses at the Legislature," *Las Vegas Review-Journal,* July 2, 1995, sec. B, p. 7.

9. Sean Whaley, "Nevada State Education Association Scorecard," *Las Vegas Review-Journal,* July 5, 1995, sec. A, p. 3.

10. Albert Deutsch, "The Sorry State of Nevada," *Collier's* 135 (March 18, 1955): 74–85. Quoted in James W. Hulse, *Forty Years in the Wilderness: Impressions of Nevada, 1940–1980* (Reno: University of Nevada Press, 1986), 88.

Chapter Six. The Nevada Legislature

1. It is worth noting that a few explicit exceptions to this rule are provided for in the constitution itself. In Article V, Section 17, the lieutenant governor (a member of the executive branch) is given the duty of serving as president of the senate with the power of a "casting vote," and the president pro-tempore of the senate (a member of the legislative branch) serves as acting governor when the governor and lieutenant governor are both absent from the state or the two offices become vacant in some other way.

2. Marsh, *Debates and Proceedings,* 144.

3. Eleanore Bushnell, "Reapportionment and Responsibility," in *Sagebrush and Neon,* ed. Bushnell, 102–3.

4. 377 U.S. 533 (1964).

5. *Dungan v. Sawyer,* 250 F. Supp. 480 (D. Nev. 1965).

6. Driggs and Goodall, *Nevada Politics.*

Chapter Seven. The Nevada Executive

1. These summaries can be found in Driggs and Goodall, *Nevada Politics.*

2. Ibid.

3. Ibid.

4. Marsh, *Debates and Proceedings,* 159.

5. Terry Reynolds, "The Executive Veto in Nevada," 4. Quoted in Bushnell and Driggs, *The Nevada Constitution,* 115–16.

6. Driggs and Goodall, *Nevada Politics.*

7. 82 Nev. 53, 410 P.2d 748 (1966).

Chapter Eight. The Nevada Judiciary

1. Bakken, *Rocky Mountain Constitution Making,* 9.

2. Bancroft, *History of Nevada, Colorado, and Wyoming,* 121.

3. Marsh, *Debates and Proceedings,* 642.

4. Driggs and Goodall, *Nevada Politics.*

5. Bakken, *Rocky Mountain Constitution Making,* 40.

6. Michael W. Bowers, "The Impact of Judicial Selection Methods in Nevada: Some Empirical Observations," *Nevada Public Affairs Review* no. 2 (1990): 5.

Chapter Nine. City and County Governments

1. John F. Dillon, *Commentaries on the Laws of Municipal Corporations,* 5th ed. (Boston: Little, Brown, 1911), 448.

2. *County of Clark v. City of Las Vegas,* 97 Nev. 260, 628 P.2d 1120 (1981).

3. Bushnell and Driggs, *The Nevada Constitution,* 156.

4. Driggs and Goodall, *Nevada Politics.*

Chapter Ten. State and Local Finance

1. John Gunther, *Inside U.S.A.* (New York: Harper and Brothers, 1947), 31. Quoted in David R. Berman, "Financing State and Local Government," in *Politics and Public Policy in the Contemporary American West,* ed. Clive S. Thomas (Albuquerque: University of New Mexico Press, 1991), 305.

2. John Gallant, "Nevada's Tax Load Lighter," *Las Vegas Review-Journal,* December 28, 1993, sec. A, p. 1.

3. Ed Vogel, "Worker Pay Is Seventh in Nation," *Las Vegas Review-Journal,* September 4, 1995, sec. A, p. 1.

4. Berman, "Financing State and Local Government," 310.

5. *Matthews v. State of Nevada, ex rel. Nevada Tax Commission,* 83 Nev. 269 (1967).

6. Berman, "Financing State and Local Government," 322.

Chapter Eleven. Nevada: Past, Present, and Future

1. Hulse, *Forty Years in the Wilderness.*

2. Quoted in Lillard, *Desert Challenge,* 224.

3. Ostrander, *Great Rotten Borough,* 46.

4. Elliott and Rowley, *History of Nevada,* 153.

5. *State of Nevada v. Daniel E. Eastabrook,* 3 Nev. 173 (1867). The legislature acted even before the decision by the court, in part because it assumed the revenue act would be struck down.

6. House, "Railroad Wrongs in Nevada," *Congressional Record,* 46th Cong., 3d sess., 2, pt. 3, Appendix: 181–90. Quoted in Elliott and Rowley, *History of Nevada,* 158.

7. Quoted in Hulse, *The Silver State,* 130.

8. Elliott and Rowley, *History of Nevada,* 161–64.

9. Ibid., 160.

10. Russell R. Elliott, *Servant of Power: A Political Biography of Senator William M. Stewart* (Reno: University of Nevada Press, 1983), 64.

11. Leonard Arrington, "The New Deal in the West: A Preliminary Statistical Inquiry," *Pacific Historical Review* 38 (August 1969): 311–17.

12. Michael W. Bowers and A. Costandina Titus, "Nevada's Black Book: The Constitutionality of Exclusion Lists in Casino Gaming Regulation," *Whittier Law Review* 9 (1987): 315.

13. Del Papa, *Political History,* 114.

14. Driggs and Goodall, *Nevada Politics.*

15. H. Josef Hebert, "Mining Law Forces Cheap Sale of Potentially Rich Land," *Las Vegas Review-Journal,* September 7, 1995, sec. D, p. 9.

16. "Nevada Parole Rate Rises," *Las Vegas Review-Journal,* September 7, 1995, sec. B, p. 5.

17. Hulse, *The Silver State,* 295.

18. Ibid., 291–92.

Selected Bibliography

Angel, Myron, ed. *History of Nevada, 1881, with Illustrations.* Oakland: Thompson and West, 1881. Reissued, Berkeley: Howell–North, 1958; New York: Arno Press, 1973.

Bakken, Gordon Morris. *Rocky Mountain Constitution Making, 1850–1912.* Westport, Conn.: Greenwood Press, 1987.

Bancroft, Hubert Howe. *The Works of Hubert Howe Bancroft.* Vol. 25, *History of Nevada, Colorado, and Wyoming, 1540–1888.* San Francisco: History Company, 1890. Reprinted, in part, as *History of Nevada, 1540–1888.* Reno: University of Nevada Press, 1981.

Bowers, Michael W. *The Nevada State Constitution: A Reference Guide.* Westport, Conn.: Greenwood Press, 1993.

Bushnell, Eleanore, ed. *Sagebrush and Neon: Studies in Nevada Politics.* Rev. ed. Reno: Bureau of Governmental Research, 1976.

Bushnell, Eleanore, and Don W. Driggs. *The Nevada Constitution: Origin and Growth.* 6th ed. Reno: University of Nevada Press, 1984.

Davis, Samuel P., ed. *The History of Nevada.* 2 vols. Reno: Elms Publishing Co., 1913.

Del Papa, Frankie Sue. *Political History of Nevada, 1990.* 9th ed. Carson City: State Printing Office, 1990.

Driggs, Don W. *The Constitution of the State of Nevada: A Commentary.* Carson City: State Printing Office, 1961.

Driggs, Don W., and Leonard E. Goodall. *Nevada Politics and Government: Conservatism in an Open Society.* Lincoln: University of Nebraska Press, in press.

Edwards, Jerome E. "Gambling and Politics in Nevada." In *Politics in the Postwar West,* edited by Richard Lowitt. Norman: University of Oklahoma Press, 1995.

———. *Pat McCarran: Political Boss of Nevada.* Reno: University of Nevada Press, 1982.

Elliott, Russell R. *Servant of Power: A Political Biography of Senator William M. Stewart.* Reno: University of Nevada Press, 1983.

Elliott, Russell, and Helen J. Poulton. *Writings on Nevada: A Selected Bibliography.* Reno: University of Nevada Press, 1963.

Elliott, Russell, with the assistance of William D. Rowley. *History of Nevada.* 2d ed., rev. Lincoln: University of Nebraska Press, 1987.

Glass, Mary Ellen. *Nevada's Turbulent '50s: Decade of Political and Economic Change.* Reno: University of Nevada Press, 1981.

———. *Silver and Politics in Nevada, 1892–1902.* Reno: University of Nevada Press, 1969.

Howard, Anne Bail. *The Long Campaign: A Biography of Anne Martin.* Reno: University of Nevada Press, 1985.

Hrebenar, Ronald J., and Clive S. Thomas, eds. *Interest Group Politics in the American West.* Salt Lake City: University of Utah Press, 1987.

Hulse, James W. *The Silver State: Nevada's Heritage Reinterpreted.* Reno: University of Nevada Press, 1991.

———. *Forty Years in the Wilderness: Impressions of Nevada, 1940–1980.* Reno: University of Nevada Press, 1986.

Johns, Albert C. *Nevada Politics.* Dubuque, Iowa: Kendall/Hunt Publishing Co., 1973.

Johnson, David A. "A Case of Mistaken Identity: William M. Stewart and the Rejection of Nevada's First Constitution," *Nevada Historical Society Quarterly* 22 (fall 1979): 186–98.

———. *Founding the Far West: California, Oregon, and Nevada, 1840-1890.* Berkeley: University of California Press, 1992.

Jonas, Frank Herman, ed. *Politics in the American West.* Salt Lake City: University of Utah Press, 1969.

Lillard, Richard G. *Desert Challenge: An Interpretation of Nevada.* New York: Alfred A. Knopf, 1942.

Mack, Effie Mona. *Nevada: A History of the State from the Earliest Times Through the Civil War.* Glendale, Calif.: Arthur H. Clark, 1935.

Mack, Effie Mona, Idel Anderson, and Beulah E. Singleton. *Nevada Government: A Study of the Administration and Politics of State, County, Township, and Cities.* Caldwell, Idaho: Caxton Printers, 1953.

Magnaghi, Russell M. "Virginia City's Chinese Community, 1860–1880," *Nevada Historical Society Quarterly* 24 (summer 1981): 130–57.

Marsh, Andrew J. *Official Report of the Debates and Proceedings in the Constitutional Convention of the State of Nevada.* San Francisco: Frank Eastman, 1866.

Miller, William C., and Eleanore Bushnell, eds. *Reports of the 1863 Constitutional Convention of the Territory of Nevada.* Carson City: Legislative Counsel Bureau, 1972.

Miranda, M. L. *Out of the Shadows: A Critical First Look at the Ethnohistory of Hispanics in Nevada* (working title). Reno: University of Nevada Press, in press.

Moehring, Eugene P. *Resort City in the Sunbelt: Las Vegas, 1930–1970.* Reno: University of Nevada Press, 1989.

Ostrander, Gilman M. *Nevada: The Great Rotten Borough, 1859–1964.* New York: Alfred A. Knopf, 1966.

Rusco, Elmer R. *Minority Groups in Nevada.* Reno: Bureau of Governmental Research, 1966.

———. *"Good Time Coming?" Black Nevadans in the Nineteenth Century.* Westport, Conn.: Greenwood Press, 1975.

Rusco, Elmer, and Sue Fawn Chung, eds. "Ethnicity and Race in Nevada," *Nevada Public Affairs Review* 2 (1987).

Thomas, Clive S., ed. *Politics and Public Policy in the Contemporary American West.* Albuquerque: University of New Mexico Press, 1991.

Titus, A. Costandina, ed. *Battle Born: Federal-State Conflict in Nevada During the Twentieth Century.* Dubuque, Iowa: Kendall/Hunt Publishing Co., 1989.

Index